AF600063

PARAOCHIAL RELATIONS AND CO-OPERATION OF THE RELIGIOUS AND THE SECULAR CLERGY

The writing of this dissertation was conducted under the direction of the Rev. Romaeus W. O'Brien, O.Carm., J.C.D., as major professor, and was approved by the Rev. Meletius M. Wojnar, O.S.B.M., S.T.L., J.C.D., and the Rev. John J. McGrath, A.B., LL.B., J.C.D., as readers.

THE CATHOLIC UNIVERSITY OF AMERICA
CANON LAW STUDIES
No. 401

Parochial Relations and Co-operation of the Religious and the Secular Clergy

A Historical Synopsis and a Commentary

A DISSERTATION
SUBMITTED TO THE FACULTY OF THE SCHOOL OF CANON LAW OF THE CATHOLIC UNIVERSITY OF AMERICA IN PARTIAL FULFILLMENT OF THE REQUIREMENTS FOR THE DEGREE OF DOCTOR OF CANON LAW

BY THE
REV. DAVID O'CONNOR, M.S.SS.T., J.C.L.
PRIEST OF THE CONGREGATION OF THE MISSIONARY SERVANTS OF THE MOST HOLY TRINITY

THE CATHOLIC UNIVERSITY OF AMERICA PRESS
WASHINGTON, D. C.
1958

NIHIL OBSTAT:

STEPHANUS QUINN, M.S.SS.T., J.C.D.
Censor Deputatus

IMPRIMI POTEST:

THOMAS O'KEEFFE, M.S.SS.T.
Custos Generalis

Silver Spring, Md., die 28 maii, 1958

NIHIL OBSTAT:

ROMAEUS W. O'BRIEN, O.CARM., J.C.D.
Censor Deputatus

IMPRIMATUR:

✠ PATRICIUS A. O'BOYLE, D.D.
Archiepiscopus Washingtonensis

Washingtonii, die 16 iunii, 1958

MURRAY AND HEISTER, INC.
WASHINGTON, D. C.

PRINTED BY
TIMES AND NEWS PUBLISHING CO.
GETTYSBURG, PA., U.S.A.

TABLE OF CONTENTS

PART ONE

HISTORICAL SYNOPSIS

TABLE OF CONTENTS (Continued)

TABLE OF CONTENTS (Continued)

PART TWO

Canonical Commentary

TABLE OF CONTENTS (Continued)

TABLE OF CONTENTS (Continued)

DEDICATED TO
ALL WHO SHARE IN THE PRIESTHOOD
OF
JESUS CHRIST

INTRODUCTION

"Joyfully and gratefully we affirm and openly proclaim that this holy spirit of concord and harmony which exists between the secular clergy and the many religious orders, which by divine benediction are ever growing and so admirably ministering to our churches in the care of souls and in the education of youth, has until now been preserved unbroken in this great country of ours, through the pious moderation and temperance of all concerned; and we sincerely expect and predict that this brotherly agreement and co-operation will remain so forever."[1]

Certainly, this attestation and prediction of the Fathers of the III Plenary Council of Baltimore remains true to this day. American priests of the secular and religious clergy have displayed an admirable spirit of co-operation in the different spheres of the apostolate allotted to them by Holy Mother the Church. It is, indeed, an evident sign of God's benediction that both branches of the clergy have dedicated themselves so wholeheartedly to their common purpose—the honor and glory of God and the salvation of souls.

In our day the religious clergy has grown to the point where over fifty-two per cent of the priests in the Church are also members of religious institutes. As the religious clergy has developed over the centuries, religious priests have more and more become active participants in every phase of the apostolate and the *cura animarum*. Since their participation in the sacerdotal ministry is necessarily and intimately involved with the administration of the sacraments, with preaching, and with other matters closely associated with parish life, such as ecclesiastical burial, the parochial relationship between secular and religious priests is considered from this aspect both historically and canonically.

In his approach to the canonical history of canons 608 and 609, the writer has briefly traced the development of the clerical life

---

[1] Cf. *Acta et Decreta Concilii Plenarii Baltimorensis Tertii* (Baltimorae: Typis Joannis Murphy et Sociorum, 1886), n. 86, pp. 46-47.

and apostolate within the religious life. He has considered such historical questions concerning the ministry of the religious clergy as the right of religious to aspire to Holy Orders, their right to enter the active apostolate, and the mutual relations between the religious and secular clergy arising out of such an active sacerdotal ministry. The canonical commentary is concerned with the juridic status of the religious, the relationship of clerical religious houses with the neighboring parishes, the ministry of non-parochial religious, and the obligation of religious superiors to make their priests available for parochial assistance.

All priests, whether secular or religious, are united under the same supreme authority in the Church, they possess the same Faith, share in the same priesthood of Christ, and are working together for the same common end. In this regard, no more fitting exhortation may be considered than the words of our present and gloriously reigning pontiff, Pope Pius XII, as contained in his apostolic exhortation to the clergy of the world, *Menti Nostrae*:

> . . . We exhort all priests, both of the diocesan clergy and those belonging to the religious orders and congregations, to go forward, bound close together with bonds of fraternal charity, in union of strength and will, toward the common goal: the good of the Church, personal sanctification, and the sanctification of the faithful. All, even Religious who live apart from the world and in silence, can contribute to the efficacy of the priestly apostolate with prayer, sacrifice and also with ready and generous action, in so far as they can.[2]

The writer wishes to take this occasion to express his gratitude to the Very Rev. Thomas O'Keeffe, M.S.SS.T., Custodian General of the Missionary Servants of the Most Holy Trinity, for the opportunity to pursue the course of studies so recently completed, and to the Very Rev. Stephen Quinn, M.S.SS.T., J.C.D., and the Rev. Richard Norris, M.S.SS.T., for their fraternal interest and suggestions in the final reading of the present manuscript.

[2] Cf. Translation by the N.C.W.C. News Service, Washington, D. C., § 72, pp. 23-27.

PART ONE

Historical Synopsis

CHAPTER I

Parochial Relations Between the Religious and Secular Clergy During the First Twelve Centuries

Article 1. The Institution and Early Development of the Religious Clergy

Our Lord and Saviour, Jesus Christ, extended an invitation to all His followers to strive for a higher life both by His example and His words: *If you will be perfect, go, sell what you have, and give to the poor, and you shall have treasure in heaven; and come follow me.*[1] Many of the early Christians answered this invitation and responded by privately undertaking an ascetical life, especially through the practice of consecrated virginity and lives of retirement and prayer.[2] The early persecutions of the Christians, especially during the reign of Decius (249-251), forced many of them to flee into the desert places where a primitive form of the religious life was adopted by some. Even when the vigor of the persecutions had subsided, these anchorites remained in the deserts and secluded places in order that they might escape the distractions and the enticements of a worldly and pagan environment.[3]

The most primitive form of the religious life was that of the anchorite or hermit. Soon, however, the eremetical and solitary life of the recluse, as exemplified by St. Paul of Egypt (c. 341), began to develop and evolve into a semi-eremetical form which was instituted by one of St. Paul's disciples, St. Anthony (+ 356), and then into the communal or cenobitical life initiated by St. Pachomius (+ 347). Large numbers of the hermits sought to

---

[1] Cf. Matthew, XIX: 21; Mark, X: 17-21; Luke, XVIII: 18-23.

[2] Cf. Acts of the Apostles, XXI, 8-9; Montalembert, *The Monks of the West* (2 vols., New York: Kenedy Co., 1912), I, Bk. 2, 170.

[3] Wernz, *Ius Decretalium ad usum Praelectionum in Scholis Textus Iuris Canonici sive Iuris Decretalium* (6 vols., Romae, 1898-1913), III, n. 602 (hereafter cited: *Ius Decretalium*); Migne, *Patrologiae Cursus Completus, Series Latina* (Parisiis, 1844-1864), XXIII, 17 (*Series Latina* hereafter cited: *MPL; Series Graeca* hereafter cited: *MPG*).

imitate these holy men and became their disciples so that they might benefit by their guidance and sanctity. The gregarious nature of men inclined them to group together under a common teacher so as to mutually encourage and sustain one another as they strove for their common goal—perfection.[4]

This highly organized type of religious life spread rapidly throughout the East under the influence of St. Basil (329-379), who wrote several rules founded and inspired by contemporary rules of other monastic groups. For the first time, a full and complete cenobitical life—a truly common life in every sense—was instituted and bore similar characteristics to the religious life as we now know it. At this time, a mode of life was embraced in which a community life and vows were an essential part, as well as the adoption of a specific rule, so that it can be stated that the religious state existed as a complete and perfect way of life.[5] This monastic type of the religious life was introduced to the West by St. Athanasius of Alexandria (C. 295-373) and developed extraordinarily fast with the spread of the rule of St. Benedict of Nursia (c. 480-547).[6]

In the early stages of the religious life, it was considered to be a state to be embraced almost exclusively by lay people and not by those in, or desiring to enter, the clergy. Like the rest of the faithful, the religious were entirely subject to the bishop and they had no intention of embracing the clerical state, for it appeared not to be in harmony with their vocation. The cleric was ordained for others, as St. Paul taught in the fifth chapter of his Epistle to the Hebrews, and the religious state was assumed in order to

---

[4] Cf. Creusen, *De Juridica Status Religiosi Evolutione, Synopsis Historica* (Romae: Apud Aedes Universitatis Gregorianae, 1948), p. 4 (hereafter cited: *De Juridica Evolutione*); Beste, *Introductio in Codicem* (3. ed., Collegeville, Minn.: St. John's Abbey Press, 1946), p. 311.

[5] Thomassinus, *Vetus et Nova Ecclesiae Disciplina circa Beneficia et Beneficiarios* (10 vols., Moguntiae, 1787), Pars I, lib. III, cap. 12, n. 10 (hereafter cited: *Vetus et Nova Disciplina*); Schaefer, *De Religiosis ad Normam Codicis Iuris Canonici* (4. ed., Romae: Typis Polygottis Vaticanis, 1947), pp. 21-23 (hereafter cited: *De Religiosis*).

[6] Butler, *Benedictine Monachism* (2. ed., London: Longmans, Green & Co., 1924), pp. 17-22.

pursue more securely one's own sanctification. As religious, the monks were subject to their religious superior and not the bishop. However, in order that the sacramental life of the religious might be cared for properly, the friendly bishop often sent a priest to minister to them. If a priest was not available, the monks left their dwellings and went to the nearest church.[7]

Eventually, priests and clerics were permitted to enter the communities as members and certain monks were even selected by the religious superior and sent to the bishop to be ordained. This is evident from the rule of St. Benedict, ever cognizant of the fact that the priest was not to be considered any more a monk than his non-clerical brothers. Indeed, it appears that a priest was admitted to the monastery only with some reluctance, after serious consideration had been given to his ability to live the rule.[8]

One of the earliest documents pertaining to clerical religious is the letter of Pope Siricius (384-399) to Bishop Himerius of Tarragona. The letter was written on February 10, 385, and substantiates the fact that religious were not only ordained priests, but that it was the express will of the pontiff that suitable candidates be selected from among the monks and given Holy Orders.[9] St. Ambrose (+ 397) speaks of the monks conferring the sacra-

---

[7] Cf. Creusen, *De Juridica Evolutione,* p. 14; Abbo-Hannan, *The Sacred Canons* (2 vols., St. Louis: Herder Book Co., 1952), Vol. I, p. 485; Schroeder, *Disciplinary Decrees of the General Councils* (St. Louis: Herder Book Co., 1937), p. 189 (hereafter cited: *Disciplinary Decrees*).

[8] Butler, *Sancti Benedicti Regula Monasteriorum* (2. ed., Friburgi Brisgoviae, 1927), cc. 60-62 (hereafter cited: *Regula Monasteriorum*).

[9] "Monachos quoque quos morum gravitas et vitae ac fidei institutio sancta commendat, clericorum officiis aggregari et optamus et volumus, ita, ut qui inter tricesimum annum aetatis sunt digne in minoribus, per gradus singulas cresecentes tempore promoveantur ordinibus et sic ad diaconatus vel presbyterii insignia maturae aetatis consecratione perveniant, nec saltu ad episcopatus culmen ascendant, nisi in his eadem, quae singulis dignitatibus superius praefiximus, fuerint tempora custodita."—c. 29, C. XVI, q. 1.; Mansi, *Sacrorum Conciliorum Nova et Amplissima Collecio* (53 vols. in 60, Paris, Arnhem, Leipzig, 1901-27), III, 660 (hereafter cited: Mansi); Jaffé, *Regesta Pontificum Romanorum ab condita Ecclesia ad annum post Christum natum* MCXCVIII (2. ed. curaverunt Löwenfield, Kaltenbrunner, Ewald, 2 vols., Lipsiae, 1885-1888), n. 225 (hereafter cited: Jaffé).

ments, preaching and performing priestly works,[10] as does St. Jerome in a letter to the monk Rusticus."[11] Nevertheless, the monastic life remained one of prayer, penance and retirement. The fact that priests were permitted to enter, that certain monks were ordained and that, occasionally, a religious cleric undertook the active ministry, was rather the exception than the rule.[12] Even when the monks settled in more populated areas, the conflicts which resulted from their activity among the people and the disregard of proper ecclesiastical authority was the work of a few fanatical followers of Eutyches (+ 454) and not that of the vast majority of these holy men of God. However, such unfortunate happenings caused the Fathers of the Council of Chalcedon (451) to consider the canonical status of religious and thereby clarify the juridical relations between religious and bishops.[13]

ARTICLE 2. THE COUNCIL OF CHALCEDON (451) AND THE CANONICAL STATUS OF RELIGIOUS

The Council of Chalcedon plays an important part in the canonical history of the religious life. It was at this council that the Church began to concern herself with, and to recognize, the increasing influence the religious institutes were having on the life of the Church. To be sure, it was the misguided zeal of the followers of Eutyches, an ignorant and stubborn superior of a monastery outside of the walls of Constantinople, which occasioned

[10] "Doctos ac probos monachos, presbyteri honore dedicatos, predicare, baptizare, penitentiam dare, debita miseris relaxare, decimarum, primitiarum, oblationum vivorum et mortuorum portione justa perfui debere, moderata dispensatione commendamus . . ." c. 21, C. XVI, q. 1 [Friedberg in (h.), n. 151 lists it as of uncertain origin].

[11] "Sic vive in monasterio, ut clericus esse merearis. Multo tempore disce quae postmodum doceas, et inter bonos semper sectare meliores. Quod si populus vel episcopus te in clericum elegerit, age ea, qui clerici sunt."—c. 26, C. XVI, q. 1 [Epistle IV of Jerome to Rusticus].

[12] "Monachus non doctoris, sed plangentis habet officium, qui vel se, vel mundum lugeat, et Domini pavidus prestoletur adventum." This is ascribed by Gratian to St. Jerome—c. 4, C. XVI, q. 1 [Letter of Jerome to Riparius and Desiderius].

[13] Cf. Duchesne, *The Early History of the Church* (3. ed., 3 vols., John Murray, London, 1931), III, 24-26.

the matter to be considered, but it did juridically establish the norms governing the relationship between religious and the bishops throughout the middle ages.[14]

With the increasing numbers of religious and the lessening vigor of the persecutions, many of the less disciplined monks began to leave their monasteries and settle in the nearby populated cities and towns or their vicinity. Their fervor had been weakened and they were not subject to any proper authority, either religious or clerical. Added to this was the influence of Eutyches. Many who had merely assumed the appearances of the monastic life, now lent ready ears to the ravings of this proud monk. They began to concern themselves with affairs of Church and State, disturb the peace with their disputes and criticisms of ecclesiastical authority, and to embarrass both religious and prelate by their actions. The lack of any legislation on such matters was remedied by this General Council. Its norms, governing the relationship between religious and bishops, were to remain substantially unchanged except for the development of exemptions, until the time of Boniface VIII (1294-1303).[15]

The sixth session of the council decreed that all monks were to be subject to the bishop. They were not to remain outside their monasteries and burden themselves with ecclesiastical or worldly affairs, but they were to remain in the monastery and give themselves to prayer and penance. The bishop, however, could commission them to undertake such works as he deemed expedient. He was to exercise a strict but paternal supervision over the monasteries, with transgressors of these provisions subject to the penalty of excommunication.[16]

---

[14] Schroeder, *Disciplinary Decrees*, pp. 78-79, 92-94; Mansi, VII, 907.

[15] Cf. Flanagan, *The Canonical Erection of Religious Houses* (The Catholic University of America Canon Law Studies, n. 179, Washington, D. C.: The Catholic University of America Press, 1943), p. 2; Duchesne, *The Early History of the Church*, II, 412-413, III, 22-26.

[16] "Qui vere et pure solitariam eligunt vitam digni sunt convenienti honore. Eos vero, qui per singulas civitates seu possessiones in monasteriis sunt, placet nobis episcopo subjectos esse, et quieti operam dare, atque observare jejunia et orationes, in locis, in quibus semel se Deo devoverint, permanentes, et neque communicare ecclesiasticas, neque seculares aliquas attractare actiones, relinquentes propria monasteria, nisi forte jubeantur propter urgentes

It can be clearly observed that the Council of Chalcedon gave the religious life a definite canonical status. The establishing of the monastery and its external relations with the diocese was a matter in which the bishop was to exercise a personal interest. The internal life of the monastery was the concern of the religious superior, but even in this matter, when the seriousness of the circumstances demanded his intervention, the bishop was to interest himself. Prior to the council, the bishop had no authority over the monastery unless, perhaps, he was also its founder.[17] Neither was the explicit approval of the bishop required to establish or erect a monastery. It seems that the tacit approval was the most that was demanded, if that.[18] The religious had been completely free in their internal life, but subject as members of the faithful to the bishop in other matters. After this council, however, the bishop was to supervise the monastery, even to the extent of correcting recalcitrant religious with appropriate canonical penalties for grave infractions of the monastic discipline.

The eighth canon of the council expressly forbade all clerics to exercise their orders in churches, monasteries and oratories without the permission of the bishop. This expressly included the religious clergy in their monasteries, as well as clerics in parishes and poorhouses. All were subject to the bishop who was responsible for the spiritual ministrations to the inhabitants of these institutions. The clerics so engaged were to give an accounting to their bishop.[19] This certainly included the monastic priests as well.

---

necessitates ab ipsius civitatis episcopo. . . . Convenit vero civitatis episcopo curam et sollicitudinem necessariam monasteriis exhibere."—c. 12, C. XVI, q. 1; Bruns, *Canones Apostolorum et Conciliorum Saeculorum IV-VII* (2 vols., Berolini, 1839), I, p. 26 (hereafter cited: Bruns); Schroeder, *Disciplinary Decrees,* p. 92; Mansi, VII, 359-360.

[17] "In monasteriis quorum Episcopus fundator et superior est, nulla quaestio de dependentia oritur."—Creusen, *De Juridica Evolutione,* p. 17.

[18] Cf. Wernz, *Ius Decretalium,* III, n. 616; Schmalzgrueber, *Ius Ecclesiasticum Universum* (5 vols. in 12, Romae, 1843-1845), lib. III, tit. 36, nn. 28-30; Suarez, *Omnia Opera* (ed. nova, 28 vols., Parisiis, 1856-1878), Vol. XVI, *De Statu Religioso.*

[19] "Clerici in parochiis, monasteriis aut martiriis constituti sub potestate sint eius, qui in ea civitate est episcopus, secundum traditionem sanctorum Patrum, neque per presumptionem recedant a suo episcopo."—c. 10, C. XVIII, q. 2; Bruns, p. 27; Mansi, VII, 361-362.

Canon 28 was directed primarily against the unruly clerics and monks who abandoned their duties and without the permission of their proper superiors betook themselves to Constantinople where they engaged in scandalous activities. It gave to the ordinary of the diocese the right to expel such recalcitrants and force them to return to their proper residences. The worldly lives of such men had created much disorder in the Church so that stern measures were necessary.[20]

The twenty-fourth canon of the Council of Chalcedon was cognizant of the evils being inflicted on the monasteries by unscrupulous and avaricious men, often the very ones entrusted with their care and protection. As the monasteries grew in wealth, they became the pawns of such men who desired to enrich themselves. The canon, therefore, demanded that consecrated churches and monasteries remain so in perpetuity and that their property not be taken from the monks and secularized. Canonical penalties were to be inflicted on those who permitted such actions to take place.[21]

At this time, it was perfectly licit and an accustomed practice to ordain qualified monks to Holy Orders. The fact that they were affiliated to a monastery would constitute their *titulus ordinationis*. Likewise, the gradual practice by the monks of adopting the recitation of the canonical hours as lectors, was, in time, to bring about the acceptance of their monastic profession as the equivalent of minor orders.[22]

In this manner the Council of Chalcedon juridically outlined the mutual relations between the religious and the bishops. The bishops were recognized as having jurisdiction over the monks and as the guardians of monastic discipline. The monks could readily be ordained, but they were not to give themselves to activities outside the cloister and were to busy themselves with the acquisition of perfection according to the rules of their monastic constitutions. When the necessity arose, however, the

---

[20] Cf. c. 17, C. XVI, q. 1; Bruns, I, 31; Mansi, VII, 367-368.

[21] Cf. Hardouin, *Acta Conciliorum et Epistolae Decretales ac Constitutiones Summorum Pontificum* (12 vols., Parisiis, 1714-1715), Tom. II, col. 622 (hereafter cited: Hardouin); Bruns, I, 31.

[22] Cf. Thomassinus, *Vetus et Nova Disciplina,* Pars I, lib. III, cap. 36, n. 16.

bishop could grant them permission or commission them to engage in secular or ecclesiastical activities. Like all clerics, the religious priests were subject to the bishop in their exercise of priestly orders. Those who left his monastery or diocese, without permission of the bishop, and engaged in such activities, could be expelled from the diocese where they journeyed. Canonical penalties could be inflicted not only on such recalcitrant clerics, but also on those who sought to enrich themselves with monastic property. The rights and obligations of both monastery and bishop were given consideration by this Fourth General Council of the Church, but the main intention of the Fathers of the Council was to legislate on matters pertaining to the recognition and enforcement of proper ecclesiastical authority.

ARTICLE 3. PARTICULAR LEGISLATION CONCERNING THE RELIGIOUS CLERGY FROM THE FIFTH TO THE TWELFTH CENTURY

Section 1. The Early Development of Exemptions from the Episcopal Jurisdiction

The Council of Chalcedon had subjected religious to the jurisdiction of the local bishop.[23] From this time on, there was a growing tendency of the religious to be free from this jurisdiction in one way or another, usually occasioned by the excesses and injustices of some of the prelates. However, exemption as a canonical institute did not truly exist nor become commonplace until the twelfth century. It evolved slowly and developed from the concessions and privileges granted to individuals, single monasteries, and to certain groups of religious, until whole orders eventually enjoyed this by papal grant. The primary reason for these concessions was to protect the religious from the greed and injustice of layman and prelate alike. This had already been stated in the admonitions of the twenty-fourth canon of the Council of Chalcedon,[24] and such precautions would not always keep avaricious men from desiring the property of monk and bishop, rather,

---

[23] C. 10, C. XVIII, q. 2.

[24] Hardouin, I, 622; Bruns, I, 31.

with the passage of time, the ever growing wealth of monastic property only fanned their greedy desires.[25]

Certainly the monks remained generally subject to the jurisdiction of the bishop in whose diocese their monastery was located. But when the internal rule of the monasteries was upset more often than safeguarded by the harsh and exacting acts of many a prelate, the pontiffs themselves tried to protect the monks without undermining the lawful authority of the local bishop. Pope Gregory the Great (590-604), a former monk himself, in a letter to Maximian, Bishop of Ravenna (c. 597), stipulated that the monks had a right to choose their abbot by lawful election, and that the bishop was not to interfere in the temporal administration, revenues, property or documents of the monastery. Neither should the bishop tax the monastery nor invade it with fraudulent action. The episcopal visitations were to be performed with great charity so that no harm would befall the monastery.[26]

At the same time, Pope Gregory safeguarded the rights and prerogatives of the bishop. He in no manner went contrary to the existing law which subjected the religious to the episcopal jurisdiction. The pontiff reminded the prelates that they were pastors of the religious as well as the other members of their flock and would have to answer to God for their conduct. The bishop was the competent judge in all judicial matters concerning the monks and nuns and it was his duty to correct, punish and supervise their conduct.[27]

---

[25] "Optimates et opulentissimi quique monasteriorum fundatores, post immensas opes in eorum structuram et dotem effusas, cum aliquandiu ipsi cum prole voluptatem fructumque cepessent ex eis, jus tandem suum omne non raro in episcopos, et in ecclesias cathedrales transferebant."—Thomassinus, *Vetus et Nova Disciplina,* Pars I, lib. III, cap. 27, n. 4.

[26] "Visitandi exhortandique gratia ad monasterium, quotiens placuerit, ab antistite civitatis accedatur; sed sic charitatis officium illic impleat episcopus, ut gravamen aliquod monasterium non incurrat."—c. 28, C. XVIII, q. 2; *Gregorii* I *Papae Registrum Epistolarum-Monumenta Germaniae Historica,* Epistolarum Tom. I et II (ediderunt P. Ewald et L. Hartmann, Berolini, 1891-1899), Ep. VIII, 17; cf. V, 49; III, 3; VII, 10 (hereafter cited: *MGH, Registrum Epistolarum*).

[27] Cf. *MGH, Registrum Epistolarum,* Epp. IX, 203; VIII, 8; IX, 114; X, 3, 9; XII, 6; XIV, 16.

It appears that a qualified exemption from episcopal jurisdiction was enjoyed by different religious groups from a very early period. This is evidenced by the monastic groups in Africa from as early a time as the fifth and sixth century. At a council held in Carthage (c. 525), the abbots of the African monasteries requested the assembled bishops to exempt them from the jurisdiction of all except that of the Primate. Their argument revolved about the fact that they had enjoyed this freedom traditionally and that they desired that it be legally preserved. Such exemption was granted to them at their request.[28]

In the year 628, Honorius I (625-638) granted to the monastery of Sts. Peter and Paul at Bobbio freedom from the jurisdiction of a vexatious bishop and subjected them to the jurisdiction of the Holy See, so that the monastery was responsible directly to the Roman Pontiff.[29] Subsequent pontiffs, such as Pope Zachary I (741-752), extended complete grants of exemptions to all who had serious reasons to request it, so that they were subject directly to the Holy See.[30] During succeeding pontificates there was an increased number of such exemptions because of the little security and protection enjoyed by the religious from those who claimed patronage over the monasteries and their goods. Therefore, the Holy See readily granted charters to free them from the ever growing evils of lay investiture.[31]

Section 2. The Ordination of Clerical Religious

Since religious were subject to the jurisdiction of the local ordinary, as stated in the canons of the Council of Chalcedon,[32] it is reasonable to state that they were to receive Holy Orders from him. Numerous provincial councils had insisted, even before the

---

[28] Cf. Thomassinus, *Vetus et Nova Disciplina,* Pars I, lib. III, cap. 31, n. 9.

[29] Cf. Montalembert, *Monks of the West,* I, 583; *Privilegium Bobiensi Coenbio Datum—MPL,* LXXX, 483; Jaffé, n. 2017.

[30] *Epistola XV, Zachariae Papae—MPL,* LXXXIX, 944.

[31] "Liberum est enim monasterium, suique juris, ut ne possit quidem alienari; nec ex eo ad episcopum quidquam redeat, nisi episcopalia jura. . . ." —Thomassinus, *Vetus et Nova Disciplina,* Pars I, lib. III, cap. 27, n. 7; cf. Jaffé, n. 4053 and 8428.

[32] C. 12, C. XVI, q. 1; c. 10, C. XVIII, q. 2.

Fourth General Council at Chalcedon, that the local bishop was the ordaining bishop by right. For example, canon 13 of a council held at Carthage (c. 401) stipulated that any bishop who dared ordain a monk of another monastery other than his own would incur excommunication.[33] Once the legislation became general law, it was repeated by many local councils and synods. Usually, the consent of the abbot was explicitly stated in the enactment as a requisite for the lawfulness of the ordination. The Third Council of Arles (455) stated that all monks were subject to the abbot and his consent was necessary before any of them could be raised to Orders by the bishop.[34] However, some bishops with a scarcity of priests in their dioceses did not hesitate to ordain monks when the need arose, even without the consent of the abbot, presumably for ministry in the diocese. Therefore, the Council of Agde (506), in its twenty-seventh canon, expressly prohibited the practice.[35] Yet, if the utility of the Church required it, some monks could be ordained by the bishop, but the will of the abbot had to be respected. Such legislation is expressed in the third canon of the Council of Lerida (c. 524).[36] Both of these decrees were later incorporated into the common law under Pope Lucius III (1181-1185), for the Church well realized the grave danger to the re-

---

[33] ". . . ut si quis de alterius monasterio receptum, vel ad clericatum promovere voluerit, vel in suo monasterii constituere; episcopus qui hoc fecerit, a ceterorum communione sejunctus, seu tantum plebis communione contentus sit, et ille neque clericus, neque praepositus perseveret."—Mansi, III, 971; Bruns, I, 175.

[34] "Laici porro monasterii in solius abbatis potestate essent, nec posset episcopus quemquam eorum ordinare, nisi petente abbate."—Thomassinus, *Vetus et Nova Disciplina,* Pars I, lib. III, cap. 26, n. 16.

[35] "Monachi vagantes ad officium clericatus (nisi eis testimonium abbas suus dederit), nec in parochiis, nec in civitatibus ordinentur. Si enim necesse fuerit clericum de monachis ordinari, cum consensu et voluntate abbatis presumat episcopus."—c. 33, C. XVI, q. 1; Mansi, VIII, 329; Bruns, II, 151.

[36] "Cum pro utilitate ecclesiae aliquos monachorum in clericatus officio episcopus probaverit promovendos, cum abbatis voluntate debent ordinari. Ea vero, quae in iure monasterii de facultatibus offeruntur, in nullo dioecesiani lege ab episcopis contingantur."—c. 34, C. XVI, q. 1; Mansi, VIII, 612; Bruns, II, 21.

ligious state if this was neglected.[37] If the consent was not received, some stated that the appointment of a monk to a church was gravely illicit.[38] When the Council of Lerida enacted the above legislation, it appears that the Fathers of the Council were reprehending some bishops who had ordained monks without the permission of the abbots and who were, also, demanding excessive tithes from the monks.[39]

The pontiffs, themselves, did not hesitate to speak out on this matter. Pope Gelasius (492-496) permitted a bishop to choose qualified monks as candidates for Holy Orders, as long as they were not under any impediments and were known for their virtuous lives, if a scarcity of priests existed in the diocese.[40] The same pontiff, nevertheless, required that the bishop receive the consent of the abbot even in this case, when the priests were to be employed in the diocesan ministry.[41] Pope Gregory the Great (590-604) did, indeed, permit monks to receive Orders with their abbots' permission,[42] but if the priests were to be employed by

---

[37] Cf. c. 5, X, *de temporibus ordinationum et qualitate ordinandorum,* I, 11.

[38] "Videtur ergo quod Episcopus invito Abbate, non possit monachum praeficere ecclesiae aliqui, vel facere ipsum clericum suum."—*Glossa ordinaria* ad c. 34, C. XVI, q. 1, s.v. *cum abbatis.*

[39] "Duo episcopi contra justitiam faciebant, nam sine consensu abbatum monachos ordinabant, et a monasteriis tertiam vel quartam decimarum et cathedraticum exigebant: et ideo reprehenduntur in concilio Leridensi et prohibet concilium ne de caetero talia fiant."—*Glossa ordinaria* ad c. 34, C. XVI, q. 1, s.v. *cum pro utilitate.*

[40] "Priscis igitur pro sua reverentia manentibus institutis (quae ubi nulla rerum vel temporum perurget angustia, regulariter convenit custodiri), quia eatenus ecclesiae, vel cunctis vel sufficientibus privatae sunt ministeris, ut plebibus ad se pertinentibus divina munera subplere non valeant, concedimus, ut, si quis monasterialibus disciplinis eruditus ad clericale munus accedit. . . ." —c. 1, D. LV; Jaffé, n. 636.

[41] "Si quis monachus fuerit, qui venerabilis vitae merito sacerdotio dignus prevideatur, et abbas, sub cujus imperio regi Christo militat illum fieri presbyterium petierit, ab ipso debet eligi, et in loco, quo judicaverit, ordinari, omnia, quae ad sacerdotii officium pertinent, vel populi vel episcopi electione provide ac juste acturus."—c. 28. C. XVI, q. 1; Jaffé, n. 697; Mansi, VIII, 329.

[42] "Ad ecclesiasticum vero officium nullus ex monasterio producatur nisi quem abbas loci admonitus, propria voluntate obtulerit episcopo."—c. 1, D. LVIII; Jaffé, n. 1504; *MGH, Registrum Epistolarum,* XVIII [Letter to Marinianus].

the bishop of the diocese in the active ministry, they were not to be permitted to have any authority in the monastery because of the danger to religious discipline.[43]

In the eighth century, the Second Council of Nicea (787), in its fourteenth canon, gave permission to abbots of monasteries who had received the solemn rite of benediction from the bishop, to confer tonsure and advance their subjects to the order of lector.[44] Therefore, the legislation of the era universally required the consent of the abbot before one of his subjects could be lawfully ordained. The local bishop could confer the sacrament on the religious candidates with the abbot's permission and sometimes legitimately employ them in the active ministry of his diocese. The local bishop was always the proper bishop for major orders, but sometimes abbots had the privilege of conferring the minor orders. Thus it remained until the thirteenth century, when the religious superiors of mendicant orders were given the privilege of selecting any bishop in union with the Holy See as the proper bishop of ordination. But even this privilege was by way of exception due to the missionary activities of the mendicants in distant lands.

Section 3. The Parochial Activity of the Religious Clergy

The priestly monks were subject to their religious superior in those things that pertained to the monastic life, but in the exercise of their Orders among the faithful, especially in the hearing of confessions, preaching and catechizing, they required the permission of the bishop. At one time, the bishop had been the sole pastor of his flock and personally distributed the sacraments and preached the word of God to them. With the growth of the infant Church, the bishop shared his pastoral ministry with his priests and deacons more and more, but they always required his per-

---

[43] "Ne pro cuiuslibet monachi aut abbatis promotione onus aliquod fortasse monasteria sustineant, studendum nobis est, ut, si quispiam monachorum ex quocumque monasterio ad clericatus officium vel ordinem sacrum accesserit, non ibi ulterius aliquam habeat potestatem,"—c. 37, C. XVI, q. 1; Jaffé, n. 1486.

[44] Cf. Thomassinus, *Vetus et Nova Disciplina,* Pars I, lib. III, cap. 36, n. 16; Schroeder, *Disciplinary Decrees,* pp. 150-151; Hardouin, IV, 495.

mission or commission for this work.[45] Slowly the parochial division of the diocese took form with the establishing of the *ecclesia baptismalis* which had a definite priest assigned to it so that he might care for that part of the bishop's flock.[46] Yet, with the continued expansion of the Church and dearth of sufficient priests to care for the people, the bishops did not hesitate to select worthy monks for Orders and then commission them for this ministry.[47] The monks were, however, prohibited from entering the active ministry without the command or, at least permission, of their religious superior.[48]

This was not always approved however, and at times, there was great opposition to the practice of monks engaging in the active ministry or, for that matter, of them even receiving Orders. For example, in Rome during the fifth century the small monasteries were subject to the supervision of the clergy. The monks were expressly forbidden to enter the ranks of the clergy.[49] The monks were considered to have embraced a life which did not permit them to enter the active clerical life, nor by some, to even aspire to Holy Orders. Pope Gregory the Great appears to have shared this opinion to a limited extent. He was a former monk himself and greatly desired to protect the cloister from any encroachment of the world.[50] In his desire to safeguard the monastic life, to strengthen and protect it from men of worldly ambitions, he made a sharp distinction between the clerical life and the monastic vocation. This distinction, however, would become of little consequence even during his own pontificate and certainly

[45] ". . . non licet sine Episcopo neque baptizare neque agapen celebrare." —*Ep. S. Ignatii ad Smyrnos*—*MPG,* V, 714.

[46] "Plures baptismales ecclesiae in una terminatione esse non possunt, sed una tantummodo cum cappellis suis."—c. 54, C. XVI, q. 1.

[47] "Cum pro utilitate ecclesiae aliquos monachorum in clericatus officio episcopus probaverit promovendos."—c. 34, C. XVI, q. 1—[Council of Lerida (c. 524)].

[48] "Monachi a monasterio foras egredientes ne aliquod ministerium ecclesiasticum praesumant agere prohibemus, nisi forte cum abbatis imperio." —c. 35, C. XVI, q. 1 [The Council of Tarragona (516)], Mansi, VIII, 543; Bruns, II, 17.

[49] Duchesne, *The Early History of the Church,* III, 26.

[50] Cf. *MGH, Registrum Epistolarum,* Ep. IX, 157; Montalembert, *The Monks of the West,* I, Bk. 5, 398.

afterwards. At first he believed the two states were not compatible, that one could not worthily live as both monk and cleric and properly fulfill the obligations of each calling.[51] It was his mind that the monks should give themselves to the recitation of the canonical hours, to prayer and penance.[52] Clerics who entered the monastic life could not become abbots, in fact, he did not even think that they should ordinarily be permitted to embrace the life. He feared that it would be detrimental to the spiritual life of the monastery, since he was aware of many instances where ambition had been the motivation of men who had entered the monastery and been placed in positions of authority. The Pope, therefore, insisted they refrain from exercising their clerical privileges when they donned the monks' habit.[53] Monks were certainly capable of receiving Orders, especially that they might care for the sacramental and spiritual needs of the community and not necessitate the bishop sending other priests to fulfill these ministrations.[54] When there was a sufficient number of monks present to recite the canonical hours, he permitted the abbot to offer some of his priestly subjects to assist a needy bishop. If, however, the monk was given an ecclesiastical benefice or office, he was not permitted to have authority in his monastery.[55] Yet these were apparently only general norms of action, since Gregory did not shrink in many instances from sending only monks to evangelize distant lands. Nor did he discourage bishops from calling upon the religious clergy to undertake missionary labors. He stated expressly that monks were lawfully able to preach, baptize, confer the sacraments and absolve from sins.[56]

---

[51] "Satis enim incongrum est, ut cum unum ex his pro sui magnitudine diligenter quis non possit explere, ad utrumque judicetur idoneus: sicque invicem et ecclesiasticus ordo vitae monachicae et ecclesiasticis utilitatibus regula monachatus impediat."—*MGH, Registrum Epistolarum,* Ep. IV, 21.

[52] Epp. I, 67; IV, 11.

[53] "Dum hi fingunt se religiose vivere monasteriis praeponi appetunt et per eorum vitam monasteria destruuntur."—Ep. V, 1.

[54] Ep. VI, 39-42.

[55] Cf. c. 37, C. XVI, q. 1; *MGH, Registrum Epistolarum,* Ep. VII, 40-41.

[56] "Ex auctoritate huius decreti (quod apostolico moderamine et pietatis officio a nobis est constitutum) sacerdotibus monachis apostolorum figuram tenentibus liceat praedicare, baptizare, communionem dare, pro peccatoribus orare, penitentiam imponere, atque peccata solvere."—c. 24, C. XVI, q. 1.

This matter, however, continued to be contested. Provincial councils differed in their legislation. A synod at Paris (829) and a Council at Aachen (839) prohibited monks from entering any form of the parochial ministry.[57] On the other hand, a Council of Mainz (847), during the pontificate of Pope Leo IV (847-855), permitted them to accept a parish with the consent of the bishop.[58]

The Council of Nimes (1096), in its second and third canons, not only sanctioned monks undertaking some form of the parochial ministry, but even stated that they were better qualified for such a spiritual work, more so than other priests.[59]

Gratian (+ c. 1157), having listed the various legislation of the pontiffs and the councils, concluded in his *dicta* that there was nothing contradictory and that it was certainly lawful for the religious clergy numbered among the monastic orders to undertake an active sacerdotal ministry, as long as they were properly

---

[57] *Monumenta Germaniae Historica,* Legum Sectio III, *Concilia* (Tomus II, recensuit A. Werminghoff, Hannoverae et Lipsiae, 1896), Tom. II, pars II, p. 711 (hereafter cited: *MGH, Concilia*) ; Mansi, XIV, 566.

[58] "Nullus monachorum parochias ecclesiarum accipere praesumat sine consensu episcopi."—Mansi, XIV, 907.

[59] "Sunt nonnulli nullo dogmate fulti audacissime quidem, zelo magis amaritudinis quam dilectionis inflammati, asserentes monachos, quia mundo mortui sunt et Deo vivunt, sacerdotalis officii potentia indignos, neque penitentiam, neque Christianitatem largiri, neque absolvere posse per sacerdotalis offici divinitus sibi injunctam potestatem. Sed omnino labuntur. Neque enim Beatus Benedictus, monachorum preceptor almificus, huiuscemodi rei aliquid modo fuit interdictor, sed eos saecularium negotiorum edixit expertes fore tantummodo. Quod quidem apostolicis documentis, et omninum sanctorum Patrum institutis non solum monachis, set etiam canonicis magnopere imperatur. *Nemo enim militans Deo implicat se negotiis secularibus.* Tantorum igitur Patrum instituti exemplis (quibus periculosissimum est refragari) credimus a sacerdotibus monachis ligandi solvendique officium Deo operante digne administrari, si eos digne contingeret hoc ministerio sublimari. Decertantes igitur monachiae professionis presbyteros sacerdotalis potentiae arcere officio, omnimodo praecipimus, ut ab huiuscemodi ausibus reprimantur in posterum, quia quanto magis quisque est celsior tanto illis erit potentior." —Mansi, XX, 934-935. (It may be noted that canon 3 of the council is introduced in this manner: "Quod monachi sacerdotali ministerio rectius fungi possint, quam presbyteri saeculares.")

appointed and approved for this ministry by the abbot and bishop.[60]

In the eleventh century, a new form of the religious clergy gained prominence. Whereas the monastic life had prescinded from the clerical state, this new form, termed Canons Regular, was actually a reform of the existing institution of canons who were considered to be essentially clerical as well as religious. The reason for this was that their work and purpose was concerned with the celebration of the divine mysteries, as stated by the "Angelic Doctor", St. Thomas Aquinas, in his *Summa Theologica*.[61] The Canons Regular professed sanctity and poverty. Their life was dedicated to the praises of God through the choir obligation, but, at the command of the superior, they were to give himself to the works of the ministry, principally preaching, teaching, administering the sacraments, or caring for the sick and the needy. The religious were accustomed, also, to accept the care of parishes and the public oratories that were lawfully entrusted to them. All the works compatible to the clerical and religious states would be accepted by them. However, they were primarily religious and observed a community life.[62]

Innocent III (1198-1216) stated that it was more proper for the Canons Regular to undertake the *cura animarum* because their rule of life was formed with such a ministry in mind. Nevertheless, the Canons were encouraged to live with their fellow religious when they engaged in the active parochial ministry, so that they might render one another assistance in the observation of their

[60] "His omnibus auctoritatibus perspicue monstratur, monachos posse poenitentiam dare, baptizare, et cetera sacerdotalia officia licite administrare. Quod vero populi electione, episcoporum institutione, et abbatis consensu potestatem suam exsequi valeant, Ieronimi, Gelasii, et Gregorii auctoritate probatur."—*Dictum ad* c. 25, C. XVI, q. 1.

[61] ". . . quod utraque religio, scilicet monachorum, et canonicorum regularium, ordinatur ad opera vitae contemplativae: inter quae praecipua sunt ea, quae aguuntur in divinis mysteriis: ad quae ordinatur directe ordo canonicum regularium, quibus per se competit, quod sint clerici religiosi; sed ad religionem monachorum non per se competit, ut sint clerici, . . ."—*Sancti Thomae Aquinatis Doctoris Angelici Opera iussu Impensaque Leonis* XIII, *P. M. Edita* (Romae: 1882-); *Summa Theologica,* IIa IIae, q. CLXXXIX, art. 8 (hereafter cited: *Summa Theologica*).

[62] Cf. Allaria, "Canons and Canonesses Regular," *Catholic Encyclopedia* (15 vols., Index and Supplement, New York, 1907-1922), III, 288.

rule.[63] The same pontiff justified, however, the ordination and parochial ministry of monks. The Glossator remarked that the monk, although not intended primarily for such a clerical ministry, could enter it because of a general dispensation granted by the law for the utility of the Church or because the common law permitted it.[64]

In the beginning of their foundations, the individual Canons lived in single *sui juris* religious houses in small groups. When however, many wished to join with them and adopt a common rule of life based on that of St. Augustine, new orders were instituted, such as the Premonstratensians and Crosier Fathers, and given ecclesiastical approval. A great number of priests joined these religious orders and dedicated themselves to the active parochial ministry.[65] Because of the purpose and ends of their institutes, the Canons Regular rarely met with the same type of opposition that the monastic communities did when they undertook any form of the parochial ministry. They fulfilled a need of their times and displayed the vitality of the Church in adapting itself to the circumstances of an ever changing world. The Canons

---

[63] ". . . si fieri potest, unum canonicum regularem tecum habeas, cuius in his quae Dei sunt et regularis observantiae, tam consortio quam solatio perfruaris."—c. 5, X, *de statu monachorum et canonicorum regularium,* III, 35.

[64] "Dicunt quidem, quod hodie possunt de jure communi, olim tamen ex dispensatione . . . alii dicunt quod nec hodie possunt nisi ex dispensatione. . . . Satis potest dici, quod olim monachi non poterant praefici ecclesiis, nisi ex necessitate . . . hodie possunt etiam utilitate suadente. Sed regulares, ut dicit hic, licite possunt eligi ad regimen ecclesiarum utilitatis causa, et de jure communi, ut videtur. . . . Sed in hoc est differentia inter monachos et canonicos regulares, quod monachus tenetur habere socios secum sui ordinis. . . . Sed regulares ad hoc non tenentur, nisi commode possint."—*Glossa ordinaria* ad c. 5, X, *de statu monachorum et canonicorum regularium,* III, 35, s.v. *regimen in presbyteros.*

[65] Cf. Vermeersch-Creusen, *Epitome Iuris Canonici cum Commentariis* (3 vols., Vol. I, 7. ed., 1949, Mechliniae-Romae: Dessain), I, n. 586, pp. 438-440 (hereafter cited: *Epitome*); Coronata, *Institutiones Iuris Canonici* (4. ed., 5 vols., Taurini-Romae: Marietti, 1941-1951), I, n. 509, pp. 609-610 (hereafter cited: *Institutiones*).

Regular were the first religious to dedicate themselves to the clerical life and, in a degree, to the active parochial ministry. They would be followed in succeeding ages by the mendicants, congregations and societies of priests which would more and more assume the burden of the missionary life of the Church.

CHAPTER II

Parochial Conflicts Between the Religious and Secular Clergy in the Middle Ages

Article 1. The Exemptions and Privileges of the Mendicants

The ideal of harmoniously blending the contemplative life of the monk and the activity of the apostle was providentially inaugurated in the thirteenth century with the founding of the mendicant communities. In quick succession, the Order of Preachers, founded by St. Dominic (1170-1221); the Order of Friars Minor, founded by St. Francis Assisi (1181-1226); and the Order of Hermits of St. Augustine (1294) undertook the apostolate so much in need at that time. The pontiffs saw in these religious orders the choicest of instruments to further the spiritual and missionary needs of the Church. For this reason, the Popes bestowed on them extraordinary privileges, especially concessions of sacramental jurisdiction and preaching faculties of an inter-diocesan nature. Thus, for example, Pope Gregory IX (1227-1241) granted to all Dominican preachers, selected by their religious superiors, the faculties to absolve all lay people who presented themselves as penitents before these Dominican confessors.[1] The Franciscan Fathers received similar privileges, although their Rule always required the Friars first to receive the permission

---

[1] "Quoniam habundavit iniquitas et per apostolica vobis scripta mandantes, quatinus dilectos filios Fratres Ordinis memorati, pro reverentia Divina et nostra, ad officium predicandi, ad quod deputati sunt, recipiatis benigne, ac populos vobis commissos, ut ex ore ipsorum Verbi Dei semen devote suscipiant, et confiteantur eisdem, cum ipsis auctoritate nostra liceat confessiones audire, ac penitentias iniungere, sedulo admonentes."—Const. *Quoniam*, 10 maii 1227—*Bullarium Ordinis FF. Praedicatorum* (Ripoll et Bremond, 8 vols., Romae, 1729-1740), I, 19 (hereafter cited: *Bull. Praed.*); Potthast, *Regesta Pontificum inde ab anno post Christum natum MCXCVIII ad annum MCCCIV* (2 vols., Berolini, 1874-1875), n. 7896 (hereafter cited: Potthast, *Regesta*).

of the local ordinary in whose diocese they were destined to labor.[2] The religious priests often enjoyed inter-parochial and inter-diocesan faculties as preachers and confessors. Human nature being what it is, there is little wonder that conflicts and controversies over the respective rights and privileges of the two groups mark the pages of canonical and historical works.[3] The privileges of the mendicants were the basis of the clerical disputes. They were greatly protested for many centuries by the prelates and diocesan clerics. Ignoring the fact that they were granted by the Roman Pontiffs for the good of the Church, so that the mendicants might not be hampered by limitations of jurisdiction in their revitalization of the spiritual life of the faithful, time and time again it was demanded by the clergy that the religious first must receive their permission before they might validly exercise their privileges. They made periodic demands that the Popes withdraw the privileges altogether.[4] The opposition of the prelates and their clergy to the active ministry of the religious communities was, indeed, an old one. However, it reached a particularly virulent stage during the twelfth, thirteenth and fourteenth centuries. In the early development of the religious ministry, the people had, for the most part, sought out the sacramental ministrations of the monks in their monasteries. But with the new form of apostolate founded with the "contemplative-active" mendicants, who literally went into the highways and byways of the lands in search of souls, this was considered by the secular clerics as an interference.[5]

These Papal privileges granted to religious were intimately connected with the conferring of exemptions from the jurisdiction of the local ordinaries. Exemptions had developed slowly from concessions made to individual religious and single monasteries. Eventually, Papal exemption became a canonical institution re-

---

[2] Cf. c. 3, *de verborum significatione,* V, 12, in Sexto.

[3] Cf. Const. *Non sine multa,* 30 mart. 1257, of Pope Alexander IV (1254-1261)—*Bull. Praed.,* I, 334.

[4] Cf. Const. *Cum olim,* 18 ian. 1259—*Bull. Praed.,* I, 369; Potthast, *Regesta,* n. 17452.

[5] Cf. Schroeder, *Disciplinary Decrees,* pp. 383-384; McCartney, *Faculties of Regular Confessors* (Catholic University of American Canon Law Studies, n. 280; Washington, D. C.: The Catholic University of America Press, 1949), p. 16.

moving religious from the jurisdiction of the local Ordinary and subjecting them immediately to the Holy See, which exercised its authority through the religious superiors. The Holy See in this way sought to protect the religious from the avarice and oppression of unscrupulous men. From the eleventh century onward, exemption and Papal protection became almost equivalent.[6]

In these parochial conflicts between the religious and the diocesan clergy, both groups shared the responsibility. It had not been unknown that religious had at times abused their extensive privileges to the complete disregard of the rights of the diocesan clergy. Some of the monastic and mendicant priests had ignored the rights of competent pastors who were ready and willing to distribute the sacraments to their subjects. Other religious had upset parochial functions by intentionally scheduling spiritual exercises in their own churches so as to draw the parishioners of other churches. Certainly, such practices did not endear the religious to their diocesan brothers. Unholy motives and blatant disregard for the parochial rights and lawful authority of the ecclesiastical authorities is never commendable.

On the other hand, the zeal and apostolic activity of the religious often made known the scandalous neglect and indifference of many of the diocesan clergy of that time in carrying out their pastoral duties. The religious clergy with the blessings of the pontiff were only giving the faithful the sacramental and spiritual ministrations which they were sadly in need of and so greatly appreciated. Favors bestowed upon the religious by the Holy See and faithful alike, only provoked petty jealousies and the disdain of the local clergy. Hence, when the University of Paris attempted to induce the Church to remove the religious clergy entirely from any form of the active ministry, it found many supporters among the prelates and clerics. William of St. Amour (+ c. 1272), the Master of Theology at the University of Paris, and his colleagues went so far in their criticism and diatribes against the religious,

[6] Cf. Melo, *De Exemptione Regularium* (The Catholic University of America Canon Law Studies, n. 12, Washington, D. C.: The Catholic University of America, 1921), p. 1 ff.; Schroeder, *Disciplinary Decrees,* pp. 383-384.

that they claimed that the religious were liable to eternal damnation for entering the active ministry when they were supposed to be dead to the world. Pope Alexander IV condemned all the propositions proposed by William of St. Amour by his decrees *Dilecti filii,* March 30, 1256, and *Si Filias* of April 4, 1256.[7]

Attempts were made to subject all religious completely to the jurisdiction of the local prelates and pastors. Often, these forbade them to reserve the Blessed Sacrament, to possess church bells, or to have their own cemeteries. Others demanded that religious attend the local parish church to fulfill their obligation of attending Mass and receiving the sacraments. Such opposition and demands contrary to the existing law of the Church and the rights and privileges of the religious found many defenders. Not only did the pontiffs speak out on these matters, but such geniuses and lights of the Church as St. Bonaventure and St. Thomas defended the status of the religious in the active ministry.[8]

---

[7] ". . . Ecce, sicut accepimus, vos ordinationem nostram super conservatione Studii Parisiensis editam solemni cum Fratribus nostris deliberatione praemissa, et alias litteras nostras, propter quasdam appellationes et exceptiones frivolas interjectas a vobis, obstinato animo non servantes, nostrae intentionis effectum circa ordinationem ipsam calumniosis adinventionibus praesumitis impedire; damnabile inobedientiae vitium, et judicium sententiarum, quae sunt contra vestram rebellionem auctoritate Apostolica promulgate, minime formidando; . . . quod simplicitatem vestrae multitudinis ab astuta malitia paucorum, et praecipue Magistri Guilielmi de Sanctoamore, credimus fuisse seductam, oculus vester, quem caligo superbiae nimium obumbravit virga correctionis debitae illustratus patenter agnosceret, quam stultum sit, et detestabile, Apostolicae Sedis aequissimis ordinationibus, et litteris contumaciter obviare."—Const. *Si Filias*—*Bull. Praed.,* I, 301; cf. Denifle, *Chartularium Universitatis Parisiensis* (5 vols., Parisiis, 1899-1907), I, nn. 317-344.

[8] ". . . status religionis est quoddam exercitium, quo aliquis exercetur ad perfectionem charitatis: sunt autem diversa charitatis opera, quibus homo vacare potest: . . . religionis status ordinatur ad perfectionem charitatis, quae se extendit ad dilectionem Dei et proximi: ad dilectionem Dei autem directe pertinet contemplativa vita, quae soli Deo vacare desiderat: ad dilectionem autem proximi directe pertinet vita activa, quae deservit necessitatibus proximorum: et sicut ex charitate diligitur proximus propter Deum; ita ut etiam obsequium delatum in proximos redundat in Deum; . . . unde, et huiusmodi obsequia proximis facta, inquantum ad Deum referuntur, dicuntur esse sacrificia quaedam . . . : et quia ad Religionem proprie pertinet

The Roman Pontiffs, themselves, demanded that the excessive requirements and oppressive treatment of the religious be stopped. Pope Gregory IX (1227-1241) and Pope Innocent IV (1243-1254) both published the charges brought against some of the injustices of the clergy. Listed among the charges were demands that religious confess and receive the sacraments in the manner of lay people, the practice of excommunicating the benefactors of religious, and the usurpation of all offerings collected during the celebration of Masses in religious oratories and Churches.[9]

Local councils and synods attempted to force the religious to be subject to their decrees when actually they were exempt from them. Therefore it was legislated that if prelates forced obedience in matters beyond their competence and jurisdiction, the submission of the exempt religious, even if to avoid greater difficulties, would be juridically illicit and invalid.[10] Councils and synods had jurisdiction over the religious only in those cases expressly stated in the law.[11] Pope Gregory IX in his bull *Nimis prava* ordered the prelates to cease hindering the religious with demands that they obey their synodal decrees.[12]

This did not mean, however, that the legitimate rights of the clergy were not protected and defended by the pontiffs. Pope Honorius III (1216-1227), for example, stipulated that the bishop always had the right to accept or reject a religious priest who was

---

sacrificium Deo offerre, . . . consequens est, quod convenienter Religiones quaedam ad opera vitae activae ordinetur."—*Summa Theologica,* IIa IIae, q. CLXXXVIII, art. 1-2, in corp.

[9] ". . . non desunt plerique tam ecclesiarum praelati, quam alii, qui, caeca cupiditate seducti, propriae aviditati subtrahi reputantes quidquid predictis fidelium pietas elargitur, quiete ipsorum multipliciter inquietant. Volunt namque contra regulam a Sede Apostolica approbatam et sui ordinis instituta, ipsis invitis eorum confessiones audire . . . et Eucharistiam exhibere . . . ut corpus Christi in eorum oratoriis reservetur."—Const. *"Nimis iniqua"* of Gregory IX—17 sept. 1245—cc. 16, 17, X, *de excessibus praelatorum,* V, 31.

[10] "Sane, si episcopi aliquid ab abbatibus, praeter debitam obedientiam contra libertatae ordinis a praedecessoribus nostris et a nobis indulta, exigunt, liberum sit abbatibus auctoritate apostolica quod petitur, denegare."—c. 5, X, *de excessibus praelatorum,* V, 31.

[11] Cf. c. 1, *de privilegiis,* V, 7, in Sexto.

[12] Cf. c. 17, X, *de excessibus praelatorum,* V, 31.

presented by his religious superior for appointment to a parish entrusted to the Order.[13] Although Pope Innocent IV (1243-1254), by a special papal confirmation, approved the practice of religious administering the sacraments to those lay persons who labored within the confines of the religious houses, he acknowledged the restrictions of such sacramental administrations to those who were not in any manner subject to the religious superior.[14]

The time finally arrived when, for one reason or another, many of the privileges granted religious were revoked by the Constitution *Etsi animarum* of Innocent IV on the thirteenth of November in 1254. These privileges concerned preaching and confessional faculties and certain burial rights which the prelates demanded to be withdrawn.[15] His successor, Alexander IV (1254-1261), restored many of these privileges. Mendicants could preach, hear confessions and perform other such sacramental ministrations with the permission of the Holy See, its legates or the local ordinary, without any further obligation to receive the permission of lesser prelates and the parish priests. He severely castigated those who slandered the religious, and praised the mendicants for their contributions to the Church.[16] Likewise, he rebuked those who

---

[13] "In parochialibus vero ecclesiis, quas habetis, liceat vobis sacerdotes eligere, et dioecesano episcopo praesentare, quibus, si idonei fuerit episcopus animorum curam committat . . ."—Const. *Religiosam vitam,* 22 dec. 1216—*Bull. Praed.*, I, 2.

[14] ". . . Ceterum, ut his, qui vestris immorantur obsequiis, divinae intuitu pietatis, quod in salutem animarum vertitur de vestris manibus assequantur, vobis de speciali gratia indulgemus, ut eis libere, cuncta ministrare possitis Ecclesiastica Sacramenta. . . ."—Const. *Qui Deum,* 5 febr. 1244—*Bull. Praed.,* I, 131.

[15] Potthast, *Regesta,* n. 15562.

[16] "Non sine multa cordis amaritudine animique turbatione audivimus, quod nonnulli Magistri, et Doctores, ac alii, acuentes ut gladium linguas suas, et venenum aspidum gerentes sub labiis, ad infamiam, gravamen, et dispendium innocentiam, illud in fuggillationem et laesionem dilectorum filiorum Fratrum Praedicatorum, et Minorum, nequiter vomuerunt. . . . Ad alia nihilominus prava et iniqua, in detractionem eorum, et suorum Ordinum derogationem, ora maliloqua relaxando. Cum igitur iidem Ordines fuerint dudum a Sede Apostolica, sicut sancti, clari, et conspicui approbati, ex quibus jam nonnulli Fratres ad supernam provecti patriam, in Sanctorum numero sunt adscripti . . . et duo magna luminaria in Ecclesia Dei luceant. . . ."—Const. *Non sine multa,* 30 mart. 1257—*Bull. Praed.* I, 334.

stated that the permission of the pastor was always required by a religious before he could preach or validly absolve a penitent.[17]

During subsequent pontificates, the privileges of the mendicants were extended or restricted, but the canonical atmosphere remained hazy and the parochial relationships were often stormy. Pope Clement IV (1265-1268) repeated and confirmed former privileges of the religious. Nevertheless, he restricted the power of religious confessors so that they could not absolve in cases which were reserved to the Holy See, to Legates of the Holy See, or to the local ordinaries.[18] Thus, the state of affairs continued to vacillate even to the time of the Constitution *Super cathedram* of Boniface VIII (1294-1303), which made a definite attempt to settle the disputes.[19]

---

[17] ". . . non poteratis praedicationis exercere officium, et confessiones audire sine sacerdotum parochialium licentia et assensu; Nos ad tollendam et confutandam assertionem huiusmodi . . . quod vos de licentia. . . . Legatorum sedis Apostolicae, vel Ordinariorum locorum, libere possitis praedicare populis, audire confessiones. . . ."—Const. *Cum olim,* 18 ian. 1259—*Bull. Praed.,* I, 369; Potthast, *Regesta,* n. 17452.

[18] "Nos ergo volentes assertionem tam temerariam penitus confutare, et elucidare in talibus veritatem, deliberatione provida, declaramus, quod, si vobis detur licentia, committatur, seu concedatur a Legatis predictae Sedis, aut Ordinariis locorum, nedum a Romano Pontifice, de quo procul dubio esset erroneum dubitare, an in omnes sine alicuius consensu, immo etiam invitis quibuslibet, huiusmodi possit concedere potestatem, populis, Legatis et Ordinariis subjectis eisdem, libere praedicare potestis, audire confessiones, et absolvere vobis confitentes, ac penitentias vobis confitentibus injungere salutares, aliorum inferiorum praelatorum . . . assensu nullatenus requisito, illis casibus exceptis, qui de jure, consuetudine, seu retentione, ab eis specialiter facta, Sedi, Legatis, et Ordinariis praedictis, specialiter relinquuntur, ad quos non licet vos manus extendere, nisi vobis specialiter committantur." —Const. *Quidem temere,* 20 iun. 1265—*Bull Praed.,* I, 455.

[19] "Scimus enim, et ex evidentia facti colligimus, quod non nisi in pacis tempore bene colitur pacis auctor, nec ignoramus quod dissensiones et scandala pravis actibus aditum praeparant, rancores et odia suscitant, et illicitis moribus ausum praebent."—c. 2, *de sepulturis,* III, 6, in Extravag. com.; Potthast, *Regesta,* n. 24913.

ARTICLE 2. THE CANONS OF THE GENERAL COUNCILS OF THE TWELFTH AND THIRTEENTH CENTURIES CONCERNING PAROCHIAL RELATIONS

Section 1. The First Lateran Council (1123)

On March 18, 1123, Pope Callistus II (1119-1124), convened the first general council to be held in the West—the I Lateran Council. The council gave general norms, during the course of its sessions, to govern the relations between the religious and the diocesan clergy. In the seventeenth canon of the council, an attempt was made to stem the possible encroachment of religious on the parochial rights of the pastors or the appropriation by them of the rights and privileges of the bishops. The canon strongly forbid abbots and monks to impose public penances, to visit the sick, to administer the last sacraments and to chant public masses. They were to look to the diocesan bishop in all matters involving the consecration of altars, chrism, holy oil and the ordination of their monks.[20] This statute, however, appears to have reference only to those Orders which the abbot himself could not confer. The abbot could confer minor Orders on his own subjects, as long as he was a priest and had received the abbatial benediction.[21] Although the choice of the ordaining bishop was restricted by this council, custom and indults often contravened this statute.[22]

The monastic clerics were forbidden to undertake the parochial ministry on their own authority and were ordered to respect the parochial rights and privileges of the diocesan clergy. According to canon 18 of this council, if a parish was to be consigned to them, the bishop would make this appointment and the incumbent priest would be responsible for the *cura animarum* to the bishop. The canon likewise reiterated the prohibition of earlier councils concerning the reception of tithes and churches from laymen without

---

[20] "Interdicimus etiam abbatibus et monachis publicas poenitentias dare, infirmos visitare, et unctiones facere, et publicas missas cantare. Chrisma et oleum, consecrationes altarium, ordinationes clericorum ab episcopis accipiant, in quorum parochiis manent."—c. 10, C. XVI, q. 1; Mansi, XXI, 285.

[21] Cf. Thomassinus, *Vetus et Nova Disciplina,* Pars I, lib. III, cap. 36, n. 16.

[22] *Glossa ordinaria* ad c. 3, *de temporibus ordinationem et qualitatibus ordinandorum,* I, 9, in Sexto, s.v. *indultum.*

the consent and will of the bishop.[23] Canon 19 of the council did not permit abbots and monks to acquire the possessions of churches and bishops through prescription of a thirty year period, and obliged them to continue to pay the taxes which monasteries and monastic churches had obliged them to pay from the time of Pope Gregory VII. It appears that this also bound those monasteries which were exempt to pay the annual pension to the bishop.[24]

Section 2. The Third Lateran Council (1179)

At the III Lateran Council, convoked by Pope Alexander III (1159-1181) in the year 1179, canon 9 lamented the state of church and monastic discipline. Religious, principally the Knights Templars and Hospitallers, were too frequently evading the episcopal authority by receiving churches from laymen. Likewise, they admitted to the sacraments and to ecclesiastical burial those who were excommunicated or interdicted. Too often, they appointed and removed priests from their churches without the knowledge and approval of the bishop. The abuses were the actions of the minority, but the council ordered them corrected and legislated penalties in canons 9, 14, 19 and 27 for those who were negligent in this matter.[25] The same canon stated that, unless the religious church was united *pleno jure* to the order or monastery, the religious superior was obliged to present the priest to the bishop for approval. The bishop was then capable of approving and appointing the priest to the secular parish, or he could disapprove of him and remove him at any time. The religious priest was

---

[23] Cf. Hardouin, IV (b), 1113.

[24] "Servitium quod monasteria aut eorum ecclesiae a tempore Gregorii Papae VII usque ad hoc tempus episcopis fecere, et nos concedimus. Possessiones ecclesiarum et episcoporum tricennales abbates vel monachos habere omnimodis prohibemus."—Hardouin, VIb, 1113.

[25] "Fratrum autem coepiscoporum nostrorum vehementi consequestione comperimus, quod fratres Templi et Hospitalis, alii quoque religiosae professionis, indulta sibi ab apostolica sede excedentes privilegia, contra episcopalem auctoritatem multa praesumant, . . . quod ecclesias recipiant de manibus laicorum, excommunicatos et interdictos ad ecclesiastica sacramenta et sepulturam admittant, in ecclesiis suis praeter eorum conscientiam et instituant et amoveant sacerdotes. . . ."—c. 3, X, *de privilegiis et excessibus privilegiatorum,* V, 33; Mansi, XXII, 223.

responsible to the bishop concerning the *cura animarum,* but responsible to the community in regard to temporalities.[26] This same provision was later repeated by the IV Lateran Council (1215) in its sixty-first canon.[27] It was the opinion of the Glossator that the bishop had no authority over a religious priest exercising the ministry in a parish *pleno jure* united to a religious community, but that the authority was in this instance the rightful prerogative of the religious superior or abbot.[28] Other commentators disagreed and supported the authority of the bishop even though the parish was united *pleno jure,* since, they reasoned, the bishop granted the *cura animarum* to the religious priest, and, therefore, he should have the right to appoint and remove him.[29] Finally, canon 10 stated that monks should not have any private property nor live apart from the monastery. They should not live alone in parishes, but should dwell with their brothers and not mingle among the externs.[30]

Section 3. The Fourth Lateran Council (1215)

The most important council of the Middle Ages, the IV Lateran Council, marked the zenith of ecclesiastical and papal power. It was convoked during the pontificate of Innocent III (1190-1216) and opened on November 11, 1215, in the Lateran Basilica. In its ninth and tenth canons, the bishops were strongly urged to instruct and minister to the faithful entrusted by God to their pastoral care. Canon 9 cautioned them to employ suitable men to minister to the sacramental life of the people and to preach to them by

---

[26] Cf. c. 3, X, *de privilegiis et excessibus privilegiatorum,* V, 33.

[27] Mansi, XXIV, 1049.

[28] *Glossa ordinaria* ad c. 3, X, *de privilegiis et excessibus privilegiatorum,* V, 33, s.v. *pleno iure.*

[29] Hostiensis, *Commentaria in Quinque Libros Decretalium* (3 vols., Venetiis, 1581), lib. III, tit. 37, *de cappellis monachorum et aliorum religiosorum,* c. 1, n. 1 (hereafter cited: *Commentaria*).

[30] "Monachi . . . non peculium permittantur habere, non singuli per villas et oppida, seu ad quascumque parochiales ponantur ecclesias; sed in maiori conventu, aut cum aliquibus fratribus maneant; nec soli inter saeculares homines spiritualium hostium conflictionem expectent."—c. 2, X, *de statu monachorum,* III, 35.

their word and example.[31] Since, as the council recognized, the bishops could not personally and adequately perform this ministry alone, they were instructed to provide a sufficient number of capable priests who were to preach, visit the people, instruct, administer the sacraments and care for other matters pertaining to the salvation of their souls.[32] Also because there was a general dearth of diocesan priests for the ministry, this decree of the council might well have been the basis for the extensive work of the religious, especially the mendicants, in assisting bishops in their pastoral work. Therefore, in a decretal letter of Innocent III, the monks were approved and encouraged to enter this type of parochial ministry. The pontiff stressed the fact that such a ministry, sharing in the parochial work of the bishops, was a privilege.[33] The Glossator gives the reason for calling it a privilege, namely that no one is able to exercise this ministry without being properly commissioned by ecclesiastical authority.[34]

The famous decree *Omnis utriusque sexus,* obliging all the faithful who attained the age of discretion to the annual confession and Easter communion, was contained in the twenty-first canon of

---

[31] ". . . districte praecipimus, ut pontifices huiusmodi civitatum sive dioecesum provideant viros idoneos, qui . . . divina officia illis celebrent et ecclesiastica sacramenta ministrent, instruendo eos verbo pariter et exemplo." —c. 14, X, *de officio iudicis ordinarii,* I, 31.

[32] ". . . quod episcopi propter occupationes multiplices, vel invaletudines corporales . . . per se ipsos non sufficiunt ministrare populo verbum Dei, . . . ut episcopi viros idoneos ad sanctae praedicationis officium salubriter exequendum assumat, potentes in opere et sermone, qui plebes sibi commissas vice ipsorum . . . solicite visitantes, eas verbo aedificent et exemplo, quibus ipsi, cum indeguerint, congrua necessaria ministrent, . . . Unde praecipimus . . . in . . . ecclesiis viros idoneos ordinaria, quos episcopi possint coadjutores et cooperatores habere, non solum in praedictionis officio, verum etiam in audiendis confessionibus et poenitentiis injungendis, ac ceteris quae ad salutem pertinent animarum."—c. 15, X, *de officio iudicis ordinarii,* I, 31.

[33] ". . . monachi possunt ad ecclesiarum parochialium regimen in presbyteros ordinari, ex quo debent praedicationis officium (quod privilegiatum est) exercere. . . ."—c. 5, X, *de statu monachorum et canonicorum regularium,* III, 35; Potthast, *Regesta,* n. 1329.

[34] "In hoc est privilegiatum officium praedicandi: quia nemo debet praedicare, nisi ei sit commissum ab episcopo loci, vel ab Apostolica sede et illi qui per electionem ad hoc eliguntur."—*Glossa ordinaria* ad c. 5, X, *de statu monachorum et canonicorum regularium,* III, 35, s.v. *privilegiatum.*

this council. This duty was to be fulfilled in the parish church before the *sacerdos proprius.* Therefore, only with the permission of the pastor and for a just cause could the faithful make their annual confession validly to another priest. Negligence could mean a prohibition to enter the church and the deprivation of Christian burial.[35]

This was ecumenical sanction to a practice already a part of the discipline of the Church for some time. Although, this was the first time the pastor was specifically mentioned, the discipline was foreshadowed by past legislation requiring the reception of Holy Communion at specified times.[36] Even in regard to confessional privileges of religious, received from the Holy See or the bishop, it was generally accepted that their exercise could in no way prejudice the rights of the pastor in the matter of the annual confession of his subjects.[37] Certainly, when religious were in charge of the parish, or were chaplains of religious oratories and equivalent to pastors, they would be the *proprii sacerdotes.* The religious residing there could fulfill their obligations before their own chaplains.

The legislation of the council was undoubtedly motivated by the fact that so many of the faithful were going to other confessors and thus were evading the customary practice of making their annual confessions in their own parishes. Indeed, it was not unknown that pastors would induce another's parishioners to make their Easter Communion at their church and to give them the

[35] "Omnis utriusque sexus fidelis, postquam ad annos discretionis pervenerit, omnia sua solus peccata confiteatur fideliter, saltem semel in anno, proprio sacerdoti, . . . suscipiens reverenter ad minus in Pascha Eucharistiae sacramentum; . . . alioquin et vivens ab ingressu ecclesiae arceatur, et moriens Christiana careat sepultura. . . . Si quis autem alieno sacerdoti voluerit justa de causa sua confiteri peccata, licentiam prius postulet et obtineat a proprio sacerdoti, cum aliter ille ipse non possit solvere, vel ligare."—c. 12, X, *de poenitentiis et remissionibus,* V, 38; Mansi, XXII, 1007.

[36] Cf. cc. 1, 17, 19 D. II, *de consecratione.*

[37] ". . . privilegium non aequiparat eos illis, qui a populo sunt electi, vel illis qui ab episcopo populo praeficiuntur, et dat eis solam executionem, et ita necessaria est adhuc licentia proprii sacerdotis, ut hic dicitur. . . . Nec Papa per talem indulgentiam intendit praeiudicare proprio sacerdoti."—*Glossa ordinaria* ad c. 12, X, *de poenitentiis et remissionibus,* V, 38, s.v. *alieno sacerdoti.*

customary tithes presented to the pastor on this occasion. Religious as well as diocesan priests were involved in such practices.[38]

In its fifty-sixth canon, the council forbade both secular and religious clerics to be involved in any contracts concerning the payment of tithes and the choice of burial that would be prejudicial to parochial churches.[39] Canon fifty-seven stated that only members of the religious community and benefactors, who had willed their possessions to the religious during their lifetime and retained only the usufruct, could be buried by the religious during an interdict. Likewise, the canon permitted religious who had entered an interdicted territory to open only a single church and that only for a year.[40]

Abbots were forbidden to interfere in matters pertaining to the exclusive jurisdiction of the bishops. Many complaints came from the bishops concerning the grave excesses of some of these abbots who had extended their sphere of activity far beyond the monastery and into those things that concerned the episcopal office. They took it upon themselves to decide marriage cases, impose public penances, to grant indulgences and other such things.[41].

Finally, canon sixty-one of the council repeated regulations contained in canon nine of the III Lateran Council concerning lay investiture and the presentation of religious priests to the bishop by the religious superior when his priests were destined for parish

---

[38] Cf. c. 12, X, *de poenitentiis et remissionibus,* V, 38; Schroeder, *Disciplinary Decrees,* p. 262.

[39] "Plerique, sicut accepimus, regulares et clerici saeculares, interdum cum vel domos locant, vel feuda concedunt, in praejudicium parochialium ecclesiarum pactum adjiciunt ut conductores et feudatarii decimas eis solvant, et apud eosdem eligant sepulturam. Cum autem id de avaritiae radice procedat, pactum huiusmodi penitus reprobamus; statuentes, ut quidquid fuerit occasione huiusmodi pacti perceptum, ecclesiae parochiali reddatur."—c. 7, X, *de pactis,* I, 35.

[40] Cf. c. 24, X, *de privilegiis,* V, 33; Mansi, XXII, 1043.

[41] ". . . de diversis mundi partibus episcoporum querelis, intelleximus graves et grandes quorumdam abbatum exessus, qui suis finibus non contenti, manus ad ea, quae sunt episcopalis dignitatis extendunt, de causiis matrimonalibus cognoscendo, injungendo publicas poenitentias, concedendo etiam indulgentiarum litteras, et similia. . . ."—c. 12, X, *de excessibus praelatorum et subditorum,* V, 31.

work.[42] The priest had to be presented to the bishop unless he was to serve in a church united *pleno jure* to the monastery. When assigned to a church other than *pleno jure,* the religious priest had to report to the bishop on all matters pertaining to the *cura animarum,* but to the abbot on matters related to the temporal administration of the parish. These priests had to be known for their uprightness and ability, or recommended by the bishop himself.[43]

The question of the propriety of monks undertaking the *cura animarum* was still, at this time, being disputed, despite a wealth of former legislation at least condoning the practice. Pope Urban III (1088-1099) seems to have generally preferred that monks not be involved with parochial work, but that a chaplain be appointed by the bishop for the care of their churches.[44] The Third Lateran Council (1179), however, did permit monks to enter parish work as long as they were living with their religious brothers and were completely subject to the bishop in their ministry and in all matters pertaining to the *cura animarum.*[45] Granting this, the juridical foundation for this parochial ministry by the monastic groups was commented on by canonists and authors. Some thought the monks were permitted to undertake such work because the common law of the Church sanctioned it,[46] and others believed that a general dispensation was granted to them so that they might assist in the parochial life of the Church.[47]

Finally, the Fathers of the council in canon thirteen ordered all who wished to enter the religious life to select either an order

---

[42] Cf. c. 3, X, *de privilegiis et excessibus privilegiatorum,* V, 33.

[43] ". . . ne quilibet regulares ecclesias, seu decimas, sine consensu episcoporum de manu praesumant recipere laicali; . . . quatenus in ecclesiis, quae ad ipsos pleno jure non pertinent, juxta ejusdem statuta concilii, episcopis instituendos presbyteros representent, ut illis de plebis cura respondeant; . . ."—c. 31, X, *de praebendis et dignitatibus,* III, 5.

[44] C. 1, X, *de cappellis monachorum et aliorum religiorum,* III, 37 [Council of Clermont (1095)]; Jaffé, nn. 5886-5887.

[45] C. 2, X, *de statu monachorum et canonicorum regularium,* III, 35.

[46] Cf. Hostiensis, *Commentaria,* III, 35, *de statu monachorum et canonicorum regularium,* c. 5, n. 8.

[47] Cf. *Glossa ordinaria* ad c. 5, X, *de statu monachorum et canonicorum regularium,* III, 35, s.v. *regimen in presbyteros.*

or a monastic rule which had been already approved. There had been too many haphazardly establishing religious communities and attempting to receive the approval of the Holy See. Already there appeared to be a sufficient enough number and forms of the religious life approved by the Church. The canon, therefore, forbid the founding of new groups after the promulgation of its decree.[48]

Section 4. The Second Council of Lyons (1274)

The II Council of Lyons, under Pope Gregory X (1272-1276), in its twenty-third canon, not only put into effect the thirteenth canon of the IV Lateran Council, but suppressed all religious foundations established in contravention of the decree. Also, all orders which had been approved by the bishop were now suppressed and all juridical effects following the profession of vows in these communities were thereby vitiated. Henceforth, only the Holy See could approve a new religious foundation. It was no longer sufficient that the local bishops' consent be considered enough for approval of the rule.[49] The members of the suppressed orders, nevertheless, could remain in them if they wished, but the institute could accept no new members. Neither were the members able to preach to those outside their dying order, nor could they hear confessions, nor function at funerals. The Franciscans and Dominicans were explicitly excluded from this condemnation to a sure but slow death. Likewise, the Carmelites and Augustinians were permitted to remain in their then present state until considered for approval or eventual suppression. Members of the suppressed communities were permitted to transfer individually, but not in a group, to other approved communities.[50]

The conflicts between the religious and the secular clergy had

---

[48] "Ne nimia religionum diversitas gravem in ecclesia Dei confusionem inducat, firmiter prohibemus, ne quis de cetero novam religionem inveniat, sed quicumque voluerit ad religionem converti, unam de approbatis assumat. Similiter qui voluerit religiosam domum fundare de novo, regulam et institutionem accipiat de religionibus approbatis."—c. 9, X, *de religiosis domibus,* III, 36; Mansi, XXII, 1002.

[49] Cf. Bouix, *Tractatus de Jure Regularium* (2 vols., Parisiis, 1857), I, 291.

[50] Cf. c. un., *de religiosis domibus,* III, 17, in VI.

been smoldering and flaring up spasmodically. The bishops desired the complete elimination of as many of the orders as could be obtained, and the abrogation of all their privileges. The prohibition against the founding of new institutes was only a concession by the pontiff which the expediency of that particular time demanded. However, due to the services rendered the Church by the religious orders, especially their fidelity and allegiance to the Roman Pontiffs, the desires of the prelates were ultimately ineffectual.[51] Nevertheless, this matter was considered again in future Pontificates and the privileges of religious were under fire.

ARTICLE 3. THE PROVISIONS OF THE CONSTITUTION *Super Cathedram* OF BONIFACE VIII (1300) AND THE COUNCIL OF VIENNE (1311-1314)

The parochial conflicts between the bishops and prelates, on the one hand, and the religious orders, on the other, were one of the prominent issues at this time. Pontiffs and councils made frequent and sincere, if not always wise, attempts to promote harmony between these two groups in the Church, well aware of the genuine harm that would befall the Church if the conflicts were not checked. The excesses of both groups in this dispute had to be adequately restrained without undermining or abrogating the rights and privileges of either.

At this particular time, the pontiffs were lamenting the oppression of the religious orders by the prelates. The unreasonable and unjust acts of some of the latter were laid bare to serve as a rebuke to them. Religious were without reason often punished with suspension, excommunication, seizure and incarceration. If they did not obey unjust and unauthorized commands, they would be placed under interdict. Religious property was impounded and unusual and excessive exactions imposed upon them. Burdensome taxes and obligations became commonplace. Such was the tenor of the charges made known by the Roman Pontiffs and, yet, there remained a host of other injustices.[52]

---

[51] Cf. Schroeder, *Disciplinary Decrees,* pp. 352-353.

[52] Cf. c. un., *de excessibus praelatorum,* V, 6, in Clem; cc. 16, 17, X, *de excessibus praelatorum,* V, 31.

On February 18, 1300, Pope Boniface VIII (1294-1303) issued his Constitution *Super cathedram* with the intention of completely removing and eradicating the scandalous discord that existed between the religious clergy and the diocesan clergy. He attempted to clarify and smooth the relations between them by concerning himself with the issues that occasioned some of the conflicts. Therefore the constitution considered specifically preaching, burial rights and confessional privileges. Any privileges that militated against the provisions of the decree were automatically revoked.[53] The desired effects, however, were not accomplished and the constitution was entirely abrogated by his successor, Pope Benedict XI (1303-1305), through the Constitution *Inter cunctas* of February 17, 1304. It seems that the intention of Pope Benedict was to remove all the limitations placed by the former constitution on the exercise of papal privileges.[54]

When the bishops gathered together at the Council of Vienne, on October 1, 1311, they persisted in their demands that the provisions of the decretal *Super cathedram* be completely restored. Pope Clement V (1305-1314) acquiesced to their forceful insistence, but not without some reluctance in permitting the provisions of the constitution to remain completely unchanged. He considered that some of these prescriptions were far too stringent in practice, especially those concerning the parochial portion, which

[53] ". . . circa id tamen ferventibus votis intendimus, . . . ac operosae studium sollicitudinis impertimur, ut ad divini nominis gloriam, exaltationem catholicae fidei, et profectum fidelium animarum . . . inter ecclesiarum antistites . . . ceterasque personas, quas ordo clericalis includit, pacis tranquillitas vigeat, fervor caritatis exaestuet, invalescat concordiae unitas, animorum identitas perseveret. Scimus enim . . . quod dissensiones et scandala pravis actibus aditum praeparant, rancores et odia suscitant, et illicitis moribus ausum praebent . . inter praelatos . . . ac clericos parochialem ecclesiarum . . . ex una parte, et praedictorum et minorum ordinum fratres ex altera . . . gravis et periculosa discordia exstitit suscitata super praedicationibus fidelium . . . eorum confessionibus audiendis et . . . sepulturam."—c. 2, *de sepulturis,* III, 6, in Extravag. com.

[54] "Sed pro ea quam intendebat quiete, turbatio nata est, . . . Ideoque cupientes, ut ipsi gregi cura nostra eo plenior impedatur, quo amplior in agro Domini operariorum numerus operetur, super egenum intendentes et pauperem, ac novitatem per eandem constitutionem inductam. . . ." c. 1, *de privilegiis,* V, 7, in Extravag. com.; Potthast, *Regesta,* n. 25370.

made it extremely difficult for the religious clergy to support themselves and their institute adequately. Three times the pontiff begged the bishops to permit him to mitigate those provisions which had proved themselves too harsh. Nevertheless, no change would be tolerated by them. The constitution was restored by Clement to its original form. Therefore, at the third session of the council, Clement issued his own constitution, *Dudum,* on May 6, 1312, formally renewing the defunct decree of Boniface VIII.[55]

Section 1. Preaching by the Religious Clergy

One of the outstanding characteristics of the mendicant apostolate from its inception was a special dedication to preaching the word of God, a new activity for the religious orders. The monastic orders had always shied away from all forms of the active life, both in their rule and in practice. Individuals and the necessity of the times had more than once taken the monks outside the cloister. At other times they were forbidden to engage in such activities. Pope Alexander II (1061-1073) had restricted the preaching of monks to their monasteries.[56] A little over a century later, however, the pontiffs approved and encouraged this apostolate of preaching by the Friars when they recognized and approved of their foundations.[57] The very title of the Dominicans, the Order of Preachers, evidences the importance of this apostolate to their community. The Dominicans and Franciscans, and later other orders, received many privileges to assist them in carrying out this mission fruitfully. Once they had been properly commissioned by their founder, the Friars were approved to preach everywhere by the Holy See. These concessions offended the

[55] "Dudum a Bonifacio papa VIII praedecessore nostro infra scripta edita decretali, Benedictus papa XI praedecessor noster aliam illius revocatoriam promulgavit, quae quia, ut probavit effectus, nedum pacis ab auctore ipsius speratae fructum non attulit, quin immo discordiae, pro qua sedanda processerat, fomentum non modicum ministravit, nos eam omnino cassantes, aliam a praefato Bonifacio editam sacro instante et approbante concilio innovamus. . . ."—c. 2, *de sepulturis,* III, 7, in Clem.; Potthast, *Regesta,* n. 24913; cf. Schroeder, *Disciplinary Decrees,* pp. 382-382.

[56] Cf. c. 11, C. XVI, q. 1; MPL, CXVI, 363.

[57] Cf. const. *Religiosam vitam* of Honorius III (1216-1227), 22 dec. 1216 —*Bull. Praed.,* I, 2-4; Potthast, *Regesta,* n. 5403.

secular clergy and made them suspicious of the religious who were preaching freely throughout their parishes and dioceses.

Consequently, the Constitution *Super cathedram* considered the situation and required that religious preachers receive the permission of the local ordinary in certain instances, although this did not affect their many other extensive privileges. They were permitted to preach, by papal authority, in their own churches and oratories, not only to the lay people, but also to the clergy as well. They were not to preach in their own churches when the local prelates wished to preach or have someone preach in their name. However, the prelates could give the mendicants permission to preach even in this case. Although the religious were accustomed to preach in religious houses of study to the secular clergy on certain feast days and at funerals, they were obliged to refrain from this when the prelates convoked clerical gatherings. Finally, the religious were not to dare to preach in the parish churches of the secular clergy without receiving the proper permission, or unless they were invited to do so by the bishop or higher prelate.[58]

The provisions of this constitution were later applied also to the Augustinians and Carmelites by the Constitution *Frequentes* of Pope John XXII (1316-1334). Transgressors were to be punished with severe penalties, even with *ipso facto* excommunication.[59]

Section 2. Religious Confessors

The IV Lateran Council (1215) had made the pastor the exclusive confessor for his parishioners at least once a year.[60] Religious, unless they were pastors of a parish, were not to be considered equally competent concerning this obligation without the permission of the proper pastor.[61] The mendicants were, never-

---

[58] Cf. c. 2, *de sepulturis,* III, 7, in Clem.

[59] Cf. c. 3, *de poenis,* V, 8, in Clem.

[60] "Omnis . . . postquam ad annos discretionis pervenerit, omnia sua solus peccata confiteatur fideliter, saltem semel in anno, proprio sacerdoti. . . ." —c. 12, *de poenitentiis et remissionibus,* X, V, 38.

[61] ". . . privilegium non aequiparet eos illis . . . necessaria est adhuc licentia proprii sacerdotis, . . ."—*Glossa ordinaria* ad c. 12, X, *de penitentiis et remissionibus,* V, 38, s.v. *alieno sacerdoti.*

theless, given generous and extensive grants of jurisdiction by the pontiffs to absolve penitents wherever their apostolate might take them.[62] The Friars freely exercised these jurisdictional privileges with few limitations. They absolved from reserved cases, since no limitation was placed on their extensive privileges and because, at times, they had received express permission to do so.[63] The use of these privileges was called an "abuse." Therefore, many of the prelates desired their complete revocation.

Pope Benedict XI (1303-1305) revoked the constitution of Boniface VIII, *Super cathedram,* and stated that if the religious confessor was approved by his own superior, he could absolve the faithful anywhere without being presented to the bishop for approval by him.[64] When, however, Clement V restored the provisions of *Super cathedram,* the constitution required a religious priest to receive the approbation of the bishop for the confessions of the faithful. These confessors were to be priests of virtue and fitted for this work. The number selected were to be in proportion to the number of faithful and clergy to be served. If religious priests presented to the bishop were not acceptable to him, others could be similarly presented by their religious superior. If the necessary faculties were again refused, then the religious would be automatically approved and receive jurisdiction to freely and licitly hear the confessions of the faithful by an act of papal power. It was not, however, the intention of the constitution to grant more extensive jurisdiction than was conceded by law to the diocesan clergy. Nevertheless, the prelates were free to suggest that more extensive jurisdiction be granted to religious confessors ministering in their dioceses.[65]

---

[62] ". . . cum ipsis auctoritate nostra liceat confessiones audire, ac poenitentas iniungere, . . ."—const. *Quoniam* of Gregory IX, 10 maii 1227—*Bull. Praed.,* I, 19.

[63] Cf. const. *Animarum salute,* 21 mart. 1233—Potthast, *Regesta,* nn. 9130, 9184, 9196.

[64] ". . . praecipimus, ut provinciales priores . . . per se vel per alios verbo vel scripto eis significent, se fratres ad huiusmodi confessionum audiendarum et poenitentiarum injungendarum officium elegisse, et non nominando, . . ." —const. *Inter cunctas,* 17 febr. 1304—c. 1, *de privilegiis,* V, 7, in Extravag. com.; Potthast, *Regesta,* n. 25370.

[65] C. 2, *de sepulturis,* III, 7, in Clem.

In a case where the prelates had refused confessional jurisdiction to the second group of religious priests presented by the superior, they would, indeed, receive faculties *ipso facto* from the Holy See. It appears, however, that the permission of the religious superior was required to validly exercise this jurisdiction, since it was not given to the individual religious, but to the order.[66] Furthermore, if a religious confessor absolved from reserved cases, when he had neither the faculties nor the privilege to do so, he would incur *ipso facto* excommunication.[67]

Section 3. The Administration of the Sacraments, Burial Rights and the Parochial Portion

The Council of Vienne decreed, repeating the legislation of the decretal *Super cathedram,* that the Friars had the privilege of free burial, namely, the right to bury all who desired to be buried in their churches and cemeteries. Since, however, the parish churches and clergy possessed this right by law, as well as to preach and hear the confessions of the faithful, the Friars were obliged by the Holy See to render the "parochial portion" when they were required to do so. This consisted in the payment of one-fourth of the income accruing from funerals and bequests, even though not established by former law or custom. This was to be understood in a strict sense, so that no more could be asked or demanded by the parochial clergy. The Friars were to pay only the fixed amount.[68]

Pope Clement V, at the same council, decreed that the religious

[66] "Particulares religiosi non possunt muneri audiendi confessiones fidelium sese sponte sua ingerere sed debent ad hoc habere consensum superiorum suorum; alias collatae ab ipsis absolutiones erunt invalidae, quia hoc privilegium datum est ipsis dependenter a voluntate superiorum, . . ."—Schmalzgrueber, *Ius Ecclesiasticum,* lib. V, tit. 38, n. 44.

[67] C. 1, *de privilegiis et excessibus privilegiatorum,* V, 7, in Clem.

[68] ". . . ut fratres dictorum ordinum in ecclesiis vel locis suis ubi libet constitutis liberam (ut sequitur) habeant sepulturam. . . . Verum ne parochiales ecclesiae et ipsarum curati sive rectores, qui ministrare habent ecclesiastica sacramenta, quibus noscitur de iure competere, praedicare seu proponere verbum Dei, et confessionis audire fidelium . . . quarta sive canonica portio dari. . . ."—c. 2, *de sepulturis,* III, 7, in Clem.

who did not acknowledge the rights and privileges of the pastor and who presumptuously administered the last sacraments, Holy Communion, or the sacrament of marriage, without the permission of the pastor, would incur the penalty of excommunication. Nevertheless, if the religious had been given permission by the Holy See to administer the sacraments to the domestics and the poor in their hospitals, this provision did not apply.[69]

The pontiff severely criticized the oppressive measures of prelates who abused the rights and privileges of religious. He listed charges concerning episcopal abuses and demanded their cessation. The list included thirty complaints, numbered among which were: the unjust incarceration of exempt religious, the severe penalizing of laymen and clerics who assisted the religious or attended their religious functions, the unreasonable prohibitions against religious chaplains concerning the celebrating of religious services for their parishioners in churches legally belonging to the orders, the excommunication, suspension and seizure of monks and secular clerics who were in the service of monasteries, unwarrantedly demanding obedience of exempt religious and then interdicting them for not obeying, the imposition of excessive taxes and burdens on parish churches of religious, the constant refusal of bishops to ordain worthy candidates in religious orders, the appropriation of their rights and the unjust seizure of their property, revenues and benefices.[70]

[69] "Religiosi, qui clericis, aut laicis sacramentum unctionis extremae, vel eucharistiae ministrare, matrimoniane solemnizare, non habita super his parochialis presbyteri licentia speciali . . . excommunicationis incurrant sententiam ipso facto, per sedem apostolicam dumtaxat absolvendi. . . . Sane, religiosis illis, quibus est ab apostolica sede consessum, ut familiaribus suis domesticis, aut pauperibus in hospitalibus suis degentibus, sacramenta possint ecclesiastica ministrare, nullum ex praemissis volumus quo ad hoc praejudicium generari."—c. 1, *de privilegiis et excessibus privilegiatorum,* V, 7, in Clem.

[70] "Frequens et assidua nos quorundam religiosorum querela circumstrepit, quod plerique episcopi, et eorum superiores, ac ceteri ecclesiarum praelati, ipsorum religiosorum quietem injuste in subsequentibus multipliciter inquietant. Quidam enim exemptos capiunt, et incarcerant, in casibus non concessis a jure. Quidam per gravium interminationem poenarum impediunt . . . neve aliqui Missas eorum audiant . . . molentes in molendis . . . vel alios qualitercumque contrahentes et participantes cum ipsis suspendunt,

Schroeder states that this decree was probably read at the third session of the Council of Vienne, but not included in its canons because it was not submitted to a vote and did not have the usual formula attached to it, namely, *sacro approbante concilio.* Later, it was included in the *Clementinae* as promulgated by Pope John XXII. He notes, also, the strange fact that Pope Clement added no sanctions for failure to observe its provisions, unlike the severe penalties that would be inflicted on or incurred by the religious for their excesses, which were often less reprehensible than those of the prelates listed in the present decree.[71]

Religious had long enjoyed the use of their own churches and oratories. They were not obliged to leave their monasteries and convents to go to the divine services in the parish churches, although some had desired that this be the rule at one time or another.[72] When, however, it became a common practice to admit lay people to their churches, many councils of the Middle Ages required the faithful to attend their parish churches on certain feast days and on the Sundays throughout the year. Lay people were often only tolerated by the religious in their chapels and oratories. Consequently, they were not disappointed at the enactment of legislation restricting this practice. At the same time, particular laws usually requested the religious, unless they were in charge of a parish church, not to admit people on stated days and to schedule services for an hour that would not conflict with those being held in the parish churches.[73] At the time of the Council

intedicunt et excommunicant absque causa rationabili pro libito voluntatis, bona illorum interdum nihilominus illicite occupantes . . . Quidam praeterea cappellanos in ecclesiis . . . licet nulla causa subsit legitima, celebrare non sinunt, nec ministrare parochianis ecclesiastica sacramenta. Nonnulli etiam indebite abbates, monachos, et conversos exemptos . . . suspendunt, excommunicant, capiunt, et incarcerant, ac loca et ecclesias interdicunt ipsorum."—c. un., *de excessibus praelatorum,* V, 6, in Clem.

[71] Cf. *Disciplinary Decrees,* pp. 431-434; cc. 16, 17, *de excessibus praelatorum,* V, 31; c. 1, *de privilegiis et excessibus privilegitorum,* V, 7, in Clem; c. 3, *de poenis,* V, 8, in Chem.

[72] Cf. const. *Nimis iniqua,* 17 sept. 1245—*Bull. Praed.,* I, 155; c. 16, X, *de excessibus praelatorum,* V, 31.

[73] ". . . districtius inhibemus, ne religiosi in ecclesiis suis aut cappellis eos diebus Dominicis solemnitatibus praecipuis recipiant ad Divina; nec horis

of Vienne, Pope Clement V forbid the Franciscans to permit members of their third orders to enter their churches for divine services during the course of an interdict. This had caused a certain amount of scandal and disrespect for censures and penalties of the Church. Contravention of this decree brought serious penalties on the offenders.[74]

The Constitution *Super cathedram* ended with an exhortation to the prelates and the parochial clergy to hold the members of the religious orders in high esteem, not treating them harshly, but agreeably and generously. They were encouraged to enlist them as collaborators in the apostolate, especially in that of preaching the word of God. The parochial clergy as well as the religious clergy were common participants in the same apostolate and were to work for the good of the Church.[75]

ARTICLE 4. LEGISLATION SUBSEQUENT TO THE COUNCIL OF VIENNE (1311-1314) AND THE PROVISIONS OF THE FIFTH LATERAN COUNCIL (1512-1517)

The provisions of the Constitution *Super cathedram* were ordered to be strictly observed and enforced by Pope John XXII (1316-1334). The privileges and rights of both the diocesan and the religious clergy were to be mutually respected and even minor transgressions were to be proportionately punished.[76] He con-

illis, in suis locis populo publice praedicent, quibus in parochiis Missarum solemnia celebrantur." [Canon 15 of the Council of Arles (1260)]—Mansi, XXIII, 1010.

[74] ". . . quod religiosi viri fratres minores in suis recipiunt ecclesiis ad audienda divina officia tempore interdicti, fratres et sorores de ordine tertio (quem Beatus Franciscus instituit) exsistentes, qui contenentes seu de poenitentia noncupantur, scandalum aliorum. . . . Quod si fecerint, eo ipso excommunicationis sententiae se noverint subiacere . . ."—c. 3, *de sententia excommunicationis,* V, 10, in Clem.

[75] "Ceterum universos ecclesiarum praelatos . . . ac sacerdotes parochiales . . . rogamus et hortamur attente . . . fratribus ipsis . . . sed potius favorabiles, propitios, ac benignos, piaque munificentia liberales se studeant exhibere, sic eos in praedicationis officio et propositionibus Verbi Dei, ac in omnibus aliis supra dictis tamquam cooperatores eorum idoneos, et laborum suorum participes prompta benignitate recipiant, ac affectuose admittere non omittant, . . ."—c. 2, *de sepulturis,* III, 7, in Clem.

[76] Cf. c. un., *de iudiciis,* II, 1, in Extravag. com.

demned as false, erroneous and contrary to Catholic teaching, the propositions of John de Polliaco (+ 1322), Doctor of Theology at the University of Paris, concerning the confessional faculties of the religious and the power of the Roman Pontiff. De Polliaco claimed that all confessions heard by the religious confessors, who had received general permission and faculties through a special grant of the Roman Pontiff were invalid and had to be resubmitted by the penitents to their proper pastor for valid absolution. He had based his conclusions on a false interpretation of the decree *Omnes utriusque sexus* of the IV Lateran Council concerning the obligation of the annual confession to the *sacerdos proprius.*[77] Likewise, he questioned the very authority of the Roman Pontiff to grant such a general permission and concession of jurisdiction. Hence Pope John XXII condemned these false teachings in his decree *Vas electionis* issued on the twenty-first day of July in the year 1321.[78] This condemnation was later repeated by Pope Eugene IV (1431-1447).[79] Also, Pope John XXII finally approved and extended the ministry privileges to the Augustinians and Carmelite Fathers.[80]

When the Council of Constance was opened on November 5, 1414, during the "Western Schism," its first canon attempted to restrict all exemptions granted to the religious. These exemptions were considered to be derogatory to the jurisdiction of the local ordinaries. Therefore, all exemptions from the episcopal jurisdiction which were granted since the death of Pope Gregory XI to

---

[77] Cf. c. 12, X, *de poenitentiis et remissionibus,* V, 38.

[78] ". . . quod illi qui praedictis fratibus confitentur, non magis teneantur eadem peccata confiteri iterum, quam si ea alias confessi fuissent eorum proprio sacerdoti juxta consilium generale, . . ."—c. 2, *de hereticis,* V, 3, in Extravag. com.

[79] Cf. const. *Gregis nobis,* 16 ian. 1446—*Bull. Praed.,* III, 217; Denziger-Bannwart-Umberg, *Enchiridion Symbolorum Definitionum, Declarationum de Rebus Fidei et Morum* (22-23 ed., Friburgi-Brisgoviae: Herder, 1947), n. 492.

[80] ". . . Eremitarum Sancti Augustini et Carmelitarum ordinum fratribus, in cuius ordinis dictorum Eremitarum personis . . . per omnia voluit postmodum integraliter et inconcusse servari, et ad quem praedictorum Carmelitarum fratrum ordinem nos subsequenter constitutionem eandem quoad omnia in ea contenta duximus extendendam, . . ." const. *Frequentes* 23 ian. 1327—c. un, *de iudiciis,* II, 1, in Extravag. com.

churches, monasteries, benefices, convents, priories and other places, were completely revoked by the Council. Those exemptions that were granted before this time were not affected by the decree. Also, the constitution intended that exemptions would be highly restricted and reluctantly granted thereafter.[81]

Pope Sixtus IV (1471-1484), in his bull *Regimini universalis,* confirmed and added many privileges to the religious orders.[82] Also, in his decree *Vices illius* of the seventeenth of June, 1478, Pope Sixtus again concerned himself with parochial discord existing between the mendicants and the parochial rectors, this time in Germany. The decree demanded that both groups cease these disputes. The parish clergy was not to impute heretical teaching to the religious, who were illuminating and presenting the truths of the Faith, nor were the religious to tell the people that they were in no manner obliged to hear Mass in their own parishes on Sundays and Feast Days. However, the Roman Pontiff did state that the faithful were free to attend Mass elsewhere as long as they had a reasonable cause. Both groups were warned not to induce the people to select their churches for ecclesiastical burial. The mendicants likewise were warned not to preach that parishioners need not consider themselves obliged to make their Easter confession to their proper priests. The secular clergy were reminded to respect the rights and privileges of the religious concerning confessional practices. Both were to observe the accepted customs in regard to preaching, chanting the divine office and the ringing of the church bells and the time for performing these functions. Neither group was to deviate from the customary time, unless the consent of the interested party was received.[83]

---

[81] Cf. Schroeder, *Disciplinary Decrees,* pp. 453 ff.

[82] Const. 31 aug. 1474—*Bullarium Franciscanum* (Nova Series, Prope Florentiam, Ex Typographia Collegiii S. Bonaventurae, Vol. III, 1949, collegit et edidit, Fr. Joseph M. Pou Y. Marti, O.F.M.), III, 626, pp. 266-273 (hereafter cited: *Bull. Fran.*).

[83] ". . . mandavimus . . . videlicet quod ipsi parochiani sacerdotes de cetero non dicant a Mendicantibus haereses processisse, cum in veritate fides nostra sit illuminata, et ecclesia exaltata per eosdem, et praesertim per ordines Praedicatorum, et Minorum, ut jura testantur. Quodque, fratres Mendicantes non praedicent, populos parochianos non teneri audire Missam in eorum parochiis diebus festivis et dominicis, cum jure sit cautum, illis diebus

During his pontificate, Pope Leo X (1513-1521) assured the faithful, mindful of their tender consciousness, that they did satisfy their obligations to attend Mass on Sundays and Holy Days of obligation when they assisted at Mass celebrated in the churches of religious. This was promulgated in his decree *Intelleximus* of November 13, 1517, and was a definite and radical change from the tenor of former law demanding attendance at the parochial church on such days.[84] Also, by the time of his pontificate, the communication of privileges between the religious orders was an approved and established practice.[85] Pope Sixtus IV had confirmed and extended the privileges of the Franciscans to other orders,

---

parochianos teneri audire Missam in eorum parochiali ecclesia, nisi forsan ex honesta causa ab ipsa ecclesia se absentarent. Quodque etiam nec fratres, nec curati inducant aliquo modo laicos ad eligendum sepulturam apud eos, et bene caveant propter poenas, quas imponunt canones, cum sit libera. Quod etiam ipsi Mendicantes desistant praedicare, quod parochiani non sint obligati saltem in Paschate, proprio confiteri sacerdoti, quia de jure tenetur parochianus saltem in Paschate proprio confiteri sacerdoti. Per hoc tamen ipsi fratres Mendicantes non censeantur exclusi, quo minus secundum juris communis et privilegiorum eisdem concessorum dispositionem, confessiones audire, et poenitentias injungere valeant. Quod etiam de cetero inter ipsos fratres Mendicantes et curatos quo ad effectum praedicandi, horas cantandi, et campanas pulsandi, servetur consuetudo antiqua, . . ."—c. 2, *de treuga et pace,* I, 9, in Extravag. com.

[84] "Intelleximus quosdam in dubium revocare, et perinde timoratis conscientiis scrupulum iniicere, si Christifideles, qui Dominicis, et Festis diebus extra Ecclesias suas Parochiales, Missas audiunt in Ecclesiis Fratrum Ord. Mendicantium, Ecclesiae praecepto de Missa audienda satisfaciat. Nos enim . . . auctoritate Apost. tenore praesentium notum facimus, omnes Christifideles utriusque sexus (qui non contempto proprio sacerdote Parochiali) in Ecclesiis Fratrum Ordinum Mendicantium, Dominicis, et Festis diebus Missas audiunt, satisfacere praecepto Ecclesiae de Missa audienda, nec in aliquam labem mortalis peccati poenamve incurrere."—*Codicis Iuris Canonici Fontes* (cura Emi. Petri Card. Gasparii editi., 9 vols., Romae [postea Civitate Vaticana]; Typis Polyglottis Vaticanis, 1923-1938. [Vols. VII-IX ed. cura et studio Emi. Iustiniani Card Serédi.]), n. 73 (hereafter cited: *Fontes*).

[85] Cf. A. Vasto, *De Communicatione Privilegiorum praesertim inter Religiones* (Schola Iuris Canonici Pontificiae Universitates Gregorianae, Aquilae in Vestines-Italia, 1936), p. 14 (hereafter cited: *De Communicatione*).

by his bull *Regimin universalis* on August 31, 1474.[86] Such extension of privileges was repeated by other pontiffs, such as Pope Julius II (1503-1513) in his decree *"Alias ad supplicationem"* of June 1, 1509,[87] and, therefore, it is little wonder that this matter would be brought up by those gathered at the Fifth Lateran Council (1512-1517) and attempts made to curtail it.

At the time of the convocation of the V Lateran Council, there was genuine need for a serious reformation in the Church. The Protestant revolt was imminent and the discipline of the clergy was at a low ebb. Nevertheless, Pope Leo X was a weak and troubled pontiff and he found it easier to cater to a worldly and selfish gathering of prelates who ignored the scandalous practices of the times and saw no need for a reform except in the religious orders. The privileges of the religious presented an ever growing obstacle to the increasing sources of revenue for the prelates. They urged the pontiff to revoke entirely the privileges of the religious, especially those of the mendicants, and to subject them directly to the common law and the authority of the local bishop. The rights of the religious were defended by the superiors general of the Dominicans and the Augustinians—the famous Cajetan and Aegidus of Viterbo.[88]

In the eleventh session of the council, Pope Leo X issued the bull *Dum intra* which was concerned directly with the controversies between the prelates and the religious communities. It applied to all religious privileges, but those which were not expressly mentioned remained unchanged.[89] The constitution decreed many things concerning the mutual relations of the two groups involved. The provisions pertained to the parishes in charge

---

[86] Cf. *Bull. Fran.*, III, 266-276.

[87] ". . . quodque in praedicta privilegiorum . . . communicatione . . . fratribus facta, eaque quoad absolutionem, dispensationem, vel alias . . . ad Priores Conventuales, idest praelatos singularum domorum Ordinis Praedicatorum, et eorum Vicarios similiter spectant, ad Guardianos, et eorum Vicarios Ordinis Minorum. . . ."—*Bull. Praed.*, IV, 258.

[88] Cf. Schroeder, *Disciplinary Decrees*, pp. 485-487; Thomassinus, *Vetus et Nova Disciplina*, Pars I, lib. III, cap. 39, n. 5; A. Vasto, *De Communicatione*, pp. 19-22.

[89] Cf. const. *Dum intra*, 19 dec. 1516—*Fontes*, I, n. 72; Mansi, XXXII, 970-976.

of religious, the administration of the sacraments by religious, contracts between the secular clergy and religious, burials, ordination of religious candidates, the consecration of churches, etc. Bishops were ordered to conduct a visitation of the parishes entrusted to religious. The visitation was to pertain to all matters concerning the *cura animarum,* but without any pecuniary expense placed upon the religious order. If the visitation found the religious priests negligent, then they were to be punished according to the penalties stated in the rule of their order.

Religious superiors were required by the constitution of Pope Leo X to present to the bishop or vicar general, when they requested it, all the religious priests destined to hear confessions in their dioceses. The bishop, or his representative, was free to examine the candidates for faculties concerning their competence as confessors, and he was free to accept or reject them. The approved religious confessors, however, could not absolve secular clerics or laymen from *ab homine* censures which were incurred *latae sententiae.* Even if the religious confessor had heard the confession of a penitent who was infirm and dying, the priest could not give him the last sacraments, unless the *sacerdos proprius* had illicitly refused to fulfill this pastoral function. The religious priest who conferred the last sacraments under the above conditions was obliged to prove such negligence by the proper priest through the presentation of witnesses or a statement made before a public notary. Religious, however, were permitted to administer all the sacraments to their subjects and employees as long as they were in their service.

The religious priest could not enter a parish church with a cross and transfer the remains of persons who had selected a religious church or cemetery for burial, unless the pastor was requested beforehand for the proper permission. Nevertheless, an ancient and uncontroverted customary usage to the contrary warranted the non-observance of this prescription.

The consecration of churches, cemeteries and altars, and the laying of cornerstones pertained exclusively to the local ordinary. When he unreasonably refused to perform these services, after being requested three times by the religious, he lost the right and the religious were permitted to invite any other bishop they wished. When any censures were published and imposed by the bishops, they were to be also published in the religious churches, if the bishops requested this. Religious confessors and preachers were obliged to remind the faithful of their obligation to pay tithes and if the penitents refused, the religious confessor was to deny them absolution.

Dum intra also stated that, all things considered, secular priests were to be permitted to celebrate Mass in the churches of religious, unless they were excommunicated. All contracts *pro tempore* between the religious and the secular clerics were to be considered valid, unless a subsequent provincial or general council abolished them. Solemn processions held by the bishop, required the religious to be present when requested, unless their monastery was more than one mile from the city. If church bells were rung at the prohibited times, the offenders could be fined.

In the same session of the V Lateran Council, Pope Leo X published his Constitution *Supernae maiestatis* on December 19, 1516. The decree concerned the preaching of secular and religious priests. Both groups were required, notwithstanding any customs, rights, or privileges to the contrary, to be carefully examined in regard to their fitness, age, knowledge, virtue and other qualifications by their superiors. This being done, the local ordinary was to be notified of this by authentic letters or other legitimate means. This same decree, renewed and confirmed all the matter contained in the constitution of Pope Clement V, *Religiosi,* concerning the administration of the sacraments by religious.[90]

---

[90] Cf. c. 1, *de privilegiis et excessibus privilegiatorum,* V, 7, in Clem.

CHAPTER III

Parochial Co-operation of the Religious and Secular Clergy from the Council of Trent (1545-1563) to the Code of Canon Law (1918)

Article 1. The Council of Trent and the Ministry of Religious

Pope Paul III (1534-1548) convoked the Council of Trent in order to initiate the internal reform of the Church, a reform already too long delayed. The Protestant Revolt forced the Fathers of the Council to consider possible reforms on every level of the Church's organizational structure. Therefore, it was obvious that the relationship of the secular clergy and the religious clergy would be given serious consideration and clarification, especially on the parochial level. Special importance was laid on the privileges and faculties of religious, long an occasion of dispute and parochial conflicts. The disciplinary measures that came from the sessions of the Council, stretching over an eighteen year period, became the fundamental legislation of the Church until the promulgation of the Code of Canon Law in the year 1918. Pope Pius IV (1559-1565) ratified the decrees of the Council in the year of its final session.

The importance of the parochial unit and the rights of the pastor were confirmed and strengthened by the Fathers of the Council. The privileges of the religious clergy, which had been lavishly bestowed upon them by pontiffs, had accumulated, grown and been extended and communicated over the centuries, and now had to be pruned. This was necessary to increase the importance of the parochial life and to safeguard the rights of the pastor who enjoyed exclusive jurisdiction over his people. The pastor was to have jurisdiction over a definite group of people dwelling within a determined parish boundary line. It was his right and duty as pastor to exercise his authority in the spiritual care of his parishioners.[1]

[1] ". . . the holy council commands the bishops that, for the greater security of the salvation of the souls committed to them, they divide the people into definite and distinct parishes and assign to each its own and permanent

Through the famous *Tametsi* decree, the pastor was designated as the exclusive official witness of marriages. It became his right alone to assist at marriages. Matrimony could be validly contracted only in the presence of the pastor or a priest delegated by him and two or three witnesses. The bestowing of the nuptial blessing was also his exclusive right, abrogating all contrary customs.[2]

The parochial portion was enforced so that any privileges granted to monasteries, hospitals, or other pious places, whereby they might receive the "parochial portion" in place of the parish church, were abrogated. Therefore, if the church had for forty years the custom of paying the parochial portion to the parish church, it was to be rendered despite any subsequent privileges to the contrary. The Council did not wish the custom of paying this portion to the cathedral and parish churches to be impaired in the future.[3]

At the same time, the fact that religious were engaged in the active ministry was accepted by the Council as a long established and certainly approved practice. This is taken for granted in the pertinent decrees of the Council. The religious priests exercising the *cura animarum* were in all things pertaining to it, as well as in the administration of the sacraments, completely subject to the jurisdiction, visitation and correction of the local ordinary. The prescripts of the Council required bishops to conduct a visitation of all churches attached to monasteries which exercised the *cura animarum* over lay people not of the household of the monastery. No one was to be appointed to the *cura animarum* except with the consent of the bishop after a previous examination by him or his vicar. An exception to this was made in favor of the Abbey of Cluny and its territories. Likewise, exceptions were made for monasteries and places in which abbots, superior generals or heads of orders had their principal residence, and for other monasteries and houses in which abbots or other superiors of regulars exercised

---

parish priest, who can know his people and from whom alone they may licitly receive the sacraments. . . ."—Schroeder, *Canons and Decrees of the Council of Trent* (St. Louis: Herder Book Co., 1941), p. 204; Sess. XXIV, *de ref.*, c. 13

[2] Sess. XXIV, *de ref.*, c. 1.

[3] Sess. XXV, *de ref.*, c. 13; cf. c. 8, X, *de sepulturis*, III, 28.

episcopal and temporal jurisdiction over the parish priests and parishioners.[4] Likewise, all appeals, privileges and exemptions to the contrary notwithstanding, the local ordinary was to make an annual visit to all benefices held by monasteries which had the *cura animarum* attached to them. He was to see that the responsibilities of the respective vicars were properly fulfilled.[5] This annual visitation was to be made to all churches, even exempt, with apostolic authority. The bishop was to provide for the repairing of churches. Appropriate penalties were to be inflicted on delinquents who neglected this matter. He was to make sure that no one was defrauded of the *cura animarum* if annexed to the church, nor of any other services due them.[6]

The Council reminded bishops of their serious and personal obligation to preach to the people. If they were legitimately impeded from doing so personally, competent substitutes were to be supplied. All priests who had churches to which was attached the *cura animarum* were similarly obliged. Negligence was to be properly punished through the infliction of censures by the competent ordinary. Exempt churches with the *cura animarum* were no less obliged to have preaching on Sundays and solemn feasts. Metropolitans were required to see that the parochial churches in their provinces which were subject to monasteries fulfilled this obligation. In this matter, the Metropolitans were to act as delegates of the Apostolic See and no custom, exemption, appeal, protest or counteraction was to interfere with the execution of this decree. All regulars had to be properly examined by their superiors concerning their life, morals and competence before being approved as preachers in the churches of their respective orders. In all other churches, nevertheless, they were not only required to be approved by their superiors, but they also personally had to present themselves before the local bishop and receive his blessing. If this was not done, they could not preach outside their own churches. The bishop, however, was to give this *beneplacitum* or permission gratuitously without any remuneration.[7] This decree

[4] Sess. XVI, *de regularibus,* c. 11.

[5] Sess. VII, *de ref.,* c. 7.

[6] Sess. VII, *de ref.,* c. 8.

[7] Sess. V, *de ref.,* c. 2.

effectively terminated any dispute about the right to preach in parochial churches. The obligation of religious to receive the permission of the bishop was clear and no contrary custom or privilege was to be tolerated. No one, secular priest or religious priest, was to presume to preach, even in the churches of his own order, if this was positively against the will of the bishop.[8]

Although the Fathers of the Council acknowledged that all priests receive the power to absolve from sins by the fact of their reception of priesthood through sacred ordination, they forbid priests, secular and religious, to absolve laymen or priests without first being "approved" by the bishop for confessions, or unless the priest had a parochial benefice. Before being "approved," the priestly candidate was to be examined or judged competent in some other fashion, if this was considered necessary. If the "approval" was given by the bishop, it was to be completely gratuitous.[9]

This decree expressly abrogated any and all contrary privileges, for it was necessary for the validity of the absolution that the confessor enjoy a parochial benefice or receive the approbation of the bishop. If the priest was a pastor, he had faculties to absolve by reason of the fact that he received this jurisdiction from his office, that is, he enjoyed ordinary jurisdiction. If he received the approbation of the bishop, the secular priests received delegated jurisdiction, but the religious, since they already had papal jurisdiction, received only the permission of the local bishop to exercise it validly.[10]

Hence, the approbation of the bishop was not synonymous with the granting of jurisdiction, but the effect was the same, since there could be no valid absolution without it. The term did not even infer the granting of jurisdiction implicitly, but referred only to a necessary condition, a prerequisite for the valid exercise of a jurisdiction already enjoyed. This has been the standard explanation asserted and maintained until the time of the Code.[11]

---

[8] Sess. XXIV, *de ref.*, c. 4.

[9] Sess. XXIII, *de ref.*, c. 15.

[10] Cf. const. *Quoniam,* 10 maii 1227—*Bull. Praed.*, I, 19.

[11] Cf. Ferraris, *Prompta Biblotheca, Canonica, Iuridica, Moralis, Theologica necnon Ascetica, Polemica, Rubricistica, Historica* (9 vols., Romae, 1885-1899), s.v. *approbatio,* art. 1, nn. 1-3 (hereafter cited: *Bibliotheca*).

ARTICLE 2. POST TRIDENTINE LEGISLATION—THE STRENGTHENING AND SAFEGUARDING OF PAROCHIAL PREROGATIVES

Section 1. Non-Parochial Churches and Oratories of Religious

In the years following Trent, the prerogatives of the parish clergy began to crystalize more and more. Matters concerning the hearing of confessions and preaching the word of God had been definitely determined by the Fathers of the Council. However, the non-parochial churches and oratories of religious, the carrying on of funeral and devotional processions, burial rights and other such matters occasionally created disputes between the parish clergy and the regular clergy. Some of this was due to the conflicting statements issued at various times by the Sacred Congregations in their responses to numerous questions submitted to them over a long period of time.

Pope Clement VIII (1592-1605), in his Constitution *Quoniam* of July 23, 1603, had stated that the local bishop was to investigate and consult any religious houses in the area concerning any newly proposed religious foundation, in order to determine whether it would be prejudicial to the rights and privileges of the existing religious communities.[12] Since the constitution also stated that the bishop should consult "*et aliis interesse habentibus*" it was the opinion of some that the pastor was certainly an interested party and should, at least be consulted before a new religious house was erected within his parish boundaries.[13] Others asserted that not only was a consultation necessary, but that the consent of the pastor was required for the validity of the proposed religious house.[14] Bouix maintained that the bishop need not bother even to consult the local pastor if it was clear that his rights would in no manner be harmed.[15]

---

[12] *Fontes,* n. 190; *Bullarum Diplomatum et Privilegiorum Sanctorum Romanorum Pontificum Taurinensis Editio* (25 vols. Augustae Taurinensis, 1857-1872), XI, n. 320 (hereafter cited: *Bull. Rom. Taur.*).

[13] Cf. Reiffenstuel, *Ius Canonicum Universum* (7 vols., Venetiis, 1735), lib. III, tit. 36, n. 33; Pignatelli, *Consultationes Canonicae* (11 vols., Coloniae Allobrogorum, 1700), I, consult. 179, nn. 52-58.

[14] Cf. Schmalzgrueber, *Ius Ecclesiasticum Universum,* lib. III, tit. 36, n. 35.

[15] *Tractatus de Jure Regularium,* I, pars II, sect. 2, cap. 4.

Pope Gregory XV (1621-1623) repeated the legislation in his Constitution *Cum alias* of August 27, 1622 and put into practice the requirements of the Constitution *Quoniam. Cum alias* gave the right to appeal to the Sacred Congregation of Bishops and Regulars if anyone considered that their interests had been prejudiced by the erection of a new religious foundation. Certainly, this could definitely include the pastor if he believed that his parochial rights were in any fashion harmed.[16] Pope Urban VIII (1623-1644), by his Constitution *Romanus Pontifex* of August 28, 1624, affirmed the precepts of the two previous constitutions and abrogated all contrary customs, privileges or exemptions in this matter.[17]

The Council of Trent had forbidden all regulars and seculars to celebrate Mass in private houses or outside the churches and oratories dedicated solely for divine worship and subject to the designation and visitation of the local ordinary.[18] Since the oratories of religious houses were never considered to be private oratories, the permission of the Holy See did not have to be sought so that the Holy Sacrifice might be offered there. The decree did require, however, that the churches and oratories be designated and visited by the ordinary. In the past, many religious communities had obtained the privilege of erecting oratories anywhere within their established monasteries, without obtaining the permission of the bishop, nor with any requirement that these oratories be subject to his visitation. Since the decree completely abrogated these privileges, the churches and oratories of the religious had to be designated by the ordinary before Mass might be offered in them. Very soon after this explicit legislation, however, the Holy See began to grant privileges and exemptions in this matter,[19] so that soon the right to visit the oratories and churches of religious applied only to those burdened with the care of souls.[20]

---

[16] *Bull. Rom. Taur.*, XII, 719.

[17] *Fontes*, n. 389.

[18] Sess. XXII, *Decretum de observandis et evitandis in celebratione missae.*

[19] Cf. Ferraris, *Bibliotheca*, s.v. *Regulares*, art. 2, n. 6.

[20] Cf. const. *Inscrutabile*, 5 febr. 1622—*Fontes*, n. 199; const. *Firmandis*, 6 nov. 1744—*Fontes*, n. 349.

The people were free to attend Mass and devotions in the churches and oratories of religious without the obligation to hear Mass in their parish churches. The bishops were to admonish their people to attend their own parish church, where it could be conveniently done, to hear the word of God preached.[21] This admonition to attend the parish church frequently applied principally to Sundays and Feast days.[22] Yet, this obligation to attend Mass at the parish church had certainly been mitigated to a mere counsel.[23] Moreover, Pope Benedict XIV (1740-1758) stated that the faithful were free to attend the sacred mysteries in any church whatsoever, as long as it was not a private oratory. Contrary custom had completely abrogated the precept of attending the parochial Mass. So greatly had the legislation changed in this matter, that the pontiff furthermore stated that a bishop could not order his subjects to assist at the parochial Mass, since the custom had obtained the nature of a common law.[24]

Therefore, it can be understood that a pastor might consider that his parochial rights were being prejudiced by the establishment of a clerical community of religious within his parish limits. Such a consideration in a given case might be purely imaginary, but the constitutions governing the erection of religious houses did give him the right to speak his opinion and appeal to the Sacred Congregation if he desired to do so.

The Sacred Congregation of Rites gave many responses to questions concerning such matters. A cursory glance at some of the decrees of the Congregation sheds light on the matters of controversy in the years between the Council of Trent and the Code. It should be noted that pastors could not interfere nor prohibit regulars from celebrating Masses in their own oratories, especially on Feast days, even though they were scheduled before the paro-

---

[21] Sess. XXIV, *de ref.*, c. 4.

[22] Sess. XXII, *Decretum de observandis et evitandis in celebratione missae.*

[23] Schmalzgrueber, *Ius Ecclesiasticum Universum,* lib. III, tit. 29, n. 11.

[24] Benedictus XIV, *De Synodo Dioecesana* (3 vols., Romae, 1783), Vol. I, lib. 9, c. 14, n. 10: Barbosa, *Collectanea Doctorum in Varia Concilii Tridentine et Canones* (Lugdini, 1657), sess. XXII, *de observandis et evidandis in celebratione missae,* n. 21 and *De Officio et Potestate Parochi Descripto,* C. XI, nn. 14 ff. (hereafter cited: *Collectanea Doctorum*).

chial Mass.[25] Religious were instructed to abide by the existing customs in regard to the ringing of church bells in order to announce parochial functions.[26] Pastors were to be permitted to enter all churches and oratories situated within their parish boundaries, even those which were exempt, in order to obtain Holy Viaticum in cases of necessity.[27] Religious superiors were given the privilege of offering Mass on Holy Thursday in the oratories of their houses (and even in the religious church if no oratory was had, but with the proviso that the doors of the church remain closed to the public), so that Holy Communion might be distributed to the religious and they could thereby fulfill their Paschal precept.[28] This was done to encourage the lay people to fulfill this Paschal precept in their own parish churches. The Council of Trent[29] had in no way retracted the provisions of the decree *Omnis utriusque sexus* of the Fourth Lateran Council which required each parishioner to receive the Paschal Communion at his own parish church. On the contrary, the prescripts were repeated by the Council and by future pontiffs.[30] In order that they might fulfill this obligation elsewhere, the parishioner required the permission of the bishop or the proper pastor.

The celebration of marriages and the conferring of solemn baptism were strictly parochial functions and never posed a problem in the relations between religious and the parish clergy. Permission to perform these functions, however, could be given to other priests by the special permission of the bishop, although this apparently was not commonly requested or granted.[31]

---

[25] S.R.C., *Neapolitana.,* 21 aprilis 1635—*Decreta Authentica Congregationis Sacrorum Rituum* (6 vols., Romae: Ex Typographia Polyglotta, 1898-1927), n. 620 (hereafter cited: *DA*); S.R.C., *Fanen.,* 23 mart. 1641—*DA,* n. 745.

[26] S.R.C., *Calaguritani Praeeminentiarum.,* 24 maii 1664, DA, n. 1281.

[27] S.R.C., *Venetiarum.,* 22 aug. 1705—*DA,* n. 2159.

[28] S.R.C., *Tertii Ordinis S. Francisii.,* 31 aug. 1839—*DA,* n. 2799; S.R.C., *Comen.,* 9 dec. 1899—*DA,* n. 4049.

[29] Sess. XVI, *de ref.,* c. 8.

[30] Cf. c. 12, X, *de poenitentiis et remissionibus,* V, 38; Clemens X, const. *Superna,* 21 iun. 1670—*Fontes,* n. 246; Benedictus XIV, const. *Magno cum,* 2 iun. 1751—*Fontes,* n. 413; Pius X, const. *Tradita ab antiquis,* 14 sept. 1912 —*Fontes,* n. 698.

[31] Cf. const. *Magno cum,* 2 iun. 1751—*Fontes,* n. 413.

Certainly, the other sacerdotal functions that were strictly parochial could not be undertaken by the religious clergy of a non-parochial church or oratory. The blessing of the baptismal font, the blessing of homes and the procession on Holy Saturday, and the celebration of the solemn Mass on Holy Thursday were listed by a decree of the Sacred Congregation of Rites as parochial rights.[32] The last mentioned, however, was eventually extended as a privilege to all religious oratories, so that the religious might receive the Blessed Sacrament and have the opportunity of fulfilling their Paschal Obligation.[33]

Therefore, all non-parochial functions could be celebrated in the religious church or oratory, independently of the pastor's permission. The blessing of and distribution of ashes, candles, palms, and the blessing of women *post partum,* as well as the exposition of the Blessed Sacrament and the Forty Hours devotions, were non-parochial functions and were certainly permissible. As long as the religious priests were approved, they could likewise hear confessions and preach in their oratories and churches.[34]

Although the non-parochial churches had almost unlimited freedom in the performance of those functions in no manner reserved to the pastor, the basic welfare of souls and the good of the Church demanded consideration. Hence, where certain celebrations caused unusual harm to the parochial life, measures to correct this were certainly recommended. Such extraordinary occurrences that occasioned parishioners to remain away from their parish catechetical and doctrinal instructions were roundly disapproved by Pope Benedict XIV in his Constitution *Etsi minime.* It appears that certain non-parochial churches, especially those of regulars, in some cities unnamed by the pontiff, were celebrating some feasts with great solemnity and pomp. On such feast days, the people would not attend their doctrinal instructions given in the parish church unless they were scheduled early in the morning, but would flock to the celebrations and often miss the

---

[32] S.R.C., *Urbis et Orbis.,* 12 ian. 1704—*DA,* n. 2123.

[33] S.R.C., *Tertii Ordinis S. Francisii,* 31 aug. 1839—*DA,* n. 2799; S.R.C., *Comen.,* 9 dec. 1899—*DA,* n. 4049.

[34] Cf. S.R.C., *Placentina.,* 22 nov. 1710—*DA,* n. 2208; S.R.C., *Perusina,* 2 iul. 1718—*DA,* n. 2251; S.R.C., *Romana,* 21 nov. 1893—*DA,* n. 3813.

Catechism to their ultimate detriment. Although, the pontiff determined no standard ruling concerning what was to be done, he left it to the prudence and discretion of the local bishops and other such circumstances.[35]

Section 2. Burial from Religious Churches

During this period, numerous decrees emanated from the Sacred Congregations regarding funeral processions, burial rights and the proper procedure in conducting funerals. The questions and responses concerned such things as whether the permission of the pastor was required before the religious chosen by the deceased could enter the home of the deceased parishioner and transport the body to their church;[36] whether the pastor had a right to recite the office of the dead over a parishioner who selected a religious church for burial;[37] and whether regulars were permitted to bury tertiaries associated with their order even though they had not selected their church for burial?[38]

---

[35] "Saepe enim contingit, in aliis ecclesiis, ac praesertim Regularium, solemni ritu, magnaque populi frequentia, festum aliquem diem celebrari: ideoque si in ecclesia parochiali, summo mane, aut statim a prandio Catechismus habeatur, aut nemo, aut pauci admodum sunt, qui eidem catechismo intersint, quique praescriptos horas non causentur. Sin vero, captentur horae civitatis commodo magis appositae, usu compertum est, populum ad ecclesiam confluere, in qua festus dies agitur; et celebritate pompae illectum, Doctrinam Christianam non sine gravi animae detrimento deserere. In hoc articulo quia certa, et communis regula praescribi non potest, id totum relictum esse volumus prudentiae vigilis ecclesiae antistitis, qui attenta loci, temporis, personarum qualitate, expensisque rerum omnium momentis, ita studeat solemnis diei celebritatem cum Doctrina Christiana componere, ne alteri altera sit impedimento. Quod si Regulares, et exempti contradixerint, et sanctum hoc Doctrinae opus, licet ab episcopis prius admoniti, suis functionibus perturbare praesumpserit, Nostram locorum Ordinariis auctoritatem, qua potimur in exemptos, pollicemur: nec alia pontificiae vigilantiae deerunt remedia, ne parochiales ecclesiae debitis fraudentur obsequiis."—7 febr. 1742—*Fontes,* n. 324.

[36] Cf. S.R.C., *Tornacen.*, 25 sept. 1649—*DA,* n. 924; S.R.C., *Baren.*, 1 dec. 1657—*DA,* n. 1042; S.R.C., *Vestana.*, 2 mart. 1647—*DA,* n. 1503.

[37] Cf. S.R.C., *Firmana.*, 26 ian. 1641—*DA,* n. 731; S.R.C., *Messanen.*, 10 maii 1642—*DA,* n. 793; S.R.C., *Novarien.*, 20 nov. 1677—*DA,* n. 1604.

[38] S.C. Ep. et Reg., *Senogallien.*, 22 nov. 1580—*Fontes,* n. 1374; S.R.C., *Spoletana Terrae De Viso.*, 20 iun. 1609—*DA,* n. 271; S.C. Ep. et Reg., *Parmen.*, 11 aug. 1702; ad 4—*Fontes,* n. 1819.

Many of the questions arose from the Constitution *Dum intra* of Pope Leo X (1513-1521) which forbade the religious clergy to enter and remove the bodies of the deceased, but allowed them to enter in procession only after consulting the pastor. Yet, the constitution provided that if the pastor refused to conduct the body to the religious church, or when custom gave them the privilege, the religious could enter and remove the body to their church for the obsequies.[39] The responses determined that the religious clergy could not enter the parish of the deceased who had chosen to be buried from their church without the permission of the pastor, but the pastor was to receive the body and conduct the procession to their church. If he refused, the regulars could enter and remove the remains. Likewise, if the pastor did not conduct the body to the religious church and the religious had waited a reasonable time after the hour set for the funeral, they could enter the parish territory and remove the body.[40] In the funeral procession, the cross of regulars was used when the funeral was to be conducted at their church.[41] The same decree stated that the proper pastor was to lead the procession and wear his stole and the procession could freely pass through all the parishes on the route to the funeral church. At the religious church, only the religious clergy had the right to conduct the services.[42]

Although the pastor was to conduct the body from the house of the deceased to the door of the religious church, the religious performed the remaining ceremonies which included the office of the dead, the requiem Mass and the interment of the body. In the procession from the church to the cemetery, the pastor was to accompany the body when any great solemnity was involved.[43] If, however, the procession proceeded directly to the cemetery with little solemnity, the religious clergy were to pass without

---

[39] 19 dec. 1516—*Fontes,* n. 72.

[40] Cf. S.C. Ep. et Reg., *gen. dec.* 12 ian. 1604—*Fontes,* n. 1627; S.C.C., *Tusculan.,* 22 nov. 1732—*Fontes,* n. 3398; S.R.C. *Messanen.,* 24 febr. 1680, ad 11—*Fontes,* n. 5634; S.C. Ep. et Reg., *Volturarien.* 13 mart. 1744, ad 3, 4—*Fontes,* n. 1860; S.C.C., *Nullius Messanen.,* 19 dec. 1857—*Fontes,* n. 4159.

[41] S.R.C., 23 apr. 1895—*Fontes,* n. 6243.

[42] Cf. S.C. Ep. et Reg., *Minorum Observantium,* 27 nov. 1671—*Fontes,* n. 1808; S.R.C., *Neritonen.,* 12 sept. 1884, ad 1—*Fontes,* n. 6159.

[43] Cf. Ferraris, *Bibliotheca,* s.v. *Sepultura,* n. 36.

any hindrances from the pastor and the presiding priest could wear the stole in the procession. In passing the parochial churches, the cross of the religious did not have to be lowered.[44]

There is no doubt that the parochial church was the proper place of burial for a parishioner unless the deceased had chosen to be buried elsewhere or there was a family tomb in which they were to be placed. This was accepted and freely asserted by all the authors until the time of the Code.[45] Therefore, there was no difficulty involved when the deceased had expressly chosen to be buried from the religious church or in their cemetery. Questions arose about those who had not chosen a place of burial but were associated with the religious order in some manner, such as tertiaries, servants, guests, etc. Unless they had selected a place for burial, tertiaries who wore only the cord of the habit and lived at home like other lay people were to be buried from their parish church.[46] Lay members of confraternities associated to the religious order,[47] lay persons who died in a religious house and even those servants of religious who did not live within the monastery and labor there under obedience to the religious superior, were to be buried by their proper pastor, unless they chose to be buried by the religious.[48] Parishioners from another diocese could choose to be buried by the religious situated in a diocese other than that of the parishioner.[49]

---

[44] Cf. S.C.C., *Ordinis Praedicatorum.*, 24 ian. 1846—*Fontes,* n. 4091; S.R.C., *Neritonen.*, 12 sept. 1884—*Fontes,* n. 6159; S.C. Ep. et Reg., *Caven. et Sarnen.*, 17 sept. 1880—*Fontes,* n. 2006.

[45] Cf. Pirhing, *Ius Canonicum Nova Methodo Explicatum* (5 vols., Dilingae, 1674-1678), lib. III, tit. 28, nn. 5-8 (hereafter cited: *Ius Canonicum*); Reiffenstuel, *Ius Canonicum Universum,* lib. III, tit. 28, n. 2; Schmalzgrueber, *Ius Ecclesiasticum Universum,* lib. III, tit. 28, n. 9; Barbosa, *De Officio et Potestate Parochi Descriptio* (ed. U. Giraldi a S. Cajetaneo, Romae, 1783), C. XXVI, n. 1; Many, *De Locis Sacris* (Parisiis, 1904), n. 170.

[46] S.C. Ep. et Reg., *Senogallien.*, 22 nov. 1580—*Fontes,* n. 1374; S.C. Ep. et Reg., 15 mart. 1606—*Fontes,* n. 1638.

[47] Cf. const. *Ex iniuncto,* 22 febr. 1645—*Fontes,* n. 230.

[48] S.C.C., *Sarzanen.*, 28 apr. 1674—*Fontes,* n. 2835; S.C.C., *Lauden.*, 14 apr. 1685, ad 3—*Fontes,* n. 2885; S.C.C., *Spoletana.*, 19 apr. 1692, ad 3—*Fontes,* n. 2928.

[49] S.C.C., *Auximana seu Lauretana,* 8 iul. 1752 and 24 mart. 1753—*Fontes,* n. 3621, 3626.

When the funeral services and burial of a parishioner were performed in a religious church, the parochial portion or *quarta funeraria* was to be rendered by the religious to the pastor of the deceased parishioner.[50] Some maintained, however, that it need not be rendered if the religious church had the privilege or custom from time immemorial of not rendering it.[51] Nor were the pastors, according to the Constitution *Cum sicut dilectus* of Pope Urban VIII (1623-1644), to ask and receive more when a parishioner selected a religious church for his burial, than when the funeral services were held in the parochial church.[52] The free choice of burial was a right asserted and protected by the Holy See.[53] Therefore, if a pastor prevented the parishioner from selecting a religious church for his burial, the pastor was to be punished by law.[54]

Section 3. Religious Confessors and Preachers

The whole tenor of the decrees of the Council of Trent left no doubt that it was the intention of the Fathers of the Council to centralize and strengthen the parochial unit and the importance of the pastor. In matters pertaining to the *cura animarum,* the religious clergy was entirely subject to the local ordinary in much the same fashion as the secular clergy. Faculties to hear confessions and to preach outside the religious churches were to be received from the local ordinary.[55] The prescripts of the council implicitly encouraged the employment of religious in the active ministry. This is especially true in regard to preaching and the hearing of confessions, for which they were always considered particularly qualified. The decrees of the council stressed the importance of preaching and caring for the spiritual needs of the people. This

[50] Cf. const. *Ex iniuncto,* 22 febr. 1645—*Fontes,* n. 230; S.R.C., *Novarien.,* 31 maii 1670—*DA,* n. 1400.

[51] Cf. Ferraris, *Bibliotheca,* s.v. *Quarta Funeralis;* S.R.C., *Theatina Terrae Buccanici.,* 11 dec. 1627—*DA,* n. 448.

[52] 2 mart. 1638—*Fontes,* n. 218.

[53] Cf. C.S. Ep. et Reg., *Maceraten.,* 7 oct. 1575—*Fontes,* n. 1317; S.C.C., *Lauden.,* 2 maii 1711, ad 3—*Fontes,* n. 3101; S.C.C., *Vilnen.,* 15 dec. 1792, ad 1—*Fontes,* n. 3883..

[54] S.C.C., *Lauden.,* 2 maii 1711, ad 3—*Fontes,* n. 3101.

[55] Sess. XXV, *de regularibus,* c. 11.

was the basic responsibility of the bishop and he was commanded to fulfill this grave duty at least through the selection of competent substitutes and delegates.[56] The pertinent decrees of the council concerning the *cura animarum* evidently show that the religious clergy within the bishop's diocese were to be his assistants in the spiritual care of the people.[57]

Therefore, once a religious priest was approved by the bishop for the hearing of confessions, all could approach him without fear of infringing on the rights of the pastor, nor with any obligation upon the penitent to seek the permission of the pastor. Some canonists, however, disputed this point. Schmalzgrueber (1663-1735) contended that the parochial subjects of the pastor had to be absolved by him for the validity of the confession and, unless the pastor had given his consent, the absolution of another priest was ineffective.[58] Van Espen (1648-1728) asserted that the faithful could freely approach any approved confessor, but with the sole exception of being required to confess to his proper pastor once a year during the Lenten or Easter seasons, unless the permission of the pastor was given, at least tacitly, or could be legitimately presumed.[59] The approbation of the bishop, however, rendered every priest the *sacerdos proprius* required by the IV Lateran Council for the Easter confession.[60] This was unquestionably settled by Pope Clement X (1670-1676) when he formally decreed that all who made their Easter confession to a religious confessor approved by the bishop, certainly satisfied this obligation. Therefore, the validity of other confessions was, *a fortiori*, substantiated.[61]

Pope St. Pius V (1566-1577) temporarily made exceptions for the religious clergy and set aside the provisions of Trent which required them to receive the approbation or permission of the

---

[56] Sess. V, *de ref.*, c. 2.

[57] Cf. sess. VII, *de ref.*, cc. 7-8; V, *de ref.*, c. 2; XXIV, *de ref.*, c. 4; XXIII, *de ref.*, c. 15; XVI, *de regularibus*, c. 11.

[58] Cf. *Ius Ecclesiasticum Universum*, lib. III, tit. 29, n. 2.

[59] *Compendium Iuris Ecclesiastici* (2 vols., Bassani, 1784), I, tit. 6, cap. 6, n. 58 (hereafter cited: *Compendium*).

[60] Cf. c. 12, X, *de poenitentiis et remissionibus*, V, 38.

[61] Const. *Superna*, 21 iun. 1670—*Fontes*, n. 246.

bishop to preach and absolve. He listed twenty-six obstacles placed in the way of the apostolate of the orders by the bishops. These hindered the approved aims of the religious and were harmful to the ends of the Church and souls entrusted to its care. The pontiff stated that too often the religious had been unjustly refused faculties by those who acted from improper motives, sometimes with demands for pecuniary payments as a condition for the granting of such faculties. Therefore, he permitted the religious to preach in their churches and absolve as confessors without need of the bishop's permission, as long as the religious cleric had the approval of his superior general or provincial.[62] Later, however, the same pontiff reenacted the decrees of Trent and revoked his former exemption, so that the religious clerics were again required to obtain the proper faculties from the local ordinaries. Too many abuses had occasioned this revocation by the Roman Pontiff.[63]

Pope Gregory XV (1621-1623) repeated the decree of the Council of Trent regarding the necessity of holding a parochial benefice or of receiving the approbation of the bishop before the confessions of lay people could be heard.[64] Further decrees emphasized the power of the bishop to control the faculties of the religious and secular clerics alike. Pope Clement X (1670-1676), in his Constitution *"Superna,"* reiterated the necessity of the bishop's approbation in these matters.[65] At the same time, the Holy See strongly disapproved of and ruled against the practice of suspending religious priests from confessions and preaching—even whole convents and monasteries of clerics—without sufficient reasons. This was done to the great scandal and spiritual loss of the faithful. Hence, the suspended religious were ordered to be reinstated by the ecclesiastical authorities and not to be suspended again except for new causes which concerned the sacrament itself or for the violation of an interdict. Moreover, every religious

---

[62] Cf. const. *Etsi mendicantium,* 16 maii 1567—*Fontes,* n. 121.

[63] Cf. const. *Romani Pontificis,* 6 aug. 1571—*Fontes,* n. 139.

[64] Cf. const. *Inscrutabili,* 5 febr. 1662—*Fontes,* n. 199.

[65] Cf. const. *Superna,* 21 iun. 1670—*Fontes,* n. 246.

priest in a given house was not to be suspended without first consulting the Holy See.[66]

In a controversy, however, between the *Society of Jesus* and a bishop in the West Indies, the Holy See stated that even when a bishop had unjustly refused faculties, the religious priests could not validly absolve, nor were they able to preach in their own churches without the *beneplacitum* of the local ordinary. If they did preach after a denial of faculties, the bishop had a right to censure them with appropriate ecclesiastical penalties. Likewise, if the religious taught that such approbation of the ordinary was not necessary, they would incur the penalty of excommunication *latae sententiae*. On the other hand, the bishop was reminded of the fruitful labors of the Society of Jesus and was exhorted to treat them with Christian charity.[67]

The Constitution *Superna* of Pope Clement X stated that the religious clergy who wished to preach in their own churches were required to seek the *beneplacitum* of the local ordinary. Nevertheless, they could preach if the permission of the bishop was sought and not positively refused by him. If it was definitely refused, they could not preach even in their own churches. Transgressors could be punished, but the bishops were not to refuse the grant of faculties to the religious without a just and reasonable cause. Once given, permission was not to be retracted without a similar reason and, generally speaking, the mind of the Church was that regulars were to be given faculties and not prohibited by the bishops.[68]

The same constitution stated that religious confessors who were approved in one diocese, were not by that fact approved for all other dioceses. Likewise, a priest was required to have special

---

[66] S.C. Ep. et Reg., 20 nov. 1615—*Fontes,* n. 1667; Bizzarri, *Collectanea in usum Secretariae Sacrae Congregationis Episcoporum et Regularium* (Romae, Ex Typographia Rev. Camerae Apostolicae, 1863), p. 22 (hereafter cited: *Collectanea*).

[67] Const. *Cum sicut accepimus,* 14 maii 1648—*Fontes,* n. 232; S.C.C., *Angelopolitan.,* 14 maii 1648—Pallottini, *Collectio Omnium Conclusionum et Resolutionum Congregationis Concilii ab anno 1564 ad annum 1860* (18 vols., Romae, 1868-1893), s.v. *Sacramentum Poenitentiae,* n. 131 (hereafter cited: Pallottini).

[68] 21 iun. 1670—*Fontes,* n. 246.

faculties for the confessions of nuns. Once the religious confessor was approved, however, he was not to be limited by the bishop as regards the time, person or locale. Moreover, the religious confessor could hear the confessions of the sick and absolve them without any permission of the local pastor being required. Yet the religious confessor so doing was obliged to inform the pastor of this fact, at least by letter. This notification of the pastor could be enforced even under threats of suspension from hearing confessions.[69] The constitution definitely confirmed the fact that the obligation of making the Easter confession, as stipulated by the decree *Omnis utriusque sexus* of the IV Lateran Council, was satisfied by confession to a religious priest *simpliciter* approved for confessions. This cleared up the dispute which concerned this obligation and stated in clear terms that the parishioner was not required to confess to his proper pastor for the validity of the Easter confession.[70]

Restrictions on the jurisdiction of religious confessors were not uncommon but the Holy See did not approve of them. Similar to the statements made in *Superna,* the Sacred Congregation of Bishops and Regulars had instructed bishops not to exclude the sick from the jurisdiction of Regular confessors. Nevertheless, the bishops were permitted to require the religious to notify the pastor of the sick parishioner after one of them had absolved a person sick and confined to his home.[71] Pope Gregory XVI (1831-1846),

[69] ". . . semel autem simplicter approbatos posse in dioecesi episcopi approbantis quovis anni tempore, etiam paschali, et quorumcumque etiam infirmorum confessionis audire absque ulla parochorum, vel ipsius episcopi licentia. De qua tamen confessione teneri dictos religiosos eorumdem infirmorum parochum illico certiorem reddere. Et hoc posse illis ab episcopo sub poena suspensionis a facultate audiendi confessiones praecipi: sufficere tamen, ut certioratio huiusmodi fiant saltem per scripturam apud ipsum infirmum relinquendam."—*Fontes,* n. 246; Pirhing, *Ius Canonicum,* lib. I, tit. 31, n. 145.

[70] "Et eos, qui dictis religiosis simplicter approbatis Paschali tempore confessi fuerint, Constitutioni, quae incipit, 'Omnis utriusque sexus,' quo ad confessionem dumtaxat satisfecisse censendos."—*Fontes,* n. 246.

[71] "Sacra Congregatio Cardinalium negotiis Regularium praeposita, inhaerens declarationibus alias desuper editis, censuit Regulares praedictos a locorum Ordinariis ad audiendas personarum saecularium confessiones approbatos, non posse ab iisdem Ordinariis prohiberi, ne earumdem personarum

in his epistle *Allatum isthinc* to Denis, Archbishop of Paris, deplored the fact that the Archbishop had placed unreasonable restrictions on Jesuit confessors, so that they could absolve only at stated times and only in parochial churches. Such restrictions, according to the pontiff, were without utility and injurious to the faithful as well as the religious. He desired that the restrictions be removed and that no such limitations be placed on the religious confessors without consultation with the Holy See.[72]

Until the time of the Code of Canon Law (1918), there was really no doubt concerning the subjection to the local ordinary of religious in exercising the *cura animarum.* Instructions reiterated the fact that the faculties to preach and absolve the faithful were to be received from the local ordinary.[73] If the religious priest had received faculties from the local ordinary but was suspended from hearing confessions by his religious superiors or not given approval by them, he was still able to absolve validly though unlawfully.[74]

Section 4. The Administration of the Sacraments by the Religious Clergy

The Council of Trent had expressly legislated that the parish priest was to know his people and that they were to receive the sacraments licitly from him alone.[75] The pastor was to have a definite territory as his parish with definite parishioners com-

---

aegrotantium in propriis illarum domibus confessiones audire possint absque licentia parochorum; dummodo relinquant schedulam, vel notificent ipsis parochis, quod paenitentiae Sacramentum huiusmodi fuerit ab iis ministratum."—S.C. Ep. et Reg., 13 sept. 1611—Bizzarri, *Collectanea,* p. 27.

[72] 12 oct. 1843—*Fontes,* n. 501.

[73] ". . . multa constituit circa debitam a Regularibus erga episcopos locorum Ordinarios observantiam et subjectionem; tam in petenda eorum licentia et benedictione pro Verbi Dei praedicatione in ecclesiis etiam suorum respective Ordinum habenda, quam in approbatione et facultate ab eisdem obtinenda pro administrando secularibus poenitentiae sacramento."—Const. Benedicti XIV *Firmandis,* 6 nov. 1744—*Fontes,* n. 349.

[74] S.C. Ep. et Reg., *Ordinis Praedicatorum,* 2 mart. 1866—*Acta Sanctae Sedis* (41 vols., Romae, 1865-1908), I (1865), 683-684 (hereafter cited: *ASS*).

[75] Sess. XXIV, *de ref.,* c. 13.

mitted to his care. It was his right to assist at the marriages of his people,[76] to preach the word of God and administer the sacraments to them, especially on Sundays and feasts of precept.[77] Those religious priests who were assigned to parish work in parochial churches entrusted to their religious community certainly enjoyed the same rights and had the same obligations over their subjects as the secular priests engaged in parochial work. The extent, however, to which religious priests not engaged in parish work might administer the sacraments was limited. If they were assigned to a monastery, religious house or some other non-parochial religious institution, they did not have the same rights and obligations as parish priests.[78]

The sacraments of Confirmation and Holy Orders played no part in the parochial relations between the religious clergy and the parish clergy. These sacraments were administered exclusively by the bishop and principally in the cathedral church. Also, the sacraments of matrimony and solemn baptism were generally recognized as parochial functions from the time of the Council of Trent.[79] The sacrament of penance has been discussed.[80] There remain only the sacraments of the Holy Eucharist and Extreme Unction.

The Council of Trent had stressed the importance of the relationship between the pastor and his parishioners and that the latter were to receive the sacraments licitly from the pastor alone.[81] The Holy See continually defended the pastor's prerogatives to administer the sacraments to his people.[82] The Council of Vienne (1311-1314) had stated that any religious who administered Holy Communion, the last sacraments or the sacrament of matrimony without the special permission of the pastor, would incur *ipso*

---

[76] Sess. XXIV, *de ref.*, c. 1.

[77] Sess. XXIV, *de ref.*, c. 4; sess. XXII, *Decretum de observandis et evitandis in celebratione missae.*

[78] Schmalzgrueber, *Ius Ecclesiasticum Universum,* lib. III, tit. 37, nn. 4-5.

[79] Sess. XXIV, *de ref.*, c. 1; S.R.C., *Oveten.*, 31 aug. 1872—*Fontes,* n. 6064; S.C.C., *Gen. Dec.*, 1891—*ASS,* XXIV (1891-1892), 358.

[80] Cf. *supra,* pp. 64-69.

[81] Sess. XXIV, *de ref.*, c. 13.

[82] Cf. S.C. de Prop. Fide., 13 iun. 1662—*Fontes,* n. 4450; S.C.C., *Romana,* 27 aug. 1667—*Fontes,* n. 2802; S.C.C., *Asculana,* 7 iun. 1698—*Fontes,* n. 2962.

facto an excommunication reserved to the Holy See.[83] Pope Pius IX (1846-1878) in his Constitution *"Apostolicae Sedis"* repeated the censure, but omitted all mention of sacraments other than Extreme Unction and Holy Viaticum.[84] The latter condemnation certainly did not include the administration of the last sacraments to a dying Catholic when his proper pastor could not be reached and it could be reasonably presumed that he would grant the required permission. Therefore, in a case of necessity, as this evidently would be, there was no fear of incurring any censure.[85] Also, some authors believed that the permission of the pastor could always be legitimately presumed in the administration of Holy Communion, except when it was given as Holy Viaticum or in fulfillment of the Paschal precept.[86] Nevertheless, commentators unanimously agreed that the administration of the last sacraments was the right of the pastor.[87]

Restrictions as to whom the sacraments might be administered did not apply to those who were exempt from the parochial jurisdiction. Therefore, members of an exempt religious community and lay people who habitually dwelled within the religious house and labored there as subjects of the religious superior, looked to the religious superior and not the local pastor for the administration of the sacraments. The Council of Trent required that the

---

[83] "Religiosi, qui clericis aut laicis sacramentum unctionis extremae, vel eucharistiae ministrare, matrimoniane solemnizare non habita super his parochialis presbyteri licentia speciali . . . excommunicationis incurrant sententiam ipso facto, per sedem apostolicam dumtaxat absolvendi."—C. 1, *de privilegiis et excessibus privilegiatorum,* V, 7, in Clem.

[84] "Excommunicationi latae sententiae Romano Pontifici reservatae subiacere declaramus: . . . Religiosos praesumentes clericis aut laicis, extra casum necessitatis, sacramentum Extremae Unctionis aut Eucharistiae per Viaticum ministrare absque parochi licentia."—12 oct. 1869—*Fontes,* n. 552.

[85] Pirhing, *Ius Canonicum,* lib. I, tit. 31, nn. 143 et 152.

[86] Cf. Schmalzgrueber, *Ius Ecclesiasticum Universum,* lib. III, tit. 29, n. 5; Barbosa, *De Officio et Potestate Parochi Descripto,* pars II, C. XX, n. 7.

[87] Cf. Pirhing, *Ius Canonicum,* lib. I, tit. 31, nn. 143 et 152; Schmalzgrueber, *Ius Ecclesiasticum Universum,* lib. III, tit. 29, n. 10; Barbosa, *De Officio et Potestate Parochi Descripto,* pars II, C. XXII, n. 2 et C. XX, n. 2; Van Espen, *Compendium,* I, tit. 8, cap. 3, n. 26 et tit. 4, cap. 5, n. 34; Wernz, *Ius Decretalium,* III, pars II, tit. 39.

lay people employed by the religious house actually dwell habitually within the religious house. If they labored there but lived elsewhere, they could not look to the religious superior for these sacramental administrations, but to the local pastor.[88] This was repeated by Pope Gregory XIII (1572-1585) in his Constitution *Circumspecta.*[89] Such provisions reflect similar ones stated in the Council of Vienne (1311-1314).[90]

The Sacred Congregation of the Council in one of its responses stated that if lay people visiting the monastery became so ill as to require the last sacraments, the local pastor was to be called if at all possible.[91] The same Congregation repeated the requirement that laborers in the religious house must live there day and night before they be considered as part of the religious family and qualified to receive the sacraments from the religious.[92] Tertiaries associated with a religious community did not fall under this exemption from the parochial jurisdiction. Therefore, if they became ill and in the danger of death, the religious were to administer the sacrament of penance and, if possible, wait for the pastor to come and administer the sacraments of Holy Viaticum and Extreme Unction.[93] It is evident that the Holy See carefully safeguarded the rights of the individual pastor. Unless exempt, all who had a domicile within the parish limits were subject to the pastor's jurisdiction. Even visitors to the territory were to look to the local pastor and not to others for the sacramental administrations. When questions arose concerning the pastor's rights, any infringement upon them or exemption from them was to be

---

[88] Sess. XXIV, *de ref.*, c. 11.

[89] 6 nov. 1580—*Fontes*, n. 1954.

[90] "Sane, religiosis illis, quibus est ab apostolicae sede concessum, ut familiaribus suis domesticis, aut pauperibus, in hospitalibus suis degentibus, sacramenta possint ecclesiastica ministrare, nullum ex praemissis volumus quod ad hoc praeiudicium generare."—C. 1, *de privilegiis et excessibus privilegiatorum,* V, 7, in Clem.

[91] S.C.C., *Monopolitana,* 27 sept. 1670—Ferraris, *Bibliotheca,* s.v. *Eucharistia,* n. 19.

[92] S.C.C., *Vratislavien.*, 25 ian. 1738—*Thesaurus Resolutionum Sacra Congregationis Concilii* (167 vols., Romae, 1718-1908), VIII, 17.

[93] S.R.C., *Spoletana Terrae de Visso,* 20 iun. 1609—*DA,* n. 271, et *Fontes,* n. 5248.

strictly interpreted.[94] A good example of this is a controversy that occurred in the seventeenth century between the *Society of Jesus* and the bishop of the diocese of Holy Angels in the West Indies. The religious were instructed by the Sacred Congregation of the Council not to administer the sacraments within the parish limits without the permission of the ordinary or the local pastor. This was the answer to the question submitted by the Jesuits to the Holy See. At the same time, however, the Congregation encouraged the bishop to be mindful of the high esteem the Society of Jesus enjoyed in the Church. The Congregation praised the missionary labors of the Society and exhorted the bishop to treat them with Christian charity.[95]

The IV Lateran Council (1215) enacted the decree *Omnis utriusque sexus* which required the faithful to receive the Paschal communion in their own parish church.[96] This was left intact by the Council of Trent.[97] Religious could administer Holy Communion to the faithful in their churches on all the days of the year except Easter Sunday. This was to encourage the faithful to fulfill more readily the Paschal precept in their own churches.[98] The religious, however, were not impeded in the administration of the other sacraments in their churches during Holy Week. Likewise, the decree *Exponi Nobis* of Pope Innocent X stated that the Paschal precept could be fulfilled at another time in the religious churches.[99] Although the obligation binding the faithful

---

[94] Cf. Benedictus XIV, const. *Inter omnigenas,* 2 febr. 1744—*Fontes,* n. 339; Pius IX, const. *Apostolicae Sedis,* 12 oct. 1869—*Fontes,* n. 552; S.C. Ep. et Reg., 21 iul. 1876—*ASS,* X (1877), 405.

[95] "Utrum regulares, etiam partes Jesuitae, in suis praediis, opificinis aliisque suis domibus saecularibus, sitis intra limites parochialium ad se non spectantium, possint administrare sacramentum baptismatis, sollemnis matrimonii, extremae unctionis et eucharistiae in festo Paschatis famulis, mercennariis, rusticis, sive aliis id genus hominibus saecularibus, absque Ordinarii vel parochi licentia?—Respondit, non posse." S.C.C., *Angelopolitan.,* 14 maii 1648—Pallottini, s.v. *Sacramentum Poenitentiae,* n. 131 et const. *Cum sicut accepimus,* 14 maii 1648—*Fontes,* n. 232.

[96] (C. 21) C. 12, X, *de poenitentiis et remissionibus,* V, 38.

[97] Sess. XIII, *de Eucharistia,* c. 9.

[98] Cf. Pius V (1566-1572), const. *Etsi mendicantium,* 16 maii 1577, n. 23 —*Fontes,* n. 121.

[99] 7 febr. 1645—*Bull. Rom. Taur.,* XV, 32.

with regard to the Paschal precept was continually repeated by the Holy See,[100] Pope St. Pius X (1903-1914) finally removed the prohibition of administering the Blessed Sacrament to the faithful on Easter Sunday in non-parochial churches so that the obligation could be fulfilled there also.[101] In non-parochial churches and public oratories established by the ordinary, Holy Communion could always be distributed during Mass independently of the proper pastor's permission.[102]

ARTICLE 3. THE CO-OPERATION OF THE RELIGIOUS AND THE SECULAR CLERGY

Until recent times in the life of the Church, the mission apostolate has been almost the sole burden of her sons and daughters in the religious life. Although the rule or constitutions of the monastic communities generally made no provision for missionary labors, as such, the pontiffs and missionary bishops relied on the monks and encouraged them to undertake some form of the apostolate when their monasteries were situated in mission lands. Hence, the pagans of the distant lands of the world were more influenced by the life and example of the monks than any direct evangelical approach. The very expediencies of the time and place forced the monks to enter the mission apostolate in some limited degree.

The mendicant communities entered the active life with the added zeal of having this as one of the ends of their institutes. Their life and constitutions were based on the concept of the "mixed life," partially contemplative and partially active. Since so many mendicants were engaged in the mission apostolate under the direction of missionary bishops who had few of their own priests to assist them, Pope Clement VIII (1592-1605) published

---

[100] Cf. S.C.C., *Farrarien.*, 15 dec. 1703—*Fontes*, n. 3011; S.C.C., *Mediolanen.*, 22 iun. 1715—*Fontes*, n. 3145; const. *Magno cum*, 2 iun. 1751—*Fontes*, n. 413.

[101] 28 nov. 1912—*Acta Apostolicae Sedis, Commentarium Officiale* (Romae, 1909-1929; Civitate Vaticana, 1929-), V (1912), 726 (hereafter cited: *ASS*).

[102] S.C.C., *Comen.*, 17 maii 1749, ad 4—*Fontes*, n. 3605.

his Constitution *Religiosorum Quorumcumque* to establish the rules to govern this form of co-operation.[103]

The pontiff commended the labors of the Franciscan missionaries in India, especially for their assistance to those bishops who had few secular priests under their jurisdiction. By a special Apostolic indult, the religious superior was to nominate certain priests of his community. The religious so selected and approved by the bishop were then to be deputed for work in the *cura animarum*. Since the religious were living *extra claustra* for long periods of time during their mission labors, they were instructed by the constitution of Pope Clement to return to their religious houses at stated times so that they might place themselves under obedience to their religious superiors and not become too accustomed to being away from their religious life. In the *cura animarum* the religious missionaries were to be subject to the bishop, but in all other things they were to remain subject to their religious superiors from whom they were to receive permission to leave the religious house.[104]

The growth of the religious clergy and their active apostolate in the life of the Church is especially noteworthy from the time of the Council of Trent. The decree of Pope Innocent III at the IV Lateran Council (1215), that no new religious communities were to be founded without the approval of the Holy See,[105] was in no manner altered by the Council of Trent. Yet, the continued prac-

[103] 6 nov. 1601—Vermeersch, *De Religiosis Institutis et Personis—Supplementa et Monumenta* (4. ed., Brugis, 1909), tit. 15, pp. 579-580 (hereafter cited: *De Religiosis*).

[104] ". . . ob penuriam Sacerdotum saecularium, ex Apostolicae Sedis speciali indulto deputari soleant, qui ab eorum Superioribus nominati, ac a locorum Ordinariis seu eorum officialibus approbati prius fuerint; cumque, sicut accepimus, Fratres sic ad curam animarum deputati, licet extra claustra in locis in quibus pro tali administratione deputantur morentur, nihilo minus certis cuiusque hebdomadae diebus ad conventus quos in locis principalibus habent accedere debeant, et Commissarios Generales, aliosque superiores quibus subsunt et oboediunt et a quibus visitantur habeant, ita ut extra claustra religionis morari minime dici possint: . . . Fratres . . . ad animarum curam exercendam, ut praefertur, deputatos, in concernentibus curam animarum Ordinario loci subesse, . . . sed suis superioribus subjectos remanere de quorum licentia extra claustra degunt."—*Loc. cit.*

[105] C. 1, *de religiosis domibus,* III, 36.

tice of the bishops of approving the founding of new religious communities with the tacit approval of the Holy See, apparently instituted a custom contrary to the law.[106] Shortly before Trent, in the year 1534, St. Ignatius Loyola founded the *Society of Jesus,* an institute that would take the fore in the counter-reformation of the sixteenth century. Pope Paul III (1534-1549) approved the Society by his Constitution *Regimini militantis Ecclesiae.*[107]

In the years following the Council of Trent, numerous new religious communities were founded for different phases of the apostolate which would extend the Church to distant lands and strengthen it in those territories already established in the Faith. Both congregations of simple vows and societies of priests were founded and approved for the active life, a fact that would bring them into close co-operation with the secular clergy. The *Oratorians,* founded in 1575 by St. Philip Neri (1515-1595),[108] and the *Eudists,* founded by St. John Eudes (1601-1680),[109] were especially active in the giving of parochial missions. The *Vincentians* were approved by Pope Urban VIII (1623-1644) and the *Redemptorists* by Pope Benedict XIV (1740-1758). The French Revolution had been the occasion for the civil authorities to suppress the work of the secular clergy and that of the older religious orders. The newly founded congregations and societies of priests were, however, able to carry on a limited apostolate and this greatly inclined the Holy See to look with a most benign attitude on their particular form of the religious life. Because of this, like institutes more readily received papal approval for all forms of the active apostolate.[110] So numerous were the religious communities founded in this period, that Pope Leo XIII (1878-1903) began the practice of classifying them as congregations of simple vows with pontifical approval, or congregations of diocesan right when they had as yet only received the approval of the local ordinary.[111]

---

[106] Bouix, *Tractatus de Jure Regularium,* I, 210.
[107] 27 sept. 1540—*Bull. Rom. Taur.,* VI, 303-306.
[108] Const. *Copiosus,* 15 iul. 1575—*Bull. Rom. Taur.,* VIII, 541.
[109] Const. *Christifidelium,* 24 febr. 1612—*Bull. Rom. Taur.,* XII, 36-37.
[110] Creusen, *De Iuridica Evolutione,* pp. 36-39.
[111] Const. *Conditae a Christo,* 8 dec. 1900—*ASS,* XXXIII (1900), 341.

Even at this late date, there were some who looked with disfavor on religious engaged in the active life. As early as Pope Gregory XIII (1572-1585), the active apostolate of the religious clergy was recognized and defended by the pontiff,[112] as many had done before him.[113] In the eighteenth century, Pope Pius VI (1775-1799) condemned the provisions of the Jansenistic Synod of Pistoia which attempted to proclaim the complete incompatibility of the religious life and the clerical ministry.[114] The false and pernicious decrees of this Synod of Pistoia (1786) demanded a vast reform in the existing practice of permitting religious to be raised to the holy priesthood. The number of priests in a monastery was to be limited so that the majority of religious should never be ordained and that the priests should remain in the minority. Even the ordained religious were not to exercise their priestly powers, but were to remain in their monasteries in silence and solitude. Holy Mass was to be offered but once or twice a day in religious houses. Most probably these propositions—as well as those that maintained that bishops were not to employ religious priests in any form of the ministry unless there happened to be a dearth of secular priests and necessity required the temporary assistance of religious—originated with the controversies emanating from the University of Paris in the thirteenth century.[115]

In his encyclical *Ubi primum,* Pope Pius IX (1846-1878) praised the apostolate of the religious clergy and exhorted their supreme moderators to work with the secular clergy in a spirit of unity and peace towards their common goal. Likewise, the pontiff encouraged the development of a spirit of concord and charity between the two branches of the clergy.[116] Similar statements were made by Pope Leo XIII (1878-1903) in his Constitu-

---

[112] Const. *Ascendente Domino,* 25 maii 1584—*Fontes,* n. 153.

[113] Cf. Honorius III, const. *Religiosam vitam,* 22 dec. 1216—*Bull. Praed.,* I, 2-4; Gregorius IX, const. *Quoniam,* 10 maii 1227—*Bull. Praed.,* I, 19: *Ioannes* XXII, const. *Frequentes,* 23 ian. 1327—c. un., *de iudiciis,* II, 1, in Extravag. com.

[114] Const. *Auctorem Fidei,* 28 aug. 1794—*Fontes,* n. 475.

[115] Cf. const. *Non sine multa,* 19 oct. 1256—*Bull. Praed.,* I, 369; Denifle, *Chartularium Universitatis Parisensis,* I, nn. 317-344.

[116] 17 dec. 1847—*Fontes,* n. 506.

tion *Romanos Pontifices.*[117] The Third Plenary Council of Baltimore (1884) quoted the statements of *Ubi primum* and joyfully noted the concord and peace that existed between the secular clergy and the religious clergy of the United States. Due to the pious moderation and temperance of all concerned, the Fathers of the Council confidently expected and predicted that the brotherly co-operation and harmony that existed in the past among the American clergy would continue to the end.[118] Finally, in a letter to Cardinal Richard, Archbishop of Paris, Pope Leo XIII praised the religious life and the good which their active apostolate was accomplishing. In his letter *Au milieu,* the pontiff noted that the scope of the religious vows was twofold: first to acquire personal perfection and secondly to prepare the religious, to purify and strengthen him, in order that he might enter the active ministry and comfort suffering humanity.[119]

---

[117] "Concordiam hanc postulat paterna caritatis Episcoporum in adiutores suos, et mutua Cleri in Episcoporum observantia; hanc concordiam flagitat finis communis qui situs est in salute animarum iunctis studiis ac viribus quaerenda; hanc eamdem exigat necessitas iis resistendi qui catholico nomine infensi sunt."—8 maii 1881—*Fontes,* n. 582.

[118] "Gaudenti et grato animo testamur et alte proclamamus, sanctam hanc concordiam, pia omnium moderatione ac temperantia, hactenus in hac qua late patet regione illaesam servatam fuisse inter clerum saecularem et plures illos ac benedictione divina crescentes ordines religiosos, tam laborantes pro ecclesiis nostris in ministerio animarum et in juventutis educatione; atque fraternum hoc foedus ac voluntatum consensionem perpetuam fore merito confidimus ac praesagimus."—*Acta et Decreta Concilii Plenarii Baltimorensis Tertii* (Baltimorae: Joannis Murphy et Sociorum, 1886), n. 86, pp. 46-47.

[119] "Le but de ces engagements est double: d'abord élever les personnes que les émettent à un plus haut degré de perfection: ensuite les préparer, en épurant et en fortifiant leurs âmes, à un ministère extérieur qui s'exerce pour le salut éternel du prochain et pour le soulagement des miseres si nombreuses de l'humanité."—8 dec. 1900—*Collectanea Sacrae Congregationis de Religiosis, Enchiridion de Statibus Perfectionis* (Romae: Typis Polyglottis Vaticanis, 1949), n. 242.

PART TWO

Canonical Commentary

CHAPTER IV

The Juridic Status of the Religious Clergy

ARTICLE 1. THE CLERICAL RELIGIOUS INSTITUTE

The religious life was first recognized as a canonical state at the Council of Chalcedon in the year 451.[1] As a canonical state for achieving perfection, it has flourished over the centuries and has developed into many different forms and various types of religious communities. The Code of Canon Law gives the different categories into which religious are placed by the Church. In canon 488, many terms affecting the religious state are defined.[2] Number 4 of this canon states what is to be understood by the term *religio clericalis*" or clerical institute: "*Religionis clericalis, religio cuius plerique sodales sacerdotio augentur; secus est laicalis.*" This basic distinction between a clerical and a lay institute does away with the former distinction of the pre-Code commentators who distinguished rather between a clerical and a monastic order.[3] They probably did this because the monastic life never accentuated clerical dignities or sacerdotal activities. The primitive monastic foundations had prescinded entirely from the clerical state and had only a limited number of priests and these merely for reasons of necessity. The spirit of monasticism with its stress on retirement, contemplation, prayer and penance seems to have created an apparent conflict with the sacerdotal activities of the clerical apostolate in the minds of many authors. Therefore, the commentators considered the monastic order and the clerical institute as being two distinct

---

[1] C. 10, C. XVIII, q. 2; cf. Schroeder, *Disciplinary Decrees*, pp. 78-79.

[2] *Codex Iuris Canonici Pii X Pontificis Maximi iussu digestus, Benedicti Papae XV auctoritate promulgatus, Praefatione, Fontium Annotatione et Indice Analytici-Alphabetico ab Emo Petro Card. Gasparri Auctus* (Romae: Typis Polyglottis Vaticanis, 1917; reimpressio, 1934).

[3] Cf. Augustine, *A Commentary on the New Code of Canon Law* (8 vols., Vols. VI-VIII, 2. ed., 1923-1924; Vols. III-V, 3. ed., 1922-1923; Vols., I-II, 4. ed., 1921-1923, St. Louis, B. Herder Co.), III, p. 58 (hereafter cited: *Commentary*).

forms of the religious state. Now, however, the monastic order can be classified as a clerical institute as long as it fulfills the requirements of canon 488, n. 4.

The expression *"plerique sodales sacerdotio augentur"* has lent itself to various interpretations. Before considering these, it is best to be familiar with the definitions considered by the Commission of Cardinals assigned to compile the present codification of Church law, while they were in the process of drawing up the present canon 488, n. 4, of our Code. It can be observed from examination that the definition was gradually narrowed to the present canon, yet broadened in its application.

In the years preceding the final draft and promulgation of the Code, many tentative definitions were submitted to this Commission. After consideration and discussion the Commission oftentimes made changes in order to clarify the intention of the legislator and the meaning of the canon.

In the year 1912 a redaction appeared that stated: *"Religio quae ex proprio fine tendit ad opera, quae sacerdotium requirunt aut pleriosque sodales ad sacerdotium disponit, clericalis est."* The redaction that followed in 1914 substituted the conjunction *"et"* for the *"aut"* of the previous definition. The one that appeared in 1916, the year before the promulgation of the Code, stated briefly: *"Nomine religionis clericalis intelligitur religio cuius plerique sodales, etsi non omnes, sacerdotio augentur."*[4]

The present canon has reduced the definition to the simple fact that if *"plerique sodales sacerdotium augentur,"* then the institute may be considered clerical.[5]

This broad definition encompasses more than some authors are willing to state. Though narrowed to this simple statement, it does not exclude other characteristic notes of a clerical religious institute. It is not correct to state that this canon is to be interpreted so as to mean that the majority of the members of the

[4] Cf. Schaefer, *De Religiosis,* n. 208, p. 85; Larraona, "Commentarium Codicis,"—*Commentarium pro Religiosis et Missionarii* (Romae, 1935-; *Commentarium pro Religiosis,* Romae, 1920-1934), II (1921), 284 (hereafter cited: *CpR*).

[5] Can. 488, n. 4.

religious institute must be priests, as some authors assert,[6] nor, as others claim, that the majority must even be destined for the holy priesthood.[7] The correct interpretation appears to be in the common opinion of the authors, namely, that a notable part of the members of an institute, at least, must be in training and destined for the priesthood.[8] Therefore the term *"plerique"* is best interpreted as meaning *many,* rather than the *majority,* or *most* of the members of the institute.[9]

Canon 488, n. 4, definitely refers to some numerical part of the community being destined for the priesthood, that is, the notable part. Since the canon is apparently stating the minimum requirement to constitute a community as clerical, it is not altogether proper to set this aside and state that it is sufficient that the lay members of an institute be subordinate to the clerical members in the constitution and government of the institute in order to classify it as clerical.[10] Neither would it be sufficient if a limited number of the community were destined for the priesthood by way of

---

[6] Cf. Woywod-Smith, *A Practical Commentary on the Code of Canon Law* (Revised and Enlarged Edition, 2 vols., New York: Joseph F. Wagner, Inc., 1948), I, p. 205 (hereafter cited: *Practical Commentary*): Augustine, *Commentary,* III, 58.

[7] Cf. Bouscaren-Ellis, *Canon Law, A Text and Commentary* (Milwaukee: The Bruce Publishing Co., 1946, 3. printing, 1949), p. 232 (hereafter cited: *Canon Law*); Creusen, *Religious Men and Women in the Code* (5. ed. revised and edited by Adam Ellis to conform with the sixth French edition, Milwaukee: The Bruce Publishing Co., 1953), n. 10, p. 12 (hereafter cited: *Religious in the Code*).

[8] "Plerique significat potiorem notabilem partem, quam constituunt qui iam sacerdotio aucti sunt sacerdotium destinantur et praeparantur."—Wernz-Vidal, *Ius Canonicum ad Codicis Normam Exactum* (7 vols. in 8, Romae: Apud Aedes Universitatis Gregorianae, 1923-1938, Vol. III, *De Religiosis,* 1933; Vol. IV, *De Rebus,* 1935), III, n. 42, p. 44 (hereafter cited: *Ius Canonicum*); Schaefer, *De Religiosis,* n. 162, p. 67; Beste, *Introductio in Codicem,* p. 314; Papi, *The Government of Religious Communities* (New York, Kenedy, 1919), n. 8, p. 12.

[9] Cf. Coronata, *Institutiones,* I, n. 503, p. 598.

[10] ". . . non sufficit . . . etsi classis sacerdotalis tantum habet vim, ut sacerdotibus ipsius regimen reservatum sit."—Schaefer, *De Religiosis,* n. 208, p. 85; the contrary opinion appears to be maintained by Vermeersch-Creusen, *Epitome,* I, n. 590, p. 442.

exception, even if at one time or another the clerics were in the majority.[11]

It must be remembered, however, that the canonical definition of the clerical institute is intended to be a broad one and is merely stating the basic norm to be used in determining whether or not a particular institute is clerical or lay. It does not thereby exclude other distinctive characteristics of a clerical community. Consequently, mere accidental changes in the number of clerics would not alter the character of the institute. If the ends of the community are sacerdotal, or if the government of the institute is placed in the hands of the clerical members, there is no doubt that the Church is erecting the community as a clerical one, even though at one time or another the lay members happen to be more numerous than the clerics.

ARTICLE 2. THE JURIDIC STATUS OF A CLERICAL INSTITUTE

All clerical religious institutes are progeny of the Church. They are moral collegiate persons given existence and sustained only through the approbation of legitimate ecclesiastical authority.[12] Some institutes may enjoy the privilege of exemption, but they always remain completely subject to the authority of the Roman Pontiff and owe him obedience even in virtue of the vow of obedience taken by their members.[13] Pope Pius XII (1939-) expressly noted this fact in opposition to the false assertion made by those who claim exemption to be contrary to the principles of the constitution given to the Church by God as well as contradictory to the law that a priest owes obedience to his bishop.[14]

---

[11] ". . . non aliqui tantum et quasi per exceptionem, sed plurimi, idest vel maior pars, vel saltem notabilis pars solalium *clerici* debent esse, et concorditer ad instituti naturam."—Fanfani, *De Iure Religiosorum* (3. ed., Rovigo: Istituto Pandano di Arti Grafiche, 1949), n. 5(D), pp. 9-10.

[12] Cans. 100, § 1; 488, n. 1; 498; 531.

[13] Can. 499, § 1.

[14] Cf. Allocution on the *Religious life* to the General Congress of Religious at Rome in the year 1950—8 dec. 1950—*AAS,* XXXXIII (1951), 27-29; Bouscaren, *Canon Law Digest* (3 vols., Vol. I, 7. printing, 1950; Vol. II, 5. printing, 1949; Vol. III, 1954; Supplements through 1957, Milwaukee: The Bruce Publishing Co.), III, 122 (hereafter cited: *Digest*).

At the same time, all clerical religious institutes are in some limited and restricted degree withdrawn from the normal organizational hierarchy of the Church and subjected more immediately to the authority of the Holy See, as exercised through their own religious superiors and the Sacred Congregation of Religious. This disposition of law, however, does not render the clerical institute any less loyal to the diocese or mission wherein it labors. In the exercise of the *cura animarum* among the faithful, clerical religious are still subject to the jurisdiction of the local ordinary.[15] The interdiocesan character of these institutes renders them more available for various forms of the apostolate wherever the universal mission of the Church requires them. This very characteristic and their more or less immediate subjection to the Holy See has been the foundation of many of the jurisdictional faculties and privileges conferred on clerical religious institutes for their apostolate.[16]

The specific sphere of activity of each institute depends on the type of institute as well as the purpose of its foundation as outlined in its constitutions. Clerical institutes will ordinarily have some form of the external sacerdotal ministry associated with their apostolate. In those institutes that are almost totally contemplative, however, external ministry will be extraordinary. Today, nevertheless, some participation in apostolic works is not necessarily excluded. In fact the Constitution *Sponsa Christi* of Pope Pius XII envisages cases in which the supreme ecclesiastical authority may recognize some form of apostolic activity for contemplatives, according to the criteria and norms fixed by the Holy See.[17] As a general principle this constitution implies that such external activity, when undertaken with due moderation and sufficient reason, not only does no harm to the contemplative life, but may bestow on it a higher value and enlarge its effectiveness.[18]

---

[15] E.g., cans. 471; 630-631.

[16] E.g., const. *Quoniam,* 10 maii 1227, of Pope Gregory IX—*Bull. Praed.,* I, p. 19; Potthast, *Regesta,* n. 7896; const. *Non sine multa,* 30 martii 1247, of Pope Alexander IV—*Bull. Praed.,* I, 334.

[17] Cf. 21 nov. 1950—*AAS,* XXXXIII (1951), 10-11; Bouscaren, *Digest,* III, 21.

[18] Cf. Letter of Fr. Larraona—S. C. Rel., 19 martii 1952—Bouscaren, *Digest,* Supplement 1954-1957, under canon 600.

This again makes it patent that the religious state is completely dependent upon the Church. It is the Church which determines how the divine principles upon which the religious life is constructed are to be adapted to present day needs. It is the Church alone which decides what forms of life are compatible with the exercise of the holy priesthood, and that no matter the mission or environment, a completely sacerdotal life be preserved.[19]

It is quite evident that the religious life is not incompatible with the sacerdotal life and the *cura animarum*. The Holy See has been relentless in condemning such false and pernicious teachings.[20] The continuous increase of clerical communities and their participation in every form of the apostolate has been paternally encouraged by the Holy See. Each new religious institute mirrors the vitality of the Church and its ability to adapt itself to the needs of the times. Once the Church has approved the rule or constitutions of a particular community, that institute is to enter the apostolate only within the confines of the specific ends outlined in its constitutions. It is the duty of religious superiors to safeguard religious discipline according to the requirements of the particular constitutions of the institute. The sacerdotal ministry of the priests of an institute must be in harmony with the religious life they have professed by entering a specific institute.

Moreover, the members of clerical institutes are not a foreign element in parish work nor mere auxiliaries to be called upon only when there is an insufficiency of secular priests.[21] Pope Pius XII has stated that it is not to be considered extraordinary or unusual,

---

[19] "L'Eglise veut avant taut, sauvegarder ce qui cónstitue la mission propre du prêtre."—Declaration of the French Bishops on "Priest-Workers"—*CpR*, XXXIII (1954), 44-45; Bouscaren, *Digest*, Supplement 1954-1957, under canon 139.

[20] Cf. The condemnations of the propositions of William of St. Amour (+ c. 1272) by Pope Alexander IV—const. *Si Filias*, 4 apr. 1256—*Bull. Praed.*, I, 301; Denifle, *Chartularium Universitatis Parisensis*, I, nn. 317-344; the condemnation of the Synod of Pistoia (1786) by Pope Pius V—const. *Auctorem Fidei*, 28 aug. 1794—*Fontes*, n. 475.

[21] Cf. Regatillo, "Relationes inter status canonicos perfectionis et alios status in Ecclesia," *Acta et Documenta Congressus Generalis de Statibus Perfectionis* (1950) (4 vols., Typis Piae Societatis S. Pauli, Romae, 1952), I, n. 67, pp. 544-555.

nor to be regarded as a temporary arrangement that religious be in parish and mission work, nor that the bishop and all the clergy of a territory belong to the regular militia of the Church. He has said that the administration of parishes and missions in the care of religious is not necessarily to be handed over to the secular clergy as soon as possible.[22]

ARTICLE 3. THE MULTIPLE VOCATION OF THE RELIGIOUS PRIEST

The Apostolic Constitution *Sedes Sapientiae* of Pope Pius XII is concerned primarily with the vocation and the training of students for the clerical religious state.[23] This constitution begins with a discussion of the divine and ecclesiastical vocation of the religious and diocesan clergy. The Holy Father states that the religious priest has a multiple vocation: religious, sacerdotal and apostolic. This divine vocation is made up essentially of a twofold element, one divine and the other ecclesiastical.[24] It is, he states, a vocation to the religious and the clerical states together, so that it is not only a call to a public life of sanctification, but also to the exercise of a hierarchical ministry in the Church. Moreover, it is a distinct vocation, so that one who has received from God the religious with the sacerdotal vocation is not to be directed incorrectly into the clerical ranks alone.[25]

The distinction between the life and the vocation of the religious

---

[22] Cf. Allocution on the *Religious life* to the General Congress of Religious at Rome in the year 1950—*AAS,* XXXXIII (1950), 28-29; Bouscaren, *Digest,* III, p. 122.

[23] 31 maii 1956—*AAS,* XXXXVIII (1956), 354-365.

[24] "Et primo quidem totius vitae sive religiosae, sive sacerdotalis et apostolicae fundamentum, quod divina vocatio appellatur, duplici veluti essentiali elemento constitui neminem ignorare volumus, divino scilicet altero, altero ecclesiastico."—*AAS,* XXXXVIII (1956), 357.

[25] "Divina enim ad religiosum et clericalem statum vocatio, utpote qua quis in Ecclesia, societate scilicet visibili atque hierarchica, ad vitam sanctificationis publice ducendum et ad ministerium hierarchicum exercendum destinetur, . . ." ". . . item ad ministerium clericale neminem promoveant, qui se religiosam solummodo vocationem divinitus recepisse demonstret; neve eos qui hoc quoque donum a Deo habuerint, ad saecularem clerum coarctent aut distrahant. . . ."—*AAS,* XXXXVIII (1956), 357-358.

priest and the secular priest does not flow from their priesthood, which is the same sharing in the priesthood of Christ, but from the fact that one of them is called to live as a priest within a specific religious institute, conforming his life to the demands of the evangelical counsels as crystalized by the Church in the rules and regulations of an approved constitution, while the other priest is not. This union of the clerical and the religious states constitutes a distinct and specific mode of life. It is a distinct vocation insofar as it is not a call to one or the other state alone, and a specific vocation insofar as it is to a particular religious institute.

The Holy Father, however, was careful to state that neither the calling of the secular priest as such, nor the vocation of the religious priest as such, is secondary and auxiliary in nature to the other. In fact, he maintains, neither of the two special forms of clerical life hold any prerogative of divine right nor has precedence over the other. Their mutual relations and the special tasks that are assigned to each depends upon the needs and conditions of each age to be decided according to the definitive decisions of the Church.[26]

In his allocution to the General Congress of Religious at Rome in the year 1950, the pontiff maintained that it is a distortion of the truth to say that the clerical state as such demands the observance of the evangelical counsels and that it must be considered a state of achieving evangelical perfection. A religious cleric is in the state of achieving evangelical perfection not because he is a cleric, but only insofar as he is a member of a religious institute approved by the Church.[27] It is for this reason that the Constitution *Sedes Sapientiae* declares that the religious priest has a greater obligation to strive for sanctification, since he is not only a priest, but has also publicly professed that he will strive for evangelical perfection. He has been constituted by his very state into an instrument for the sanctification of others, so that the salvation of souls and the growth of God's kingdom on earth depend greatly on his own personal holiness.[28]

---

[26] Cf. Allocution on the *Religious life* to the General Congress of Religious at Rome in the year 1950—*AAS,* XXXXIII (1951), 29.

[27] Cf. *AAS,* XXXXIII (1951), 28-29; Bouscaren, *Digest,* III, 122-123.

[28] ". . . quanto magis ad id tenetur, qui, non modo sacerdotio est auctus, sed ipsam perfectionem evangelicam sibi acquirendam publice professus est,

However, every priest is obliged in a special way to acquire personal holiness.[29] The mere fact of having entered a canonical state of acquiring perfection does not mean that the personal holiness of the religious priest is thereby automatically greater than that of the secular priest. Personal holiness depends on the virtue of the individual, not on the state of life he has embraced. Consequently, the person who is not in a canonical state of acquiring perfection may actually be more perfect than one who is a member of such a state.[30]

Nevertheless, the religious priest has special means at his disposal for acquiring perfection. Furthermore, he is gravely obliged to strive for perfection according to the specific norms which have received ecclesiastical approbation and which are contained in the constitution of his particular religious institute.[31] It is through these means that personal holiness can be more surely acquired, indeed will be, if he is faithful to his rule of life.

Therefore, the fact that a priest is a member of a specific religious institute specifies precisely the mode and the extent of his sacerdotal apostolate. The prescriptions of his constitutions and the precepts of his religious superiors will determine when, where, how and under what circumstances he is to enter the active sacerdotal ministry.[32] Certainly, the sacerdotal state possesses far greater dignity in degree of excellence than does the religious life. It is however to the religious life—indeed, to the specific rule of life adopted—that the religious priest must conform in the exercise of his sacerdotal powers. His whole sacerdotal life will be completely colored and channeled by the particular religious institute to which he belongs. At the same time, while the priesthood elevates

---

immo suo ipsius munere adeo ceterorum sanctificationis instrumentum constitutitur, ut ab eius sanctitate ipsa animarum salus et regni Dei incrementum non parum pendeat?"—*AAS,* XXXXVIII (1956), 300.

[29] Cf. can. 124.

[30] "En conclusion il faut donc dire: la vocation de l' individu à la sainteté ou à la perfection personnelle, l' adoption et l' exercise permanent de celle-ci ne peuvent être confondus avec la question de l' "état de perfection" au sens juridique de terme."—Letter of the Secretariate of State, July 13, 1953, to Cardinal van Roey—cf. *CpR,* XXXII (1953), 49.

[31] Can. 593.

[32] Cf. cans. 875, § 1; 1339, § 1.

and enriches the religious life, the latter strengthens and prepares the priest to give himself wholly and disinterestedly to the sacerdotal ministry.

The qualifications of the religious priest for a certain type of ministry must be considered in accordance with this intimate relationship between the religious state and the priesthood. Canon law is ever conscious of this relationship and requires religious superiors to safeguard and preserve religious discipline to that end. The demands of the sacerdotal apostolate must be considered in relation to the effect they will make on religious discipline, a discipline that will be regulated according to the prescriptions of particular constitutions and concrete situations.[33]

Consequently, since certain aspects of the ministry can be detrimental to the demands of the religious life, the Holy See may desire that secular priests be preferred to religious in regard to some particular activity. An example of such an activity in which secular priests are given preference is the assuming of military chaplaincies.[34] The demands of this ministry do not always run parallel to the prescriptions of religious discipline. Therefore, in such cases, the religious life takes precedence and the particular activity is sacrificed.

---

[33] Cf. cans. 608, § 1; 1334.

[34] "Munus cappellani militum quod a sacerdote in propria manente domo religiosa atque integris communis vitae institutis exercere non potest, sed e contrario postulet ut tota fere vita extra religiosam familiam militari quodam saecularique modo continenter ducantur, non est accipiendum nisi vera cogit necessitas, scilicet cum cappellani e clero saeculari desiderantur."—S. C. de Rel., 2 febr. 1955—*AAS,* XXXXVII (1955), 93; Bouscaren, *Digest,* Supplement 1954-1957, under canon 451.

CHAPTER V

The Juridic Relationship of Clerical Religious Houses With the Neighboring Parishes

Article 1. The Erection of the Clerical Religious House

The religious house of a clerical institute is a moral person and a subdivision of the institute. It exists independently of its material buildings.[1] But there is an intimate connection between the moral person and the material dwelling, since in many instances a change of location requires a change of the moral person.[2]

All legitimately established religious houses are at least non-collegiate moral persons and, if three religious are assigned to it, the house is a collegiate moral person.[3] It can be a *"domus formata"* or a *"domus non-formata."* A house of a clerical institute must have at least six professed members, four of them priests, to be a *"domus formata."* Fewer members than six would imply as a consequence a *"domus non-formata."*[4] Whatever its classification, every religious house requires at least the permission of the local ordinary for its valid establishment.[5]

At one time in the pre-Code era there was a controversy as to whether or not the local ordinary was obliged to consult or obtain the consent of the pastor before a religious house could be erected within parish boundaries. This question evolved out of an interpretation given to a phrase in the Constitution *Cum alias* of Pope Gregory XV (1621-1623).[6]

The constitution was concerned with the erection of religious

---

[1] "Domus religiosa formaliter et proprio sensu in iure religiosorum significat religiosam communitatem. Et ubi adest propria communitas habetur, servatis servandis, persona moralis collegialis."—Schaefer, *De Religiosis,* n. 164, p. 67; cf. Abbo-Hannan, *The Sacred Canons,* I, 497.

[2] Larraona, "Commentarium Codicis," *CpR,* III (1922), n. 174, p. 47.

[3] Can. 100, § 2.

[4] Can. 488, n. 5.

[5] Can. 497.

[6] 27 aug. 1622—*Bull. Rom. Taur.,* XII, 719.

houses. It stated that if there was any doubt whether a proposed house would prejudice the rights of religious foundations already established, the local ordinary was to obtain the consent of the respective religious superiors of the latter before granting permission to erect the new house. The constitution also stated that the bishop should consult ". . . *aliis interesse habentibus*. . . ." The conclusion of some canonists was that the pastor, as an interested party, must be consulted. Other authors believed that the consent of the pastor was necessary before a proposed religious house could be erected within his parish.[7]

Cum alias, however, gave the right to interested parties to appeal to the Holy See if they considered their interests to be prejudiced. Consequently, the dispute had little practical value.[8] Nevertheless, although the pastor's consultation, much less his consent, was not necessary legally, the consultation was recommended before the bishop gave permission to the religious to erect a house, especially when there was danger that strictly parochial rights might be prejudiced.[9]

In the present discipline, the pastor is removed from all consideration as far as the validity of the erection of a religious house is concerned. Canonical equity and prudent discretion, however, may require the local ordinary to ascertain prior to the actual granting of permission to erect a religious house whether the rights of an interested party are in danger of prejudice.[10]

---

[7] Cf. *supra*, pp. 56-58.

[8] Cf. Schaefer, *De Religiosis*, n. 338, p. 142.

[9] "Quamvis autem necessarium non sit, ut parochus vocetur et audiatur, et multo minus ut consentiat, tamen si *iuribus parochialibus stricte talibus* per novam conventus fundationem damnum illatum iri existimet, integrum ipsi est a decreto episcopi, erectionem concedentis, ad Congregationem Ep. et Reg. recurrere. Imo audire debet parochus, si episcopum *ante concessam* licentiam adeat, et oppositionem faciat."—Mocchegiani, *Iuris prudentia Ecclesiastica* (3 vols., Friburgi Brisgoviae, 1904-1905), I, n. 263, p. 162.

[10] Cf. Coronata, *Institutiones*, I, n. 523, p. 621; Beste, *Introductio in Codicem*, pp. 326-327; Abbo-Hannan, *The Sacred Canons*, I, n. 496, p. 503; Larraona, "Commentarium Codicis," *CpR*, V (1924), 323-333; Creusen, *Religious in the Code*, n. 38, p. 31; Fanfani, *De Iure Religiosorum*, n. 21, p. 40.

Prümmer[11] and De Meester[12] maintain that the pre-Code papal constitutions concerning the erection of religious houses retain their force. In their opinion, these constitutions were founded on the very nature of the erection of a proposed religious foundation and, consequently, their prescriptions are to be observed even now. According to them, therefore, when the local ordinary foresees that prejudice may befall the local parish or neighboring religious houses, he is obliged to consult the pastor and the religious superiors.

Although this opinion has practical advantages with respect to safeguarding equity, canon 6, n. 6, appears to preclude its canonical necessity. Such a consultation may well be recommended to insure the proper fulfillment of canon 496, which forbids the erection of religious houses unless their financial support is prudently foreseen, but it cannot be urged for the valid or lawful erection of a religious house.[13] The final judgment as to whether a proposed religious house can be financially sustained, in accordance with canon 496, without detriment to other religious houses or interested parties pertains ultimately to the local ordinary. Moreover, if the prescriptions of canon 496 are not observed, the validity of the erection of the religious house is not involved.[14]

A canonical remedy in canon 1676 is given to interested parties who feel that their rights have been prejudiced. Canonical injury must be proved within a period of two months through an action introduced before the tribunal of the diocese where the religious house in question is located. A right of injunction is able to suspend the erection of the religious house, unless adequate measures are taken by the religious institute to restore conditions to

---

[11] Cf. *Manuale Iuris Canonici* (4. ed., Friburgi Brisgoviae), q. 181, p. 241 (hereafter cited: *Manuale*).

[12] "Etsi Codex nihil dicat de conditionibus, sub quibus Ordinarius loci hunc consensum praestare valet, tamen, videntur in vigore permanere veteres ordinationes utpote quae in ipsa rei natura fundatae sunt et ut observetur can. 496 . . ."—*Iuris Canonici Compendium* (3 vols. in 4, Brugis, 1921-1928), II, n. 941, p. 391 (hereafter cited: *Compendium*).

[13] Cf. Wernz-Vidal, *Ius Canonicum,* III, n. 75, p. 73.

[14] Cf. Schaefer, *De Religiosis,* n. 340, p. 144; Fanfani, *De Iure Religiosorum,* n. 21, p. 40; Flanagan, *The Canonical Erection of Religious Houses,* p. 43; Larraona, "Commentarium Codicis," *CpR,* V (1924), 333-334.

their original status in the event of an adverse sentence by the judge.[15] If the interested party should choose to abandon his legal right of action according to canon 1676, he can, nevertheless, have recourse to the Holy See without suspensive effect when he foresees his rights will be canonically prejudiced.[16]

Wernz-Vidal state, however, that in actual practice recourse by pastors to the Holy See rarely comes to a happy ending for the plaintiff. Attempts to prove a defect in the fulfillment of the prescripts of canon 496, or to prove that strictly parochial rights have been canonically prejudiced by the establishment of a new religious foundation, have often times availed little.[17] The decisions of the Holy See on cases instituted by pastors show their inability to impede the erection of a proposed religious house unless they can prove canonical injury to parochial rights. Apparently, the Holy See does not recognize certain complaints as constituting canonical injury. Although it has been stated that the construction of churches and oratories connected to a religious house occasion a lessening of attendance and a diminution of monetary offerings at the parish church, this complaint has not obstructed the religious foundations. Neither justice nor strictly parochial rights were thereby harmed. Consequently, a pastor or bishop presenting these objections has not been regarded as offering reasons that should have been sustained by reason of canonical worth.[18]

The suitable sustenance of a proposed religious house and of those already in existence has always been considered a matter of

---

[15] Can. 1676, §§ 2, 3; cf. Sipos, *Enchiridion Iuris Canonici* (6. ed., Romae: Orbis Catholicus—Herder, 1954), p. 340 (hereafter cited: *Enchiridion*).

[16] Cf. Larraona, "Commentarium Codicis," *CpR*, V (1924), 333-334.

[17] "At in probatione defectus congruae sustentationis vel laesionis strictorum iurium parochialium recursus parochorum ad Sedem Apostolicam raro habebit felicem exitum."—*Ius Canonicum*, III, n. 75, footnote (22), p. 73.

[18] "Econtra non potest parochus fundationem novi conventus impedire, eique sese opponere ob rationem, quia tum sibi, tum parochiali ecclesiae inferuntur praeiudicia, *iurium tamen parochialium non laesiva.* Hinc non potest sese opponere ob secuturam imminutionem concursus populi, vel ob imminutionem oblationum spontanearum, quae nempe parocho non debentur ex iustitia, sive ob alia eiusmodi praeiudicia, quae non laedunt iura parochialia *stricte talia.*"—Mocchegiani, *Iurisprudentia Ecclesiastica*, I, n. 265, pp. 162-163; cf. Bouix, *Tractatus de Jure Regularium*, I, 287.

serious concern to the Holy See.[19] For this reason, the law requires that particular attention be directed to this consideration, lest the erection of a new house be detrimental to the sustenance and support of neighboring religious houses and clergy. At the same time, the Holy See has always fostered the development and spread of religious institutes and has opposed endeavors to impede their progress or restrict their sacred ministry.[20] The practice of the Sacred Congregations has consistently favored the erection of religious houses with their adjoining churches and oratories in spite of protests that parochial prerogatives were being thereby prejudiced.

The decisions of the Holy See in pre-Code times give evidence of the fact that the erection of religious houses was often an occasion of parochial discord. It is clear from these decisions of the Sacred Congregations that objections raised by pastors were often futile and of no canonical value. The attendance of parishioners at oratories of non-parochial status and a consequent diminution of alms and offerings to the pastor were not considered prejudicial to parochial rights. This is clearly illustrated in a decision given by the Sacred Congregation of the Council in the eighteenth century. Reference is made to similar decisions given by the same Congregation and by the Congregation of Bishops and Regulars:

> Pluries, tam in ista S. Congregatione, quam in altera Episcoporum et Regularium, actum est de constructione publici oratorii. Non obstante parochi oppositione, eadem S. Congregatio Ep. et Reg. facultatem concessit aedificandi novum oratorium, in *Ianuensi.* 5 sept. 1692, salvis tamen iuribus parochialibus. Similiter in *Nucerina.* obstiterat parochus, non solum ob timorem deficientiae eleemosynarum, sed etiam ne populi frequentia imminueretur, ac interponeretur difficultas explicationi catechesis, sacrisque supplicationibus. Cum tamen episcopus in actu visitationis facultatem impertitus fuisset construendi oratorium, nonnullis adjectis conditionibus, et sine praejudicio iurium parochiali, re delata ad eamdem S. Congregationem 12 die martii 1693, rescriptum prodiit: *"Servetur disposita*

[19] Cf. Reiffenstuel, *Ius Canonicum Universum,* lib. III, tit. 48, n. 46.

[20] Cf. const. *Auctorem Fidei* of Pope Pius VI, 28 aug. 1749—*Fontes,* n. 475; Letter of Pope Leo XIII, *Au milieu,* 23 dec. 1900—*Fontes,* n. 645.

> *per episcopum."* Eademque fuit pro constructione oratorii in *Placentina* oratorii 20 maii 1697, licet parochus et episcopum dissentirent.
>
> Sacra autem Congregatio, nulla de parochi dissensu habita ratione, licentiam aedificandi oratorium concessit in *Maceratensi.* 10 maii 1687, cum obligatione congruae dotis, et salvis iuribus parochialibus. Item in *Theatina.* 29 iulii 1690, quamvis archiepiscopus dissentiret, ne villici propriam parochiam desererent. Ac demum in *Foroliviensi.* 16 ianuarii 1694, in qua parochus ob proximitatem ecclesiae parochialis contradixerat. Ex his arguit Monacellus . . . despiciendum esse praeiudicium parochiis obventurum ex imminutione concursus et eleemosynarum, cum ex praescripto concilii Tridentini (sess. XXIV, cap. 4, *de ref.*) hortandi quidem, non tamen cogendi sint fideles ad parochialem ecclesiam diebus festis adeumdam.[21]

The present legislation of the Church was enacted with full awareness of former objections to the erection of religious houses, especially those of clerical institutes. Nevertheless, the Code has even granted more generous concessions to religious and has eliminated many formalities once involved with the establishment of religious foundations and with the erection of churches and oratories. The propagation and spread of religious institutes is not to be hampered by objections without canonical value. When strictly parochial rights are prejudiced, however, measures may be taken to preclude or rectify the matter.

ARTICLE 2. THE ERECTION OF A CHURCH OR PUBLIC ORATORY OF A CLERICAL RELIGIOUS HOUSE

Section 1. The Right to a Church or Public Oratory

All clerical religious institutes are given the right by law to erect a church or public oratory in connection with a house of the institute.[22] This right is derived from the law itself and is a privilege *"per modum legis."*[23] Consequently, it cannot be re-

[21] Causa *Sarsinaten.* 19 dec. 1772—*Thesaurus Resolutionum Sacrae Congregationis Concilii,* XXXXI, 233.

[22] Can. 497, § 2.

[23] Cf. can. 72, § 4.

nounced by the religious. The issuance of such a law depends solely on the will of the legislator so that the recipient is not free to choose to accept or renounce the privilege.[24] As a general principle, it may be stated that no religious superior, not even the General, may renounce privileges granted the institute.[25]

It appears, however, that the use of the right may be renounced.[26] Nevertheless, there are many authors who contend that the religious may not renounce even the *use* of the right.[27] The church or public oratory has always been considered an integral and principal part of a clerical house and necessary for the adequate exercise of the clerical ministry. It is questioned, therefore, whether the religious may consider themselves free to set aside their right, or even their use of the right. Moreover, the authors assert that the local ordinary may not limit or restrict this right.[28]

---

[24] Cf. Cicognani, *Canon Law* (2. ed., authorized English version by Joseph M. O'Hara and Francis J. Brennan, Westminster, Md.: The Newman Press, Reprint, 1949), p. 812.

[25] Cf. Ojetti, *Commentarium in Codicem Iuris Canonici* (4 vols., Romae, 1927-1931), I, 303.

[26] "Religiosi usui facultatis vi iuris communis concessae etiam renuntiare possent."—Schaefer, *De Religiosis,* n. 342, p. 146; cf. Flanagan, *The Canonical Erection of Religious Houses,* pp. 82-83; Maroto, "Annotationes," *CpR,* V (1924), 427.

[27] "Videtur ne ipsos regulares renuntiare posse iuribus eorum ecclesiis et oratoriis publicis iure communi concessis; pactum inire valent tantum de iis, quae liberae ipsorum dispositioni sunt relicta."—Huizing, "De auctoritate Ordinarium locorum in Missa Paroeciali Propaganda,"—*Periodica de Re Morali, Canonica, Liturgica* (*Periodica de Religiosis et Missionariis,* Brugis, 1905-1919; *Periodica de Re Canonica et Morali, utilia praesertim Religiosis et Missionariis,* Brugis, 1920-1927; *Periodica de Re Morali, Canonica, Liturgica,* Brugis, 1927-1936; Romae, 1937-), XLIV (1955), 183 (hereafter cited: *Periodica*); Toso, *Ad Codicem Iuris Canonici . . . Commentaria Minora* (5 vols. in 2, Taurini-Romae, 1920-1927), II, pars 2, ad can. 497, p. 21 (hereafter cited: *Commentaria Minora*).

[28] "Hanc facultatem Ordinarius loci excludere nequit, quia iure communi conceditur; sed nec religio usui facultatis ex toto renuntiare valet, quia haec renuntiatio esset contra mentem Legislator, qui . . . facultatem concedit . . . ut animarum curam spiritualem exerceant . . ."—Tocanel, "De facultate Ordinarii loci prohibendi divina officia in ecclesiis et oratoriis religiosorum," *Apollinaris* (Romae, 1928-), XXIX (1956), 91; ". . . the religious congregation is not at liberty to relinquish the use of the privilege, since it is not conceded for its private good alone."—Lynch, *Contracts between*

It is generally conceded by the authors, however, that the religious may not renounce the right itself and that the local ordinary may not forbid the clerical institute to have either a church or an oratory attached to a house of the institute. It must be admitted, on the other hand, that the use of the right may be voluntarily set aside by the institute in the act of erecting a house of the clerical institute. Apparently, the Holy See has recognized the binding force of such contracts entered into by religious and bishops. It is a moot question whether such a contract has any canonical value apart from the approval of the Holy See. Nevertheless, there is a tendency on the part of the Holy See to recognize all agreements between religious and bishops when the rights of the parties are vindicated, especially in the act of erecting a house of the institute.[20]

The religious do not have a right to a church or public oratory until they have been given permission to erect the religious house. The local ordinary might condition his consent for the erection of a house on the voluntary renunciation by the religious of their use of the right to have a church or public oratory. If the religious

Bishops and Religious Congregations, The Catholic University of America Canon Law Studies, n. 239 (Washington, D. C.: The Catholic University of America Press, 1946), pp. 115-116 (hereafter cited: *Contracts*).

[20] Canon 9, § 1, n. 1, of the Oriental Code is concerned with the erection of monasteries. In such instances, any clauses in the decree of erection concerning the permission to have a church or public oratory, or to exercise the ministry and perform pious works seem to be binding: "Erectio monasterii vel constituendi novi monasterii permisio secumfert, si monasterium sit sui iuris vel filiale, licentiam habendi ecclesiam vel oratorium publicum et sacra ministeria peragendi, itemque pia opera exercendi monasterii ad normam statutorum propria, *salvis clausulis in ipsa erectione vel permissione appositis, . . .*" (The italics are the writer's.) On the other hand, canon 19, § 2, of the Oriental Code is almost a repetition, verbatim, of canon 497, § 2, of the Latin Code. It is the parallel canon in this matter, since canon 9 is concerned with monastic foundations and these are placed in a completely different classification in Oriental law. Consequently, apart from monastic foundations, the law is identical. Cf. *Litterae Apostolicae Motu Proprio Datae ad Venerabiles Fratres Patriarchas, Archiepiscopos, Episcopos, Ceterosque Locorum Hierarchas Ecclesiarum Orientalium, Pacem et Communionem cum Apostolica Sede Habentes*: *De Religiosis . . . cura Pontificii Consilii Codicis Iuris Canonici Orientalis Redigendo* (Romae: Typis Polyglottis Vaticanis, 1952). (Hereafter cited: Motu Proprio *Postquam Apostolicis.*)

acquiesce, the binding force of the agreement depends, eventually, on the recognition which the Holy See gives to it. Nevertheless, from what has been stated above, it appears that the contract will be binding. In such a case, the religious choose not to exercise a right, although they do not renounce the right itself, in order to receive the permission of the local ordinary to establish a house in his diocese.

The Code gives all clerical religious institutes the right to erect a church or public oratory concomitantly with the permission of the legitimate authority to establish a house. The reason for this privilege appears to be essentially associated with the clerical nature of the institute and is considered necessary for the proper exercise of the sacerdotal ministry.[30] Moreover, the faithful have an equally acknowledged right to attend churches and public oratories of religious houses, at least during the time of services.[31] For this reason, some authors maintain that the Code gives clerical religious their right to have such a church or oratory in order that the faithful may receive the spiritual and sacerdotal administrations of the religious priests.[32]

Apparently, this opinion has some merit since something less than a church or public oratory would ordinarily suffice for the use of the religious alone. Although it is asserted that the principal reason the law grants this right to clerical religious is to enable them to fulfill adequately the choir obligation,[33] this is not necessarily true since many religious communities do not have

---

[30] Cf. Lynch, *Contracts,* pp. 115-116; O'Brien, *The Exemption of Religious in Church Law* (Milwaukee: The Bruce Publishing Co., 1943), pp. 122-123 (hereafter cited: *Exemption of Religious*); Toso, *Commentaria Minora,* II, 21.

[31] Cans. 1161; 1188, § 2, n. 1.

[32] ". . . nam planum est aedificationem novae ecclesiae vel oratorii . . . maiori emolumento spirituali christifidelium, qui saepius ad religiosas ecclesias confugiunt et religiosorum directionem expostulant."—Goyeneche, *Quaestiones Canonicae de Iure Religiosorum* (2 vols., Neapoli: M. D'Auria, Pontificius Editor, 1954-1955), II, 318 (hereafter cited: *Quaestiones Canonicae*); Tocanel, "De facultate Ordinarii loci prohibendi divina officia in ecclesiis et oratoriis religiosorum," *Apollinaris,* XXIX (1956), 91.

[33] Cf. Coronata, *Institutiones,* II, n. 732 (d), p. 32.

the choir obligation.[34] Although the law gives the parish clergy the primary right and obligation to minister to the faithful,[35] this does not lessen the right of properly approved and canonically qualified priests other than the parish clergy to exercise their sacerdotal ministry in favor of the people. Consequently, it is not the exclusive prerogative of the parish priest to dispense spiritual ministrations to the faithful.[36]

The faithful are free to attend services held in any church or public oratory and they may fulfill their obligation to hear Mass on Sundays and holy days of obligation in these non-parochial places of worship.[37] The Code does not oblige them to attend their parish church and only states that they are to be exhorted to attend frequently, where this causes no inconvenience, the services and the sermons in their parochial churches.[38] As has been stated in the previous article, the Holy See has not yielded to an objection against the establishment of religious houses or of non-parochial churches and oratories on the grounds that a lessening attendance and a diminution of offerings to the parish is a probable consequence of their erection.[39] Added to this is the tenuousness of a canonical obligation on the faithful to make any pecuniary offering to their parish at any particular time, since the obligation of church support is a general one based on divine law.[40]

---

[34] Cf. Bastnagel, "Status of Religious Oratory after Waiver of Right to Public Oratory," *The Jurist* (Washington, D. C., 1941-), IV (1944), 155-156.

[35] Can. 464, § 1.

[36] ". . . sed gravis esset exaggeratio si quis affirmaret, parochum *unice* ex mente ecclesiae curam genere animarum, unde parochiani unice ad eius ecclesiam se conferre obligentur."—Beyersbergen, "De monitione facienda fidelibus ut accedant ad ecclesias paroeciales proprias,"—*Periodica,* XXIX (1940), 16-23.

[37] Cf. cans. 1161; 1188, § 2, n. 1; 1249.

[38] Can. 467, § 2.

[39] "Aliquando parochus erectioni domus religiosae se opponit, quia timet imminutionem aut concursus populi in ecclesia parochiali aut oblationum spontanearum, sed Curia Romana identidem declaravit, has rationes insufficientes esse."—Prümmer, *Manuale,* q. 181, p. 241.

[40] Cf. cans. 1186, n. 2; 1379, § 3; cf. Hannan, "The Obligation of Church Support," *The Jurist,* I (1941), 342-344; Bastnagel, "Exempting Parishioners from the Pastor's Authority," *The Jurist,* X (1950), 58-59.

In the pre-Code law, not all clerical religious had the privilege of a church or public oratory such as that granted by the present Code. Formerly, clerical institutes of simple vows had to seek further permission to have an oratory after they had first received permission to establish a religious house. The present discipline, therefore, is much more generous than the old. This has been done with full awareness of past difficulties arising from the attendance of the faithful at the sacred functions held in the churches and oratories of religious houses. The present law is more extensive and less formality is involved since the clerical house is given the right *ipso iure* with the permission to establish the foundation. Moreover, it appears that the law has granted such public places of worship to all clerical religious houses not only because of the sacerdotal character of the institutes, but also because of the many spiritual benefits that will accrue to the faithful who have a canonical right to attend sacred functions held in such a church or public oratory.

Section 2. The Site of the Church or Public Oratory

There is only one provision which the law makes in conceding a church or public oratory to an established clerical religious house. It is, namely, the obligation to obtain an additional authorization from the local ordinary to erect the sacred edifice on a certain location.[41] Although the consent of the local ordinary is not necessary in order to have the church or public oratory, since the law itself concedes this to the religious, his permission is required to build one or the other on a determined site. The reason behind this prescription appears to be that the local ordinary is thereby given the opportunity to use his discretion in selecting the most appropriate site so that he can prevent any injury or prejudice to other churches in the vicinity, harm which may not be compensated for by the spiritual benefits to the faithful arising from the new church or oratory.[42]

---

[41] Cans. 497, § 2; 1162, § 4.

[42] "Ratio praecisa est, ut ordinarius habeat opportunitatem praecavendi ne aedificatio ecclesiae novae in praeiudicium sprirituali fidelium utilitate non compensatum vergat aliarum ecclesiarum in vicina iam extantium."—Beste, *Introductio in Codicem*, p. 569.

The local ordinary may refuse permission to erect the church or oratory on a certain location when he prudently foresees that it cannot be adequately supported, or that some other grave detriment will befall the churches in the vicinity without spiritual compensation to the faithful.[43] As a general principle, however, it had always been recognized that when a place of worship is erected in connection with a religious house, its necessary financial support is presumed to be assured.[44] When there is no canonically recognized reason for refusing to approve the site of the proposed church or oratory, the local ordinary may not refuse the religious permission to build on a site.[45] Once having received permission to erect a house, the clerical religious have an acquired right which cannot be obstructed without a correspondingly serious reason.

The exact nature of the harm to be prevented is not stated in canon 1162, but it is that which may befall churches located in the area which is not compensated for by proportionate spiritual advantages that redound to the faithful. Often some minor material detriment is necessarily associated with such an enterprise. Yet, it may be offset by the greater spiritual benefit to be derived from the erection of a new church or oratory.[46] If, however, an unusually large pecuniary loss is prudently foreseen, it would appear to be a sufficient reason against the approbation of a particular site.

In order that the local ordinary might make a proper judgment concerning the prejudice that may affect the churches in the vicinity, he is to consult their rectors before approving the site.[47] Certainly the pastor is numbered among these.[48] Authors

---

[43] Cf. can. 1162, § 2.

[44] Cf. Feldhaus, *Oratories,* The Catholic University of America Canon Law Studies, n. 42 (Washington, D. C.: The Catholic University of America, 1927), p. 81.

[45] Cf. Flanagan, *The Canonical Erection of Religious Houses,* p. 84.

[46] "Detrimentum utique de quo hic agitur, est etiam detrimentum materiale seu pecuniarum; at si tale detrimentum necessarium sit vel valde conferat ad spiritualem populi utilitatem, attendi nullo modo debet, dummodo tamen inter detrimentum ex una parte et utilitatem ex altera nimia differentia non sit."—Coronata, *Institutiones,* II, n. 732, p. 31.

[47] Can. 1162, § 3.

[48] "Contra solius conventus erectionem parochus querelam facere non potest,

dispute about the necessity of this consultation and its effect upon the validity of the ordinary's approval.[49] In view of the authority of opinions on either side of the question, one can safely state that there appears to be a *dubium legis* and, consequently, the validity of the choice cannot be questioned.[50]

Furthermore, although the local ordinary does not approve a particular site for the construction of the church or public oratory, he is still obliged to approve one that is relatively convenient and acceptable to the religious.[51] Once a certain location has been approved and accepted, the religious cannot be forced to build later on some other site.[52] Since the Code gives the local ordinary the discretionary power to approve or reject the site of the church, it therefore indirectly gives him some discretion concerning the general location of the religious house itself.[53]

Canon 497, § 2, states that the permission to establish a clerical religious house also implies the right to have a church *or* a public oratory. It is generally admitted that the local ordinary may restrict this concession for a just reason to the minimum and permit the religious to have only a public oratory.[54] There is some question whether the choice of having a church or public oratory depends on the religious or the local ordinary. It appears that the religious may make the selection unless the local ordinary restricts

---

sed contra erectionem ecclesiae cum domo religiosa coniuncta si iura paroechialia diminuerentur."—Schaefer, *De Religiosis,* n. 340, p. 144; Augustine, *Commentary,* III, 80-90.

[49] E.g., Consultation does not affect the validity of the approval: Vermeersch-Creusen, *Epitome,* I, n. 299, pp. 209-210; Bouscaren-Ellis, *Canon Law,* p. 91. Invalid without the consultation: Coronata, *Institutiones,* I, n. 153, pp. 184-185; Beste, *Introductio in Codicem,* pp. 163-164.

[50] Can. 15; Bouscaren-Ellis, *Canon Law,* p. 91.

[51] Cf. Vermeersch-Creusen, *Epitome,* II, n. 478, p. 334.

[52] Cf. Larraona, "Commentarium Codicis," *CpR,* V (1924), 428.

[53] ". . . videtur Ordinario loci ius agnoscendum determinandi locum ubi ecclesia religionis clericalis erigenda sit et consequenter, indirecte etiam locum ubi domus religiosa construi debeat."—Coronata, *Institutiones,* I, n. 524, p. 624.

[54] Cf. Schaefer, *De Religiosis,* n. 342, p. 145; Larraona, "Commentarium Codicis," *CpR,* V (1924), 427, n. 369.

them for some just reason as, for example, the proximity of the parish church.[55]

The local ordinary also has the right to bless and lay the cornerstone of the sacred edifice, unless the house belongs to an exempt clerical institute. In the latter case, the right pertains to the major superior.[56] All ordinaries have the obligation to see that the prescriptions of Christian tradition and the laws of sacred art are observed in the ecclesiastical architecture. Violations of these norms in the plans of the building or in its actual construction are to be corrected.[57]

ARTICLE 3. THE USE OF THE CLERICAL RELIGIOUS CHURCH OR PUBLIC ORATORY IN RELATION TO THE PARISH CHURCHES

Section 1. The Right to Celebrate Sacred Functions

All sacred functions may be celebrated within churches and oratories which are in conformity with the law and the liturgy. The right to celebrate sacred functions is *ipso iure* granted along with and logically follows the right of clerical religious to possess a church or public oratory in connection with their legitimately erected houses.[58] Presupposing, therefore, that all the requirements of the law are complied with, there is nothing to prevent the clerical religious from administering the sacraments, celebrating Mass, and performing all those functions that are commonly associated with the power of Holy Orders. Encompassed in the notion of sacred functions are all those non-reserved sacerdotal functions which pertain to the divine cult and which are exercised for the spiritual welfare of the religious community.[59]

The local ordinary who grants permission to establish a clerical religious house can not arbitrarily impose conditions on the use

---

[55] Cf. Ojetti, *Synopsis Rerum Moralium et Iuris Pontificii* (3. ed., 4 vols., Romae, 1909-1914), I, n. 243, s.v. *aedificatio*.

[56] Cf. cans. 1153; 1163.

[57] Can. 1164, § 1.

[58] Can. 497, § 2.

[59] Cf. can. 2256, n. 1; Tocanel, "De facultate Ordinarii loci prohibendi divina officia," *Apollinaris*, XXVIII (1955), 323; Larraona, "Commentarium Codicis," *CpR*, V (1924), 428-429.

of the church or public oratory. It is not within his competence to restrict the performance of sacred functions which are permitted by the law of the Church.[60] He can not place limitations upon the clerical character of the institute, or upon the facilities and liberties conceded to religious by the common law, or, finally, upon the privileges associated with exemption.[61] The right to perform sacred functions does not flow from the privilege of exemption but from the power of Orders. It is evident from this canon that reference is made to the ordinary works of the sacred ministry, those that are common to all clerics, in so far as they may be performed in the church or public oratory of the clerical religious house.

Where jurisdiction, approbation, or permission is required to exercise the powers received by Holy Orders, it is not to be refused or restricted except within the confines recognized by law. In cases where none of these are necessary, greater reason is required to interfere with the performance of sacred functions. Accordingly, one author asserts that even though the religious accept conditions which prevent the full exercise of the sacred ministry permitted them by law, these conditions are to be considered as null and void even if agreed upon by the religious and the bishop in the very act of erecting the religious house.[62] This opinion is difficult to defend, however, in view of the fact that the Holy See appears to be very much inclined to recognize the validity and binding force of contracts entered into between religious and the bishop when establishing a new house of the institute. Of course, only those rights which may be set aside or which may have conditions appended to their exercise are able to be the matter of

---

[60] "Neque in permissione constituendae novae domus regularibus clericis dandae, vi canonis 497, § 2, Ordinarii eximere possent saltem oratorium publicum neque in illa conditiones apponere quae laederent iura superioribus quoad functiones sacras ibi celebrandas ipso iure communi concessa."—Huizing, "De auctoritate Ordinariorum locorum in Missa paroeciali propaganda," *Periodica,* XLIV (1955), 183.

[61] Cf. Ojetti, *Synopsis Rerum Moralium et Iuris Pontificii,* I, n. 243, s.v. *aedificatio.*

[62] Cf. O'Brien, *Exemption of Religious,* p. 125.

such a contract. Those rights which are granted *"per modum legis"* to a moral body may not be renounced.[63]

The final phrase of canon 497, § 2, is concerned only with the conditions which are able to be imposed by the ordinary on the religious in the very act of erecting the house.[64] As can be seen from the grammatical construction of the canon, the conditions concern neither the right of clerical religious to possess a church or a public oratory, nor the right to perform sacred functions in conformity with the law. The conditions that can be imposed by the local ordinary have reference to the pious works proper to each institute. Therefore, the local ordinary may limit, for example, the type of schools a teaching institute might conduct, but he may not altogether exclude the work of education when it is the primary aim for which the institute was erected. In view of the importance of the matter, therefore, the local ordinary should only limit or restrict pious works of the institute for some grave and reasonable cause.[65]

Any infringement on the right to celebrate sacred functions must be strictly interpreted.[66] All sacred functions may be celebrated, but the privileges, legitimate customs and rights of others must be respected and safeguarded, especially those of the parishes.[67] Liturgical law must be observed, for some sacred rites which are permitted in a church may not invariably be performed in an oratory.[68] Proper faculties are necessary for the exercise of certain sacerdotal functions such as the hearing of confessions and preaching.[69] The celebration of sacred rites in churches and public oratories connected to clerical religious houses is a right conceded by law. What the common law grants cannot be capriciously

[63] Can. 72, § 4.

[64] "Constituendae novae domus . . . ; pro omnibus religionibus, pia opera exercendi religionis propria, salvis conditionibus in ipsa permissione appositis."—can. 497, § 2.

[65] ". . . quam limitationem Ordinarius nonnisi ex gravi et rationabili causa apponere potest."—Wernz-Vidal, *Ius Canonicum,* III, n. 76, p. 74.

[66] "Leges quae . . . liberum iurium exercitium coarctant . . . strictae subsunt interpretationi."—can. 19.

[67] Cans. 497, § 2; 1171.

[68] Can. 1191, §§ 1, 2.

[69] Can. 877.

undermined or hampered by conditions and limitations that have no canonical recognition. If, however, the religious enter a contract with the bishop when their house is being established, and accept limitations on the exercise of this right, they are bound to observe such an agreement.

Section 2. The Celebration of Sacred Functions

Although, generally speaking, all ecclesiastical rites and functions may be celebrated in churches and oratories, special consideration must be given to parochial privileges, customs and rights.[70] The local ordinary, in this regard, is given the authority to determine the hour of services in sacred edifices subject to his jurisdiction, but not those which belong to exempt religious.[71] Exempt superiors must, nevertheless, be vigilant that celebrations in their churches and oratories do not interfere with the catechetical instructions and gospel explanation given in the parish churches.[72]

It is to be noted that the prescriptions of canons 609, § 3, and 1171 determine the basic relationship between the churches or public oratories of clerical religious houses and the parish churches. It matters little whether the parish churches in question are in the care of the religious clergy or the secular clergy. The prescriptions of canons 479-486, concerning the rectors of churches and their relationship to the parish clergy, do not apply to the churches and oratories of religious houses. This is quite evident from the wording of canon 479, § 1: "*Nomine rectorum ecclesiarum hic veniunt sacerdotes, quibus cura demandatur alicuius ecclesiae, quae nec . . . adnexa domui communitatis religiosae. . . .*" The local ordinary enjoys generous discretionary power to judge whether or not the parish ministry is detrimentally affected by religious services in the churches subject to rectors and he is authorized to take appropriate measures in case of conflict.[73] He

---

[70] Can. 497, § 2; 1171.

[71] Can. 1171.

[72] Can. 609, § 3.

[73] "Ecclesiae rector potest divina officia etiam solemnia ibidem celebrare, salvis legitimis fundationis legibus et dummodo non noceant ministerio paroeciali; in dubio autem utrum huiusmodi detrimentum contingat, necne, Ordinarii loci est rem dirimere et opportunas normas praescribere ad illud evitandum."—can. 482.

is not given the same extensive authority over the churches and oratories of clerical religious houses, nor do the prescriptions of canon 482 apply to them. If this is not adverted to, the restrictions which may be placed on the celebrations of sacred functions in these places will be greater than the law of the Code permits.

The specific type of harm, which the services in a church or public oratory of a religious house can occasion, is clearly indicated in the canon 609, § 3. It is only this type of harm that the local ordinary is given authority to judge and, in most cases, to correct. The harm with which this canon is concerned is any detriment to the parochial catechetical instruction or gospel explanation. The local ordinary is the sole judge in this matter, even though the church belongs to an exempt clerical institute. As can be seen, the ordinary enjoys less authority there than he does over churches in the care of rectors. In this latter case he may use any appropriate means to preclude whatever he considers detrimental to the parochial ministry.

The proper understanding of the implications of canons 609 and 1171 is aided by an examination of the legislation upon which the present canons are based. The references in the present Code compiled by Cardinal Gasparri list certain decisions of the Sacred Congregations and the encyclical letter *Etsi minime* of Pope Benedict XIV,[74] which will be referred to in order to clarify the extent and meaning of the present law. The basic intent of canon 1171 is, however, to safeguard parochial rights, privileges and lawful customs. Obviously, all strictly parochial functions reserved to the pastor by canon 462 cannot be performed outside the parish church without the permission of the pastor. Besides these reserved functions, moreover, privileges and lawful customs are to be respected. Consequently, religious may not introduce the celebration of a feast that has been celebrated from time immemorial in the parish church by great numbers of the faithful.[75] At the same time, lawful custom or privilege may introduce the right to perform some parochial functions outside the parish church, as, for example, the privilege of having a baptismal font, or of solemnly baptizing

[74] 7 febr. 1742—*Fontes,* n. 324.

[75] Cf. Ferraris, *Biblotheca,* s.v. *Festivitates,* n. 46.

a convert whom a religious has instructed in the truths of the Faith. Moreover, the Code has expressly given religious superiors of clerical houses the right to perform particular functions that are otherwise parochial prerogatives, such as the administering of the last sacraments.[76]

Section 3. Catechetical Instructions and the Celebration of Sacred Functions

Religious superiors are obliged to be vigilant lest the celebration of services in their churches and oratories conflict with the parochial catechetical instructions and gospel explanation.[77] The term *"advigilent"* is the canonical method of imposing a supervisory obligation.[78] This is an important obligation. It receives special mention in canon 1171 when the local ordinary is given the right to judge whether or not services in religious churches and oratories conflict with the parish catechetical and doctrinal instructions. This right pertains solely to the local ordinary, even in the case of exempt churches and oratories. Woywod-Smith maintain that the general exemption given exempt clerical religious institutes is limited by the right given the local ordinary in canon 609, § 3, and again cited in canon 1171.[79] Therefore, according to this opinion, the local ordinary may not positively order exempt religious to hold services at certain hours, but he may forbid them, nevertheless, to have services at those hours which interfere with the preaching of the Gospel or the catechetical instructions in a given parish church.

This opinion, however, cannot be maintained. Canon 615 is the fundamental canon governing the exemption of religious. Its prescriptions are clear: "*. . . ab Ordinarii loci iurisdictione exempti sunt, praeterquam in casibus a iure expressis.*" Consequently, unless the law expressly states that exempt religious are subject to the local ordinary in a specific matter, they are considered to be exempt. Canon 1171 expressly excludes exempt religious churches and refers only to the obligation of religious superiors to guard

---

[76] Cf. cans. 514, § 1; 462, n. 3; 938, § 2.

[77] Cf. can. 609, § 3.

[78] E.g., cans. 336, § 2; 605; 607; 865; 1261, § 1; 1349.

[79] Cf. *Practical Commentary,* I, 294-295.

against the celebration of rites which conflict with the parish instructions. Therefore, the ordinary is not given the right to regulate the functions held in exempt churches, but he does have the right to determine when these functions interfere with the parochial instructions. It is this right alone which he possesses and canons 609, § 3, and 1171 confer no other power over the exempt churches and oratories except this reserved judgment.[80]

Once the local ordinary determines that certain services in an exempt church or oratory cause detriment to these instructions, he should advise the superior of this fact and request him to make appropriate corrections. If the superior fails to rectify the matter, the ordinary should warn him that the matter will be referred to the Holy See. He cannot, however, compel the superior to regulate the hour of services nor penalize him for not so doing.[81] Although it is the reserved right of the ordinary to make the judgment concerning the question of harm befalling the parochial instructions, in practice he has no remedy except to have recourse to the Holy See. As a result, his judgment is ineffectual until the Holy See makes its investigation of the matter.[82]

It should be noted that the power of the local ordinary extends only to the judgment concerning possible harm to the parochial catechetical instructions and gospel explanation. Consequently, if harm is experienced with regard to some other parochial function as a result of parishioners attending a particular rite in the church or oratory of exempt religious, the ordinary may not direct them to rectify the matter.[83]

Canon 1171 authorizes the local ordinary to regulate the time of services for any just reason in all non-exempt churches and

---

[80] Cf. Goyeneche, *Quaestiones Canonicae,* II, 33; O'Brien, *Exemption of Religious,* p. 128.

[81] Cf. Beste, *Introductio in Codicem,* pp. 417 et 576; Berutti, *Institutiones Iuris Canonici* (5 vols., Taurini: Marietti, 1936-1943), III, n. 122, p. 275 (hereafter cited: *Institutiones*); Fanfani, *De Iure Religiosorum,* n. 329, p. 481.

[82] Cf. Huizing, "De auctoritate Ordinariorum locorum in Missa Paroeciali Propaganda," *Periodica,* XLIV (1955), 180.

[83] ". . . ob alias tamen causas praeter nocumentum explicationi Evangelii et catecheticae instructioni in regularium ecclesiis potestatem non habet Ordinarius loci aliquid decernendi."—Coronata, *Institutiones,* II, n. 472, p. 43.

oratories, especially when he judges that there exists a detrimental effect upon the catechetical instructions in a parish.[84] From the tenor of canon 609, § 3, and canon 1171, it seems that the ordinary should fix the hour of services only after a futile admonition to the religious superior to correct the matter. It is not clear whether the local ordinary is able to punish recalcitrants, or whether he should have recourse to the Holy See. Some authors maintain that the ordinary should amicably warn the religious when they fail to rectify the matter. If this fails, he may impose a precept on the superior, but not a censure.[85] Although some state that the matter should be referred to the Holy See,[86] it appears that this is only in reference to exempt religious. Non-exempt religious, however, are subject to the local ordinary in this matter and may be penalized.[87]

If the neighboring pastor feels that certain functions are detrimental to parochial instructions, he is free to ask the religious superior to consider adjusting the matter. The religious, however, need not act on his judgment since neither the pastor nor the religious superior have a right to make authoritatively this decision. Both must defer to the judgment of the local ordinary to whom canon 609, § 3, gives the reserved right to make this decision.[88]

Without doubt, the purpose of the law is by-passed when the faithful attend religious churches and oratories and do not receive any instruction at all. However, if the religious habitually give a homily on the Gospel, or catechetical or doctrinal instruction during their services, especially at Masses on Sundays and holydays

---

[84] Cf. can. 609, § 3.

[85] "Si nocumentum, loci Ordinarius superiorem religiosam primo amicaliter monere, dein praecepto (non censura) coercere potest."—Claeys Boúúaert-Simenon, *Manuale Juris Canonici* (3 vols., Vol. I et III, 5. ed., Vol. II, 3. ed., Gandae et Leodii: apud Auctores, 1939-1947), I, n. 688, p. 398.

[86] "Si Superiores ab Ordinario moniti neglexerint divina officia ita ordinare, ne catecheticae instructioni et evangelii praedicationi parochiali nocumentum afferatur, Ordinarius ad Sedes Ap. recurrere potest."—Sipos, *Enchridion,* p. 323.

[87] "In omnibus in quibus religiosi subsunt Ordinario loci, possunt ab eodem etiam poenis coerceri."—can. 619.

[88] Cf. Berutti, *Institutiones,* III, n. 122, p. 275; Fanfani, *De Iure Religiosorum,* n. 377, p. 528.

of obligation, it can be doubted whether the detriment contemplated in canon 609, § 3, is actually perpetrated. The primary reason for the law appears to be the assurance that the proper instruction of the faithful take place together with an inspiration to their devotion. It is only a secondary consideration that the instructions can be more fittingly and appropriately given in the parish churches. As Vermeersch-Creusen point out, the pastor has the obligation after the bishop to care for the spiritual life of the faithful and to see that they are properly instructed in the truths of the Faith. This obligation is clear from the prescriptions of canon 514, § 4. However, the faithful are free to attend the churches and oratories of religious and to fulfill their obligation to hear Mass on Sundays and holy days of obligation. Consequently, as long as they receive some instructions on these occasions, there is little prejudice to the parochial instructions.[89] On the other hand, there is no doubt that the law regards the parish church as the best and the most appropriate place for the instruction of the faithful. It is the serious obligation of the pastor to preach to his people and to minister to their spiritual needs.[90] The will of the legislator and the spirit of the law manifests the fact that the Church recognizes that the spiritual welfare of the faithful depends greatly on the parochial ministry. At the same time, however, the law does not consider that it is the sole right of the pastor to minister to the faithful, for it empowers the bishop to commission others to participate in this work.[91] This fact seems to have been in the mind of Benedict XIV when he authorized local ordinaries in his encyclical letter *Etsi minime* to oblige non-parochial priests and rectors to give instructions on Christian doctrine at all Masses attended by the faithful on Sundays and holy

[89] "Rursus autem integrum est religiosis fideles ad suas missas et praedicationes admittere, etsi, quo maior sit in una ecclesia frequentia populi, eo minor per se futura fuerit in aliis ecclesiis, quod tamen detrimentum multis bonis compensatur. Nam caput, tandem aliquando, est, ut populus devotione crescat, et audiat explicationem catechismi et evangelii."—*Epitome,* I, n. 767, p. 580.

[90] Cans. 1329-1332.

[91] E.g., cans. 1334-1335; cf. Beyersbergen, "De monitione facienda fidelibus ut accedant ad ecclesias paroeciales proprias,"—*Periodica,* XXIX (1940), 16-23.

days of obligation. So insistent was the pontiff that the faithful receive proper instruction, that he decreed that recalcitrant priests be obliged by way of penalties to provide such instructions.[92]

Apparently, this encyclical was motivated by an unusual situation in certain rural localities where the people became accustomed to attend public chapels, some of which were close to the parish church. As a result, they rarely attended the parish church and did not receive the customary catechetical instructions given there. Furthermore, they received no instructions in the mysteries of the Faith, the sacraments, or the commandments of God when attending these public chapels. Stressing the obligation of the pastor to administer the sacraments to his people and provide Christian instruction, the encyclical of Benedict decreed that the small public chapels near the parish church were not to offer Mass until after the time of the parochial Mass and instructions. Concerning those chapels which were removed somewhat from the parish church, the pontiff stated that their rectors could be coerced by penalties to offer instructions. Consequently, the tenor of the pontiff's encyclical was primarily to provide the faithful with the opportunity to receive proper instructions and to guarantee that they would receive suitable training in the truths of the Faith.[93]

More recently, the same concern for the proper instruction of the faithful has been manifested by the Holy See. The Sacred Congregation of the Council issued a circular letter to all the Ordinaries of Italy,[94] as well as the decree *Provido sane consilio* to the religious throughout the Catholic world,[95] encouraging the use of religious for assistance in the important matter of providing Christian doctrinal instructions for the faithful. Pope Pius XI in his Motu Proprio *Orbem catholicum* exhorted religious to cooperate in this work so dear to the pontiff and so necessary for salvation.[96] It appears, therefore, that the essential and primary purpose of the canons governing this matter[97] is to care for the

[92] 17 febr. 1742—*Fontes,* n. 324.

[93] Cf. Huizing, "De auctoritate Ordinariorum locorum in Missa paroeciali propaganda," *Periodica,* XLIV (1955), 184.

[94] S.C.C., 31 maii 1920—*AAS,* XII (1920), 299.

[95] S.C.C., decr., 12 ian. 1935—*AAS,* XXVI (1935), 145.

[96] 29 iun. 1923—*AAS,* XV (1923), 327.

[97] Cans. 609, § 3; 1171.

proper instruction of the faithful and not merely to foster parish life and unity.[98]

Consequently, if the essential purpose of the law is fulfilled, it seems that no harm can be considered to befall the parochial catechetical instructions or Gospel explanation. Nor must it be thought that when the religious provide such instructions in their church or oratory that they are, nevertheless, obliged to arrange or adjust the time of their services.[99] However, some authors maintain that the local ordinary might persuade them to make some concession in this matter even though he cannot regularly prohibit them from having services.[100] It also seems that the local ordinary can still demand that no services detrimentally affect the attendance at the principal Mass of the parish.[101]

Generally speaking, however, this prejudice is hardly verified when instructions are given in the churches and public oratories of religious,[102] even when they are given at the same hour as those in the parish.[103] The law gives the local ordinary a simple and direct method of precluding any detriment to the primary end of canon 609, § 3, by giving him the right to prescribe that all churches and oratories give a short Gospel explanation or doctrinal instruction at all the Masses attended by the faithful on Sundays and holy days of obligation.[104] Therefore, it is easy to understand why many commentators stress the moral implications of the canons, rather than their strict juridical interpretation.

---

[98] "Unde vides non inspiciendam esse utilitatem ecclesiae paroecialis sed ministerium paroeciale et prae primis populi spiritualem profectum."—Goyeneche, *Quaestiones Canonicae,* II, 317; Schaefer, *De Religiosis,* p. 819.

[99] ". . . si in ipsis regularibus ecclesiis talis instructio praebeatur, quia tunc finis legis sufficienter adimpletur."—Melo, *De Exemptione Regularium,* p. 140.

[100] "Potest hoc ab Episcopo, datis certis adiunctis, dissuaderi, sed cum principalem finem suum lex attingat, regulariter non prohibere."—Claeys Boúúaert-Simenon, *Manuale Juris Canonici,* I, n. 668, p. 369.

[101] Cf. Tocanel, "De facultate Ordinarii loci prohibendi divina officia."—*Apollinaris,* XXVIII (1955), 328.

[102] ". . . ut non verificentur abusus necesse est ut revera in ecclesiis religiosorum evangelii explicationi et catechismi opera detur."—Coronata, *Institutiones,* I, n. 615 (3), p. 794.

[103] Cf. Claeys Boúúaert-Simenon, *Manuale Juris Canonici,* I, n. 668, p. 369.

[104] Cans. 1334; 1345.

Ultimately, it is relatively unimportant whether the end of the law is fulfilled through the parish instructions or through other suitable and equivalent means.[105]

Section 4. The Scheduling of Sacred Functions

For any just reason the local ordinary may fix the hour of services in all churches and oratories except those that belong to an exempt institute.[106] It is the opinion of some authors that if the public order is involved, or if the ordinary wishes to avoid unbecoming controversy, he has a just reason for determining the hour of services in any church.[107] Since canon 1171 does not restrict the extent of the ordinary's power, he, therefore, can regulate the time of services in all churches subject to his authority, whether parochial or non-parochial, exclusive of those belonging to exempt religious. However, the just reason required by the canon should be prompted by whatever will foster the greater good of souls.[108] Schaefer states that a material utility to the church is not sufficient, but that it must be a reason associated with the spiritual welfare of the faithful.[109]

At the same time, however, the rights of other churches are to

---

[105] Cf. Huizing, "De auctoritate Ordinariorum locorum in Missa paroeciali propaganda."—*Periodica,* XLIV (1955), 191; Feldhaus, *Oratories,* p. 101; De Meester, *Compendium,* II, 466; Goyeneche, *Quaestiones Canonicae,* II, 317; Schaefer, *De Religiosis,* n. 1372, p. 819; Clayes Boúúaert-Simenon, *Manuale Juris Canonici,* I, n. 668, p. 369; Coronata, *Institutiones,* I, n. 615 (3), p. 794; Vermeersch-Creusen, *Epitome,* I, n. 767, p. 580.

[106] ". . . Ordinarius autem, praesertim horas sacrorum rituum, potest, iusta de causa, praefinire, dummodo ne agatur de ecclesia quae ad religionem exemptam pertineat."—can. 1171.

[107] ". . . horas sacrorum rituum iusta de causa (propter ordinem publicum, ad evitandas aut componendas controversias) praefinire, . . ."—Sipos, *Enchiridion,* p. 555; cf. Jone, *Commentarium in Codicem Iuris Canonici* (3 vols., Paderborn: Officina Libraria F. Schöningh, 1950-1955), II, 341 (hereafter cited: *Commentarium*).

[108] Cf. cans. 482; 1162, § 3; 2162.

[109] "Non inspicienda est utilitas materialis ecclesiae paroecialis, sed ministerium paroeciale et prae primis verus populi profectus spiritualis."—*De Religiosis,* n. 1372, p. 819.

be considered. In view of canon 19,[110] canon 1171 must be strictly interpreted. In selecting the term *"praefinire,"* the legislator intended to convey only one meaning, namely, the right to fix the time or schedule the hour of the services. This does not include the right to forbid, suppress, or limit the number of sacred functions. The legislation on which this canon is based seems to substantiate this assertion. The decisions of the Sacred Congregation of the Council, cited in the footnote to canon 1171, all concern cases where there was a conflict between the celebration of Masses in a non-parochial church or oratory and those offered in the parish church. In one decision, the Congregation stated that the bishop could not prohibit the celebration of more than one Mass in a non-parochial oratory in order to safeguard the parochial Mass.[111] In the two other cases cited,[112] the same Congregation and the Sacred Congregation of Rites responded in an identical manner. In one response given by the Sacred Congregation of the Council, references were made to many similar cases and the decision was that a religious house need not abstain from the celebration of Mass or other sacred rites until after the parochial Mass.[113]

In view of reasons such as those referred to above, Feldhaus asserts that the silence of the Code regarding the local ordinary's power to forbid the celebration of sacred functions in a church or oratory is not merely a matter of negative silence alone. It actually appears to be an intentional denial of such a power to the local ordinary.[114] Although the word *"praesertim"* in canon 1171

---

[110] "Leges quae . . . liberum iurium exercitium coarctant . . . strictae subsunt interpretationi."

[111] ". . . non potuisse episcoporum praescribere ut ibi unica tantum Missa in eadem die valent celebrari. . . ."—*Fesulana,* 23 aug. 1659, ad 2—*Fontes,* n. 2760.

[112] S.C.C., *Fulginaten.,* 7 iul. 1696—*Fontes,* n. 2955; S.C.R., *Comen.,* 11 iul. 1643—*Fontes,* n. 5431.

[113] *Squallacen.,* 8 aug. 1761—"An Religiosi Conventuales Bruneaturi moniti ab episcopo debeant se abstinere a celebrandis Missis, aliisque peragendis functionibus cum sonitu campanarum ante Missam parochialem, vel donec illa absovatur?—Negative."—*Thesaurus Resolutionum Sacrae Congregationis Concilii,* XXIX, 46-47.

[114] Cf. *Oratories,* p. 102.

implies that the ordinary may use means other than regulating the time of services, it does not appear to include the right to prohibit, suppress, or forbid religious to celebrate such functions. Moreover, the canon does not authorize him to limit the number of functions that can be performed.[115] If the local ordinary does prohibit the celebration of ecclesiastical rites in non-parochial churches and oratories in order to force the faithful to attend their parish churches, it would appear that he is assuming an authority which he actually lacks and, furthermore, he is hampering the acquired right of the rectors to celebrate sacred rites. Moreover, he is practically infringing upon the right of the faithful to attend such rites.[116]

The fact that the legislator did not give this power becomes more evident from an examination of the preparatory redactions of the Code of Canon Law. One of these redactions was published in the year 1913 and read: "*Ordinarius autem praesertim circa horas sacrorum rituum, potest, iusta de causa, aliquos terminos apponere.*"[117] It can be seen that the phrase "*. . . aliquos terminos apponere . . .*" and the infinitive "*praefinire*" of canon 1171 do not convey the same concept. The former implies the right to limit, while the latter gives only the right to schedule or to regulate. Undoubtedly, the present canon 1171 was adopted in order not to insinuate that the local ordinary may limit the number of sacred rites which may be performed in the church or oratory. Therefore, the ordinary may schedule the hour of services in all churches subject to his authority. He cannot, however, limit or suppress the number of sacred functions, nor may he directly forbid them. Yet, since he can regulate the hour of services, it appears that he is indirectly given the power to prohibit the performance of certain rites at stated times, although he cannot forbid the functions themselves. Even in the exercise of this right, the spiritual benefit of the faithful must be the primary consideration in judging whether or not a just cause is present. Regatillo indicates that restrictions

---

[115] Cf. Schaefer, *De Religiosis,* n. 1372, p. 819.

[116] Cf. cans. 497, § 2; 1161; 1171; 1188, § 2, n. 1.

[117] Cf. Jone, *Commentarium,* II, 391; Goyeneche, *Quaestiones Canonicae,* II, n. (1), p. 320.

upon the freedom of the faithful to attend devotions and religious services is often detrimental to their fervor.[118]

ARTICLE 4. THE JURISDICTION OF THE PASTOR AND CLERICAL RELIGIOUS HOUSES

Pastors have a serious obligation to exercise the *cura animarum* in behalf of their parishioners[119] and this obligation is founded on the virtue of justice.[120] The subjects of the pastor of a territorial parish are those who have a domicile or quasi-domicile there,[121] those who have neither a domicile or quasi-domicile but are actually within the parish territory[122] and, finally, those who are in the parish but who have only a diocesan domicile.[123] In certain matters the power of the pastor also extends to visitors within the parish who have a domicile or quasi-domicile elsewhere.[124]

The phrase *cura animarum* includes, especially, the right and duty of the pastor to administer the sacraments and to care spiritually and temporally for his parish. Although it does not impose an obligation on the parishioners, it necessarily implies the corresponding right of the parishioner to receive certain spiritual benefits from his proper pastor. The *cura animarum* is exercised under the authority of the local ordinary.[125] The jurisdiction the pastor enjoys can be delegated in whole or in part, exclusive of his confessional faculties.[126] Although most commentators admit that the pastor enjoys a limited jurisdiction in the external forum, they generally restrict his jurisdiction to the internal forum.[127]

[118] Cf. *Institutiones Iuris Canonici* (2. ed., 4 vols., Santander, 1946), II, n. 19, p. 17 (hereafter cited: *Institutiones*).

[119] Can. 451, § 1.

[120] "Hanc curam animarum parochus ex officio, seu ut communiter interpretantur auctores, ex iustitia exercere tenetur."—Coronata, *Institutiones,* I, n. 480, p. 567.

[121] Can. 94, § 1.

[122] Can. 94, § 2.

[123] Can. 94, § 3.

[124] Cf. cans. 1044; 1045; 1245.

[125] Can. 451, § 1.

[126] Cf. cans. 199, § 1; 873; 899.

[127] Cf. Cappello, *Summa Iuris Canonici* (4. ed., 3 vols., Romae: Aedes Universitatis Gregorianae, 1945-1955), I, 456; Beste, *Introductio in Codicem,*

Yet, there is a growing tendency to concede a greater pastoral jurisdiction in the external forum than has heretofore been recognized.[128]

Pastors have the obligation to exercise the *cura animarum* in behalf of their parishioners who are not legitimately exempted from parochial jurisdiction.[129] Although the law itself may not exempt a certain group, the bishop may exempt religious and pious groups for just and grave reasons, if their residence is within the parish boundaries.[130]

This removal from pastoral authority, whether it be by law or the will of the bishop, means an exemption for the person or persons from the jurisdiction of a particular pastor to whom they would otherwise be subject. As a correlative of this exemption, the pastor is relieved of his obligation in justice to minister to such an exempt person or group. Those privileged by the law or by this exemptive act of the bishop must look to some other designated person for those spiritual ministrations they would ordinarily receive from the pastor.

The term "exemption" is most frequently used in canon law in reference to exemption of religious. Certain religious institutes have been withdrawn from the jurisdiction of the local ordinary and placed under the immediate authority of the Holy See which governs them through superiors legitimately chosen from each institute. All regulars as well as their houses and churches are exempt from the jurisdiction of the local ordinary.[131] Certain other religious institutes also, such as the Redemptorists and Passionists, enjoy the privilege of exemption by special grant of the Holy See.[132] This exemption is not a complete withdrawal from the jurisdiction of the local ordinary, but it is such that

p. 289; Abbo-Hannan, *The Sacred Canons,* I, 447-448; Bouscaren-Ellis, *Canon Law,* p. 189; Coronata, *Institutiones,* I, 553; Vermeersch-Creusen, *Epitome,* I, n. 534, pp. 406-407; Augustine, *Commentary,* II, 511.

[128] Cf. Deutsch, *Jurisdiction of Pastors in The External Forum,* The Catholic University of America Canon Law Studies, n. 373 (Washington, D. C.: The Catholic University of America Press, 1957), pp. 174-180.

[129] Can. 467, § 1.

[130] Can. 464, § 2.

[131] Cf. cans. 615; 1230, § 3.

[132] Cf. can. 500, § 1.

those who possess this privilege are exempt in all matters except those in which the law expressly states that they are not exempt.[133] Furthermore, as a general principle, exemptive rights are always more extensive in clerical institutes than in lay communities.[134]

The question to be answered, therefore, is: what is the parochial position of a clerical religious house situated within the parish boundaries? Are the members of a clerical religious institute considered parishioners of the local pastor, or have they been removed in some manner from his authority and subjected to the pastoral care of another? It is the opinion of the writer that the latter is the position in which the law has effectively, at least, placed them. All clerical religious have been efficaciously withdrawn from the jurisdiction of the local pastor. The religious are to look to the local religious superior who is to take the place of the pastor with regard to the spiritual care of the members of the clerical house. This pertains to all clerical religious houses indiscriminately, whether they belong to exempt or non-exempt religious institutes, whether they be pontifical or of diocesan approval.

All religious men lose their proper diocese after making perpetual profession of vows,[135] and, if they be clerics, they are *ipso facto* excardinated and completely affiliated with their religious institute.[136] Their proper pastor, therefore, would ordinarily be determined by the location of the religious house to which they are habitually assigned as members.[137] Furthermore, since regulars are exempt from the jurisdiction of the local ordinary, they must logically be considered exempt from the jurisdiction of the neighboring pastor.[138] In fact, all exempt religious institutes and their

---

[133] Cf. can. 615; Beste, *Introductio in Codicem,* pp. 424-425. Herein, Fr. Beste enumerates and catalogues the exceptions to the privilege of exemption.

[134] Cf. O'Brien, *The Exemption of Religious,* p. 5.

[135] Can. 584.

[136] Can. 154.

[137] ". . . concludendum videtur *parochum proprium religiosorum,* in iis circa quae a parocho religiosi dependent, habendum esse parochum intra cuius paroeciae limites domus religiosa ad quam quis hic et nunc pertinet, sita est." —Fanfani, *De Iure Religiosorum,* n. 41, p. 76.

[138] Cf. Agius, *Summarium Iurium et Officiorum Parochorum* (Neapoli: M. D'Auria, Pontificius Editor, 1953), n. 40, p. 36 (hereafter cited: *Summarium Iurium*).

houses, whether the institutes be clerical or lay, are completely removed from the jurisdiction of the pastor and placed under the pastoral care of another priest.[139] Exempt religious are removed from the jurisdiction of the neighboring pastor with regard to the internal government of their houses and with regard to their external sacerdotal ministry and their reception of the sacraments. The exercise of the *cura animarum* in behalf of the members of the religious house pertains to the exempt clerical superior. It is clearly his right and duty to care spiritually for his subjects.[140] It is to be noted that although the Code derogates exemption in specific instances in favor of the jurisdiction of the local ordinary, it never extends this derogation in favor of the parochial jurisdiction.[141]

The juridic relationship of exempt religious to the local ordinary and to the neighboring pastor is, therefore, quite clear. However, little is mentioned by the authors concerning the relationship of non-exempt clerical religious to the jurisdiction of the pastor. Certainly, non-exempt religious are subject to the jurisdiction of the local ordinary; but are they to be considered dependent upon the neighboring pastor as his parishioners? Fanfani states that all non-exempt religious are dependent upon the pastor except in those matters which pertain to the administration of the last sacraments by clerical religious superiors and to ecclesiastical burial.[142] Schaefer also states that non-exempt clerical religious are sub-

---

[139] "Quoad subiectionem parocho haec teneas: Religiosi exempti sunt omnino liberi."—Cappello, *Summa Iuris Canonici,* II, n. 11, p. 16; cf. Schaefer, *De Religiosis,* n. 414, p. 185.

[140] Cf. Wernz-Vidal, *Ius Canonicum,* III, n. 142, p. 118; Fanfani, *De Iure Parochorum, ad normam Codicis Iuris Canonici* (Taurini-Romae, 1924), n. 392, p. 350 (hereafter cited: *De Iure Parochorum*).

[141] Cf. cans. 528; 529; 875, § 2; 1338, § 3; cf. Schaefer, *De Religiosis,* n. 414, p. 186. One of the logical inferences from this express grant of exemption from the jurisdiction of the local ordinary and, therefore, from parochial jurisdiction, is that the exempt do not participate in the *missa pro populo,* nor can the pastor absolve them in lieu of parochial jurisdiction outside his parish boundaries.

[142] ". . . si non sunt exempti, religiosi, sive clerici sive laici dependent a parocho sicut alii clerici vel laici in paroecia existentes. *Excipe* quae administrationem ultimorum Sacramentorum vel funera respiciunt. . . ."—*De Iure Parochorum,* n. 392, p. 350.

ject to the pastor except in those matters in which the law exempts them.[143] Coronata, however, maintains that all non-exempt clerical religious are exempt from the jurisdiction and care of the pastor, but he gives no reasons to substantiate this assertion.[144] This opinion seems to be preferable in view of the concessions given to all clerical religious institutes and to clerical superiors by the Code of Canon Law, as will be explained.

Clerical religious have a right to their own churches and public oratories and may celebrate sacred functions within these public places of worship.[145] Moreover, clerical superiors enjoy pastoral prerogatives in behalf of their subjects. In fact, an examination of the reserved parochial functions contained in canon 462 indicates that they have no importance with regard to the spiritual care of the members of a clerical house. Those reserved functions concerning solemn baptism, the blessing of baptismal fonts, and the conducting of certain public processions, have little practical implication with respect to the *cura animarum* of clerical religious.[146] Those functions concerning the administration of Holy Communion and the last sacraments, as well as the announcing of sacred ordinations and the conducting of funerals,[147] have express exceptions in favor of clerical religious in other canons of the Code.[148] The only remaining parochial functions, the carrying of the Blessed Sacrament publicly to the sick within the parish and the blessing of homes on Holy Saturday or at some other customary time, have no practical importance in the present consideration.[149] It can be readily seen, therefore, that the members of a clerical religious house situated within the parish limits have no need for reliance upon the local pastor's spiritual and sacramental

---

[143] *De Religiosis,* n. 416, p. 186.

[144] "A cura paroeciali et iurisdictione parochi exempti sunt omnes religiosi religionum clericalium, etiam non exemptarum, immo etiam iuris dioecesani." —Coronata, *Institutiones,* I, n. 531, p. 632.

[145] Cf. can. 497, § 2; 1171.

[146] Can. 462, nn. 1, 7.

[147] Can. 462, nn. 3, 4, 5.

[148] Cf. cans. 514; 998, § 1; 1121.

[149] Can. 462, nn. 2, 6.

ministrations.[150] They are truly independent in practice. Although it would not be entirely correct to equate the position of a pastor over his parishioners and that of a clerical religious superior over his subjects, it, nevertheless, appears that the law considers clerical religious to be exempt from the jurisdiction of the pastor and subjected to the quasi-parochial authority of the superior.[151]

One commentator, while discussing the power of non-exempt clerical superiors, maintains that many of the faculties given clerical superiors by the Code are based on a partial exemption of the religious so as to preclude the pastor's continuous interference in the domestic life of the religious house.[152] He states that these faculties are not based on the dominative power which all religious superiors possess, but pertain to the same kind of power which a pastor exercises over the faithful.[153] He implies, therefore, that

---

[150] Canon 544, § 1, requires an aspirant to the religious life to present testimonial letters concerning the reception of the sacraments of baptism and confirmation. However, if it was discovered that a religious in danger of death had not been confirmed, the pastor could certainly confirm the religious whenever the bishop was not available. The pastor has this faculty by grant of the decree *Spiritus Sancti munera.* Cf. S. C. de Sacramentis, 14, sept. 1946—*AAS,* XXXVIII (1946), 349-358; Bouscaren, *Digest,* III, 303.

[151] ". . . satis clarum apparet Codicem supponere exemptionem Congregationum clericalium a Parocho, cui ceterum praxis et doctorum auctoritas favet."—Larraona, "De potestate paroeciali relate ad religiosos," *CpR,* VIII (1927), 39.

[152] "De caetero, si considerantur rationes cur haec exemptio partialis concedatur illis Religionibus, apparet eas non esse proprias vitae religiosae seu non oriri ex natura vitae religiosae, sed potius esse ordinis practici. Haec exemptio enim non oritur ex necessitate ipsius vitae religiosae, sed ex quadam convenientia practica, ne continuo interventus parochi requiratur in rebus domesticis Religionis."—Kindt, *De Potestate Dominativa in Religione,* Universitas Catholica Louvaniensis, Dissertationes, Series II, Tomus 34 (Brugis-Parisiis-Romae: Desclée de Brouwer, 1945), p. 276 (hereafter cited: *De Potestate Dominativa*).

[153] "Unde, concludere possumus non probari has facultates referendas esse ad potestatem dominativam Superiorum religiosorum, sed pertinere potius ad potestatem eiusdem naturae ac illa qua eas exercet parochus in proprios fideles; uno verbo, quia exemptio partialis fundamentum est harum facultatum, facultates istae sunt eiusdem naturae ac si parochus eas exerceret."—Kindt, *op. cit.,* p. 277. McGrath, on the other hand, asserts that the dominative power of the local non-exempt clerical superior embraces all the various

clerical religious superiors of non-exempt institutes do enjoy some form of jurisdiction, a jurisdiction of the same nature as that enjoyed by pastors. Larraona asserts that the power of the non-exempt clerical superior is more than a merely *private* dominative power. Rather, it is a *public* dominative power which is granted to the superior by the Church through the Code and the constitutions of each religious institute.[154] Moreover, this public dominative power is an imperfect form of jurisdiction. Since all clerical religious superiors are responsible for the *cura animarum* of their religious subjects,[155] the present writer maintains that non-exempt clerical superiors enjoy this imperfect jurisdiction consequent to the intention of the legislator to remove, in effect, all clerical religious from the jurisdiction of the neighboring pastor and to subject them to the quasi-pastoral authority of the clerical superior.

Although the bishop does not expressly remove a religious house of a non-exempt clerical institute from the jurisdiction of the local pastor,[156] this exemption is quite clear from an overall consideration of the juridic status of non-exempt clerical religious. This exemption is at least a partial exemption from the pastor's jurisdiction. It is a practical consequence of privileges bestowed on clerical institutes whereby pastoral powers have been granted clerical superiors by the Code. Although it is only a partial exemption, it is sufficient to remove them from the category of

---

faculties granted by the Code to the superior. Cf. *The Local Superior in Non-Exempt Clerical Congregations,* The Catholic University of America Canon Law Studies, n. 351 (Washington, D. C.: The Catholic University of America Press, 1954), p. 58.

[154] "Ideo, potestas dominativa quatenus publica est et aliqua ex iurisdictione habet, non immerito dici potest iurisdictio imperfecta seu inchoata."—"De potestate dominativa publica in iure canonico,"—*Acta Congressus Iuridici Internationalis* (5 vols., Romae: Apud Custodiam Librariam Pontifici Utraque Iuris, 1935-1937), IV, p. 167.

[155] "Aliqua ratione ad curam animarum pertinet *ius* et *officium* Superioribus cuiusvis religionis clericalis, sive exemptae sive non exemptae. . . . Haec profecto sunt *officia pastoralia,* quae in can. 514, § 1, *expresse* ad Superiores *non—exemptos* extenduntur."—Wernz-Vidal, *Ius Canonicum,* III, n. 142, p. 118.

[156] Cf. can. 464, § 2.

parishioners. Since this exemption is not the complete exemption enjoyed by exempt clerical institutes,[157] non-exempt clerical religious may avail themselves of concessions not given to their superior, but which, however, are enjoyed by pastors by reason of their office. For example, the pastor may dispense them from the laws of fast and abstinence.[158]

Exempt clerical superiors enjoy true jurisdiction and all the pastoral powers required to care for their subjects.[159] Consequently, the members of exempt clerical institutes need not look to the pastor for his ministrations. Non-exempt superiors, on the other hand, possess only those pastoral powers given them by the Code and necessary to function in a quasi-pastoral capacity.[160] These powers, nevertheless, appear to be an implicit grant of exemption from the jurisdiction of the pastor. As a practical consequence, they amount to a complete withdrawal from parochial power and make it unnecessary for the non-exempt clerical religious to have reference to the pastor for his spiritual ministrations. Juridically, however, these powers are equivalent at best to a partial exemption. Therefore, the opinion that all clerical religious are exempt from parochial jurisdiction appears to be sustained and worthy of acceptance since the Code presupposes that the obligations involved in the *cura animarum* of clerical religious are sufficiently satisfied by the clerical superior. Moreover, this exemption protects the independent and autonomous nature of each religious house and makes it unnecessary for the pastor to interfere in the domestic life of the community, especially when his pastoral position is easily filled by a member of the particular religious institute.

---

[157] Cf. can. 615.

[158] Cf. can. 1245, § 1.

[159] Cf. cans. 873, § 2; 875, § 1; 1245, § 3.

[160] Cf. cans. 514; 998, § 1; 1121.

CHAPTER VI

Parish Life and the Sacerdotal Ministry of the Priests of Clerical Religious Houses

ARTICLE 1. RELIGIOUS CONFESSORS

Church law gives special attention to the administration of the sacrament of penance by religious priests.[1] They are considered especially qualified to act as confessors, not only because they may offer parishioners a greater liberty of conscience in approaching this sacrament, but also because of the privileges that many religious enjoy in the matter of absolving and dispensing. In the early church, especially in the east, the burden of preaching and absolving the faithful was often the special lot of those monks who had been raised to the holy priesthood and commissioned for this work.[2] Consequently, from the earliest times religious assisted the secular clergy in ministering to the spiritual needs of the faithful, especially as confessors.

Many privileges for confessors were conferred on the mendicant religious of the middle ages. The pontiffs recognized such confessors as excellent instruments to revive the wavering faith of the people. Often these religious were authorized to preach and absolve in virtue of pontifical jurisdiction alone.[3] Since their apostolate cut across the parochial and episcopal organization, it was bound to cause some friction. More than once the Holy See

---

[1] "Vicissim locorum Ordinarii ac parochi libenter utantur opera religiosorum . . . in sacro ministerio et maxime in administrando sacramento poenitentiae." —can. 608, § 2.

[2] Cf. Shuhler, *Privileges of Regulars to Absolve and Dispense*, The Catholic University of America Canon Law Studies, n. 186 (Washington, D. C.: The Catholic University of America Press, 1943), pp. 2-3.

[3] E.g., const. *Quaniam* of Gregory IX (1227-1241), 10 maii 1227—*Bull. Praed.*, I, 19; Potthast, *Regesta*, n. 7896; const. *Inter cuncta*, 17 febr. 1304 —c. 1, *de privilegiis*, V, 7, in Extravag. com.

was forced to interfere and demand that the privileges conferred on the mendicants by the pontiffs be respected.[4]

The present Code of Canon Law has not completely abrogated all the privileges which the religious enjoyed in the past. The law does state, however, that only those privileges granted by the Holy See or contained in the Code are now enjoyed by religious.[5] Moreover, all future communication *in forma aequi principali* is forbidden. Nevertheless, privileges that had been received and were still in effect at the time of the Code remain in effect unless they have been expressly revoked.[6]

Regulars, therefore, continue to enjoy many privileges conceded centuries ago. Consequently, regulars who are approved as confessors by their superior and by the local ordinary as well, may absolve from censures reserved by common law to the local ordinary. This privilege is restricted to the internal sacramental forum. Such confessors may also dispense from non-reserved vows and oaths in the internal forum, as long as there is no injury to third parties involved.[7]

The present law clearly outlines the extent to which the jurisdiction received by the religious may be exercised, whether it is with the approval of the local ordinary, of the exempt clerical superior, or with the approval of both. The local ordinary of the place where confessions are to be heard is the authority competent to grant jurisdiction for the confessions of all persons, both lay and religious, to secular and religious priests.[8]

Special jurisdiction is required for the confessions of women religious and this is received also from the local ordinary.[9] If, however, a woman religious goes to confession for peace of con-

---

[4] E.g., const. *Non sine multa* of Alexander IV (1254-1261), 19 oct. 1256—*Bull. Praed.*, I, 320; Potthast, *Regesta*, n. 1658.

[5] Can. 613, § 1.

[6] Cf. can. 4; 30 dec. 1957—*AAS*, XXX (1937), 73; Bouscaren, *Digest*, II, 172.

[7] Cf. Vermeersch-Creusen, *Epitome*, I, n. 785, pp. 595-596; Coronata, *Institutiones*, I, 619 *bis*, pp. 804-805; Piatus Montensis, *Praelectiones Iuris Regularis* (3. ed., 2 vols., Parisiis, 1906), I, p. 400.

[8] Can. 874, § 1.

[9] Can. 876, §§ 1, 2.

science to a confessor who has diocesan faculties but lacks this special jurisdiction for absolving women religious, the confessor absolves validly and lawfully.[10] Religious confessors are not to use their diocesan faculties without the permission, at least the presumed permission, of their proper superior.[11] The local ordinary should not normally grant jurisdiction for confessions to religious if they are not presented by their proper superior. Presumably, the judgment of the superior is sufficient for the local ordinary to act on.[12] He may, however, examine religious presented by a superior so as to satisfy himself regarding their qualifications to act as confessors.[13] This would be exceptional though, since he may freely abide by the attestation of the religious superior.[14]

Besides the jurisdiction which the local ordinary can grant, exempt clerical superiors may confer a limited jurisdiction for the confessions of professed religious subjects, novices, and those indicated in canon 514, § 1.[15] This latter group is made up of all those who live day and night in the religious house, either as servants, or for the purpose of education, or as guests, or on account of ill health. The proper superior may grant this jurisdiction to secular and religious priests who are not members of the institute. Unless particular law specifies otherwise, the proper superior in this matter is the local superior.[16]

When both the local ordinary and the exempt clerical superior have conferred jurisdiction on a confessor, limitations placed by either authority will not affect the jurisdiction received from the other. However, a revocation of the faculties by the clerical superior suspends the privileges to absolve from censures reserved by law to the local ordinary.[17] Those who are able to confer jurisdiction, as well as their lawful superiors and successors, may revoke

---

[10] Can. 519.

[11] Can. 874, § 1.

[12] Can. 874, § 2.

[13] Can. 877, § 1.

[14] Cf. Goyeneche, *Quaestiones Canonicae,* II, 264-265; O'Brien, *Exemption of Religious,* p. 178.

[15] Cf. can. 875, § 1.

[16] Cf. Goyeneche, *Quaestiones Canonicae,* II, 266.

[17] Cf. Shuhler, *Privileges of Regulars to Absolve and Dispense,* pp. 57-58; Fanfani, *De Iure Religiosorum,* n. 145, p. 217.

or suspend it. If jurisdiction is revoked, the absolution is invalidly conferred except in those cases in which the Code itself supplies jurisdiction, e.g., canons 207, § 2, and 209. If the confessor is merely suspended, its use is unlawful but valid.[18] Grave reason is required to suspend or revoke jurisdiction once it has been conferred.[19] In a given case, however, the local ordinary and the exempt clerical superior may determine whether or not a grave reason is present. To protect the confessor from an unjust suspension or revocation of his jurisdiction and consequent injury to his reputation, he may have recourse *in devolutivo* to the Holy See.[20] Even with grave reasons, the local ordinary should not revoke simultaneously the jurisdiction of all the confessors of a *"domus formata"* of a clerical institute.[21] Such a revocation by the bishop would be valid but unlawful, unless the local ordinary had first consulted the Holy See.[22] He need not consult the Holy See to revoke the faculties of the priests in a *"domus non-formata."* Nevertheless, such a revocation does not affect the jurisdiction an exempt religious receives from his proper superior. Although the religious superior cannot revoke the jurisdiction which a subject received from the local ordinary, he may forbid him to exercise it. This prohibition does not apply, however, when the priest in question is approached by a penitent with a request for absolution.[23]

Normally, the proper religious superior is to present his subjects to the local ordinary for the reception of diocesan faculties.[24] However, when a pastor requests the assistance of religious who do not reside in his diocese, it does not seem inappropriate for him to request diocesan faculties for the visiting priests. When religious are approved as confessors elsewhere, either by the local ordinary of another diocese or by their exempt clerical superior,

---

[18] Cf. Schaefer, *De Religiosis,* n. 1331, p. 795.

[19] Can. 880, § 1.

[20] Cf. O'Brien, *Exemption of Religious,* p. 179; Goyeneche, *Quaestiones Canonicae,* II, 266-269.

[21] Cf. can. 880, § 3; S. C. Ep. et Reg., 20 nov. 1615—*Fontes,* n. 1667.

[22] Cf. Abbo-Hannan, *The Sacred Canons,* II, 10; Schaefer, *De Religiosis,* n. 1331, p. 295; Fanfani, *De Iure Religiosorum,* n. 145 (c), p. 216; Vermeersch-Creusen, *Epitome,* II, n. 150, p. 103.

[23] Cf. can. 2261, § 2; 2284.

[24] Can. 874, § 2.

the local ordinary in question need not require the extra-diocesan priests to submit to an examination. He may abide by the attestation of the proper local ordinary or superior concerning the confessors' qualifications.[25]

Church law encourages the local ordinary and the pastor to seek the assistance of religious, especially in the role of confessors.[26] As strangers to the affairs of the local parish they may be able to offer penitents greater liberty of conscience. Moreover, religious are presumed to have special ability in the spiritual direction of souls.[27] Again, as has been mentioned, the legislator was probably not unmindful of the privileges many religious institutes enjoy in the matter of absolving and dispensing. The assistance of religious is particularly proper in the matter of appointing confessors for religious. The religious priests should possess the qualifications required of every confessor. In addition, however, he should have a better understanding of the problems and difficulties that pertain to the religious life. In his capacity as a confessor, the religious priest is given an appropriate field of sacerdotal activity in which he may assist the parish clergy and be an instrument of good for both the parochial and religious life.

ARTICLE 2. RELIGIOUS PREACHERS

Since the middle ages, preaching has been one of the most noteworthy characteristics of many religious institutes. Although, at times, restrictions were placed on the preaching activities of monks,[28] the preaching apostolate of the mendicant communities was one of the principal means of counteracting the false teachings

---

[25] Cf. O'Brien, *Exemption of Religious,* p. 178.

[26] Can. 608, § 2.

[27] "Religiosi enim, rebus paroeciarum extranei, magis liberam esse sinunt paenitentis accusationem; et, prae conditione sua, maiorem copiam consiliorum spiritualium pro animarum directione habere praesumuntur."—Vermeersch-Creusen, *Epitome,* I, n. 767, p. 579.

[28] E.g., Pope Alexander II (1061-1073) decreed: "Iuxta Chalcedonensis tenorem optimi concilii monachis quamvis religiosis, ad normam Sancti Benedicti intra claustrum morari praecipimus; vicos, castella, civitates peragrare prohibemus, a populorum praedicatione omnino cessare censuimus . . ."—c. 11, C. XVI, q. 1.

of heretics and of spreading the teachings of the true Faith. When the Fifth Lateran Council (1512-1517) instructed bishops to provide competent preachers, it was to the mendicants that they turned for priests to exercise this office fruitfully.[29] Many papal privileges were conferred on the mendicants to facilitate their missionary activities.[30] The influence of their preaching activities is felt even today. Not only do many institutes still regard preaching as one of the principal forms of their apostolate, but the obligation to provide "parish missions" can be traced to the work of the religious.[31]

The office of preaching is primarily the right of the Roman Pontiff and the bishops of the world.[32] All others need a canonical mission to lawfully exercise the ministry of preaching, unless they possess an office in which the ministry of preaching is inherent by canonical provision.[33] This commission is a grant of power akin to jurisdiction and involves approbation and permission.[34] Religious priests require the approbation of the local ordinary when they are to preach to the faithful. Approbation is required by exempt clerical religious when they are going to preach to the faithful other than those mentioned in canon 514, § 1. This approbation is conferred by the local ordinary of the place where the preaching is undertaken.[35] The local ordinary should not refuse his approval without serious reason when religious are presented by their proper superior. Neither should he revoke it, once given, especially not at one and the same time from all the priests of a religious house, except when the preachers are found to lack the necessary qualifications.[36] Preachers who are religious

---

[29] C. 5, X, *de officio iudiciis ordinarii,* I, 311.

[30] Cf. const. *Quoniam,* 21 apr. 1227—Potthast, *Regesta,* n. 7880; const. *Quidem temere,* 20 iun. 1265—Potthast, *Regesta,* n. 1921.

[31] Cf. can. 1349; Lavelle, *The Obligation of Holding Sacred Missions in Parishes,* The Catholic University of America Canon Law Studies, n. 295 (Washington, D. C.: The Catholic University of America Press, 1949), p. 110.

[32] Can. 1327, § 1.

[33] Can. 1328.

[34] Cf. Abbo-Hannan, *The Sacred Canons,* II, 566.

[35] Can. 1338, §§ 1, 2.

[36] Cf. cans. 1339, § 1; 1340.

may use the power given them only with the permission of their superior.[37] However, this permission can be legitimately presumed when it cannot be directly requested and there is no reason to doubt that it would be given by the superior.[38]

The local ordinary or the religious superior are seriously bound in conscience not to grant approbation or permission to anyone to preach unless it has been previously established that his moral life is irreproachable and, through an examination, that he is adequately learned.[39] This examination need not be given if the candidate's moral and doctrinal qualifications are known and need no proof.[40] Although religious are required to submit to an examination when they seek the approbation of the local ordinary, it appears that he may dispense with the examination and accept the attestation of the religious superior as sufficient proof of the candidate's qualifications. Moreover, since reference is made to canon 877, § 1, in the matter of conducting an examination, there seems to be no objections to having one examination suffice for both confessional faculties and preaching approbation.[41]

Strictly taken, lectures, catechetical instructions, and talks on religious subjects at conventions or schools, are not considered to be an exercise of the power of preaching. Therefore, when a priest is called upon to give talks of this nature the canonical mission is not necessary.[42] Nevertheless, if a cleric gives catechetical instructions inside a church, he should seek the proper approbation because this is considered to be a sermon.[43] Moreover, retreat conferences, even though not given in a church or oratory, cer-

---

[37] Can. 1339, § 2.

[38] Cf. Schaefer, *De Religiosis,* n. 1397, p. 883.

[39] Cans. 1340, § 1; 877, § 1.

[40] Cf. S. C. Consist., instr. 28 iun. 1917, n. 1—*AAS,* IX (1917), 328.

[41] Cf. McCarthy, "The New Regulations on Preaching," *The Ecclesiastical Review* (*The American Ecclesiastical Review,* Vols. I-XXXIII, 1889-1905; from 1905: *The Ecclesiastical Review,* Philadelphia, 1905-1943; from 1944: *The American Ecclesiastical Review,* Washington, D. C.), LVII (1917), 385.

[42] Cf. Beste, *Introduction in Codicem,* p. 669.

[43] Cf. Allgeier, *The Canonical Obligation of Preaching in Parish Churches,* The Catholic University of America Canon Law Studies, n. 291 (Washington, D. C.: The Catholic University of America Press, 1949), p. 35.

tainly appear to be an exercise of preaching. Therefore, faculties would be required.[44]

Oftentimes, religious assist parish priests by conducting missions and retreats. Ordinaries are obliged to see that all pastors provide a sacred mission for their people at least once every ten years.[45] Although the Code does not mention who are to be entrusted with this important work, the Holy See seems to give preference to priests from outside the particular parish.[46] Extra-parochial preachers may offer the parishioner a beneficial change, since the parishioner often becomes accustomed to the preaching of the parish priest. Since "missions" also offer penitents a special opportunity to avail themselves of the sacrament of penance, the extra-parochial priest will provide them with a greater liberty of conscience in this matter. Although preference is not to be given necessarily to religious priests for conducting "missions," they will be more available than other priests for this type of activity. For example, many religious institutes have mission bands that specialize in this apostolate.

When pastors invite a religious superior to designate some of his subjects to conduct a "mission" or to undertake some other preaching assignment in the parish, they should seek permission from the local ordinary if the religious are from another diocese.[47] The local ordinary may desire information from the proper ordinary of the extra-diocesan priests regarding their qualifications.[48] In the case of exempt clerical religious, the proper ordinary is the major superior,[49] whereas the local ordinary of the diocese where he is assigned is the proper ordinary for the non-exempt religious. In either case, however, it seems that the proper religious superior is competent to attest to the qualifications of his subjects and that the knowledge of the extra-diocesan priest's qualifications need not always come from the proper ordinary.

---

[44] Cf. Hannan, "Faculties for Retreat Conferences," *The Jurist,* X (1950), 391.

[45] Can. 1349, §§ 1, 2.

[46] Cf. ep. *Nostris et Nobiscum* of Pius IX (1846-1878), 8 dec. 1849—*Fontes,* n. 508.

[47] Can. 1341, § 2.

[48] Can. 1341, § 1.

[49] Can. 198, § 1.

Practically speaking, the local ordinary could prudently give pastors general permission to invite any extra-diocesan preacher they wish, as long as they are assured that he has the proper qualifications.[60] In this case, it appears that the local ordinary implicitly grants approbation to the preachers who are invited by the pastor. When religious superiors are requested by pastors to designate some of his subjects for preaching assignments, it seems preferable, however, that the superior send the names of these priests to the pastor so that if the religious do not have the approbation of the local ordinary where they are to preach, proper inquiry may be made at the ordinary's discretion. In this manner, the requirements of canon law are complied with and the bishop of the diocese is free to make his own investigation or accept the attestation of the religious superior.

ARTICLE 3. THE ADMINISTRATION OF THE SACRAMENTS

The administration of some sacraments is normally a matter of parochial concern alone. Baptism and matrimony are examples. Other sacraments may ordinarily be associated with parochial ministry, but the law makes exceptions in behalf of religious superiors in relation to their subjects. Thus he is authorized to administer the sacraments of Holy Viaticum and Extreme Unction. Finally, there are those sacraments whose administration pertains to neither group exclusively, such as the Holy Eucharist and Penance. Holy Orders and Confirmation are almost always episcopal functions and have little connection with the sacramental relationship between the parish and the clerical religious house. With the exception of Holy Orders and Penance, the latter already having been summarily treated, the remaining sacraments will be briefly considered in so far as their administration by the priests of a clerical religious house affect parish life.

Section 1. Baptism

In a case of urgent necessity, private baptism may be administered at any time and place.[61] The proper place for the ad-

[60] Cf. Vermeersch-Creusen, *Epitome,* II, n. 676, p. 472.

[61] Can. 771.

ministration of solemn baptism is the baptistry in a church or public oratory.[52] The ordinary minister is the priest and its solemn conferral is reserved to the proper pastor.[53] Another priest may confer solemn baptism with the permission of the pastor or the local ordinary and in case of necessity this permission may be lawfully presumed.[54] Every parish church is required to have a baptismal font.[55] Consequently, the conferral of solemn baptism is normally performed by the pastor in the parish church.

The pastor may permit another priest to administer solemn baptism. Any reasonable request made by a parent or priest may be honored by the pastor or the local ordinary, especially when a refusal of permission will occasion embarrassment or estrangement of the faithful. In the United States it is customary to permit the priest who instructs a convert to administer the sacrament of baptism to this person in a convenient parish church.[56] Therefore, when a religious priest instructs a convert, he may reasonably request permission of any pastor to administer this sacrament in the parish church. Many times parents request a priest who is a friend or a relative of the family to confer this sacrament on their children. Such requests appear to be reasonable and should normally be respected. Since the solemn conferral of this sacrament, however, is a reserved parochial function, the pastor has the right to safeguard his prerogatives from any possible infringements.

For the convenience of the faithful, the local ordinary may permit or command that a baptismal font be placed in some other church or public oratory within the parish limits.[57] This convenience may be suggested by reason of many circumstances. Thus, difficulty in reaching the parish church because of the terrain, climatic conditions, or distance entailed might well prompt the placing of a font in a nearby church or oratory. Yet, even in this

[52] Can. 773.

[53] Can. 462, § 1, n. 1.

[54] Can. 738, § 1.

[55] Can. 774, § 1.

[56] Cf. Conway, *The Time and Place of Baptism,* The Catholic University of America Canon Law Studies, n. 324 (Washington, D. C.: The Catholic University of America Press, 1954), pp. 106-107.

[57] Can. 774, § 2.

case, the right to administer the sacrament solemnly is still proper to the pastor, although the font be in the church of religious. For the sake of convenience, the pastor can habitually delegate the religious superior to confer this sacrament in the event that he is not readily available himself.[58] It may also happen that the pastor has occasion to use a church or oratory of religious to confer the sacrament, even though there is no baptismal font. In such a case, the request of the pastor should not be refused by the religious superior.

If a religious priest confers solemn baptism with the permission of the local pastor or the local ordinary, the obligation of registering the baptism devolves on the pastor.[59] When permission is presumed by a priest to confer solemn baptism, he is obliged to inform the proper pastor and assist him with the specific data necessary for the baptismal register.

Section 2. Confirmation

The ordinary minister of the sacrament of Confirmation is the bishop.[60] The extraordinary minister is any priest who has been authorized by the common law or by way of special indult of the Holy See.[61] The Holy See has granted power to pastors and specifically designated priests to confirm persons who are within their proper territory and in the danger of death whenever the bishop of the diocese or other Catholic bishop is lawfully impeded from conferring Confirmation in person. This faculty is contained in the decree *Spiritus Sancti munera* which became effective on January 1, 1947.[62]

Although abbots and prelates *nullius* may confirm within the boundaries of their territory during their term of office, positive law prohibits them, as well as all others who have this personal faculty, from delegating another priest to administer this sacra-

---

[58] Can. 738, § 1.
[59] Can. 777, § 1.
[60] Can. 772, § 1.
[61] Can. 782, § 2.
[62] Cf. S. C. de Sacramentis, 14 sept. 1946—*AAS*, XXXVIII (1946), 349-358; Bouscaren, *Digest*, III, 303-313.

ment. The non-parochial priest, therefore, whether religious or secular, will not have an opportunity to administer Confirmation unless he possesses this power by indult of the Holy See.

Section 3. Holy Eucharist

The Holy Eucharist is to be reserved in a church attached to the house of exempt religious.[63] It may be reserved in the principal oratory of other religious houses with the permission of the local ordinary.[64] By reason of papal privileges, however, exempt clerical religious have the right to reserve the Blessed Sacrament in their principal oratory.[65] Moreover, religious may distribute Holy Communion to the faithful at all days and hours when the celebration of Mass is permitted.[66]

The Fourth Lateran Council (1215) had required the faithful to fulfill their Paschal obligation in their own parishes.[67] This obligation had been repeated by the Council of Trent (1545-1563),[68] but abolished by Pope St. Pius X (1903-1914) when he permitted the faithful to make their Easter Communion anywhere, even in non-parochial churches and oratories.[69] Today the Code of Canon Law recommends that the faithful satisfy this obligation in their parish church,[70] but they are free to fulfill it anywhere, even though it be in a church or oratory of a religious house.

The right and duty of bringing the Blessed Sacrament publicly to the sick within the parish is the prerogative of the pastor.[71] Other priests may do so only in case of necessity or with the presumed permission of the pastor or local ordinary.[72] An exception is made in the case of a clerical religious superior. He may

---

[63] Can. 1265, § 1, n. 1.

[64] Can. 1265, § 1, n. 2.

[65] Cf. Sartori, *Jurisprudentiae Ecclesiasticae Elementa* (2. ed., Romae: Pontificium Athenaeum Antonianum, 1949), p. 58.

[66] Cf. cans. 846; 869.

[67] Cf. c. 12, X, *de poenitentiis et remissionibus,* V, 38.

[68] Sess. XIII, *de Eucharistica,* c. 9.

[69] Cf. S.C.C., 28 nov. 1912—*AAS,* IV (1912), 726.

[70] Cans. 559, § 3; 866, § 2.

[71] Cans. 462, n. 2; 848, § 1.

[72] Can. 848, § 2; cf. Vermeersch-Creusen, *Epitome,* II, n. 114, p. 77.

freely administer Holy Communion to novices or professed religious subjects confined in a hospital.[73] To preclude any problem that may arise from such parochial rights, it may be stated that any priest may carry the Blessed Sacrament privately to sick religious and laymen, either in or outside of the religious house. In such cases, the permission of the pastor is not required. Moreover, in the United States the accepted administration of the Blessed Sacrament to the sick is a private one. The II Plenary Council of Baltimore (1866) authorized this practice as a means of safeguarding reverence to the Sacrament. The Council took into consideration the fact that Catholics were in the minority of the population and that frequent public administrations of the Holy Eucharist could possibly occasion irreverence.[74]

Prior to the Code, it was questioned whether the first Holy Communion of children was a pastoral prerogative. Today there is no doubt about the matter. The Code does not confer on the pastor an exclusive right to admit subjects to the first reception of Holy Communion.[75] Accordingly, it can be said that this solemn act is not reserved to the pastor and he cannot exclusively regulate the reception of first Holy Communion. On the other hand, the pastor should be vigilant lest a child without the proper qualifications receive his first Holy Communion. If he wishes he may examine the child.[76] Actually, however, the primary right to decide upon the disposition of the child belongs to the confessor and the parents.[77] Consequently, a religious confessor could make this decision and the pastor need not question it or require the candidate to submit to an examination.

---

[73] Cf. Decision of the Pontifical Commission for the Authentic Interpretation of the Code—*AAS*, XXIII (1931), 353; Bouscaren, *Digest*, I, 294.

[74] Cf. *Concilii Plenarii Baltimorensis II. in Ecclesia Metropolitana Baltimorensis, a die VII ad diem XXI Octobris, A.D. MDCCCLXVI, Habiti et a Sede Apostolica Recogniti, Acta et Decreta* (2. ed., Baltimorae, J. Murphy, 1894), n. 264.

[75] Cans. 462; 854.

[76] Can. 854, § 5.

[77] Cans. 853; 854, § 4; cf. Abbo-Hannan, *The Sacred Canons*, I, 853-854; Vermeersch-Creusen, *Epitome*, II, n. 118, pp. 81-82.

Section 4. Matrimony

Matters pertaining to the celebration of marriage are of concern to the pastor exclusively. The publication of the banns, assistance at the marriage, and the conferral of the nuptial blessing are functions reserved to him.[78] The Code grants authorization in certain unusual cases to priests other than the pastor, since these cases by their very nature are exceptional.[79] Unless a religious priest is assigned to parish work, therefore, he will have few opportunities to concern himself with matters related to the celebration of marriage.

Any unauthorized interference here should be punished. In past ages, the religious priest who assisted at a marriage without the proper authorization was liable to the penalty of excommunication.[80] The decree *Tametsi* of the Council of Trent decreed that anyone who assisted at a marriage or bestowed the nuptial blessing without proper authorization incurred an *"ipso facto"* suspension.[81] Although these penalties are no longer sustained by the Code,[82] infringements upon the present law are strictly forbidden and, moreover, may render the marriage null and void.[83]

In relation to the subject under consideration in this study, it may be stated that there are three cases in which a non-parochial priest may be concerned with the celebration of marriage. The first of these is the case in which a particular religious may be designated by the pastor or the local ordinary to officiate at a particular marriage.[84] It is a right of the local ordinary or pastor to delegate a specific priest to assist at a marriage within his respective territory.[85] Furthermore, if the parties wish to be married in a church or public oratory of a clerical religious house, the local ordinary or the pastor may grant their request if the religious

---

[78] Cans. 462, n. 4; 1090.

[79] Cf. cans. 1044; 1098.

[80] Cf. [The Council of Vienne (1311-1314)]—c. 1, *de privilegiis et excessibus privilegiatorum,* V, 7, in Clem.

[81] Sess. XXIV, *de ref.,* c. 1.

[82] Can. 6, n. 5.

[83] Cans. 1094; 1095.

[84] Cans. 1094-1096.

[85] Can. 1095, § 2.

superior is not opposed to this practice. Although the parish church is the ordinary place for the celebration of marriage,[86] it would be false to assert that the parish church is the only place recognized by law as proper for this union.[87] For reasonable cause, the marriage may be celebrated elsewhere.[88]

The other two cases in which a non-parochial priest may licitly and validly assist at a marriage are both extraordinary. Canon 1098 authorizes a priest to officiate at marriages in danger of death and, also, at those marriages which may be celebrated during a prolonged absence of an authorized priest. If the parties cannot go to an authorized priest nor the priest come to them without serious inconvenience, and there is a reasonable prospect that this condition will last for a month, any priest at hand may officiate. If this priest can obtain delegation from the local ordinary or pastor, he should do so before assisting at the marriage. In any case, the priest who assists at a marriage performed in the danger of death or on account of the prolonged absence of proper ecclesiastical authority should arrange to have the marriage registered as soon as possible.[89]

Section 5. The Last Sacraments

The pastor has the right and duty to give the last sacraments to all persons dying within his parish boundaries.[90] This administration of the last sacraments is a matter, ordinarily, of territorial rather than personal jurisdiction. It has been a parochial prerogative since the fourteenth century. The Council of Vienne (1311-1314) stated that a priest who dared administer the last sacra-

---

[86] Can. 1109, § 1.

[87] "Specialis tamen prohibitio celebrandi matrimonium in ecclesiis vel oratoriis religiosorum non habetur, quinimmo cum religiosas nominatim exclusit, religiosos exclusos hac speciali norma evidenter noluit legislator."—Goyeneche, *Quaestiones Canonicae,* II, 305; Fanfani, *De Iure Religiosorum,* n. 377, p. 529.

[88] Cf. can. 1109; Abbo-Hannan, *The Sacred Canons,* II, 367-368; Wernz-Vidal, *Ius Canonicum,* V, n. 579, p. 731.

[89] Can. 1103, § 3.

[90] Cans. 848, § 2; 938, § 2.

ments without permission from the pastor or local ordinary would incur an excommunication.[91] Pope Pius IX (1846-1878) repeated the censure but made an exception for their administration in case of necessity with the presumed permission of the pastor or local ordinary.[92]

It was understood that none of the prohibitions had reference to the administration of the last sacraments to his subjects by a clerical religious superior. Pope Gregory IX (1227-1241)[93] and Pope Clement V (1305-1314)[94] permitted clerical superiors to give the last sacraments to their subjects and *familiares.* The latter group included all those who lived at the religious house and were subject to the superior. The Council of Trent (1545-1563) repeated this concession[95] and stated that the term *familiares* referred to the members of the faithful who resided day and night within the religious house and who were subject to the superior.[96]

Prior to the Code, clerical superiors were not permitted to administer the last sacraments to lay people who were guests or resided at the religious house for reasons of education.[97] Many clerical institutes, however, received the privilege to administer these sacraments even to this group. Very often other institutes received this privilege by the medium of the communication of privileges.[98] Even with this privilege, when a guest became seriously ill, the pastor was to be called to the monastery to give the last sacraments if time permitted. The clerical superior was not to give the last sacraments in such a case when the pastor was available.[99]

The Code has retained many of the prescriptions and privileges

---

[91] Cf. c. 1, *de privilegiis et excessibus privilegiatorum,* V, 7, in Clem.

[92] Cf. const. *Apostolicae Sedis,* 12 oct. 1869—*Fontes,* n. 552.

[93] C. 16, X, *de excessibus praelatorum et subditorum,* V, 31.

[94] C. 1, *de privilegiis et excessibus privilegiatorum,* V, 7, in Clem.

[95] Sess. XXV, *de regularibus,* c. 11; cf. Melo, *De Exemptione Regularium,* p. 62.

[96] Sess. XXIV, *de ref.,* c. 11.

[97] S. C. Ep. et Reg., *Zagabrien.,* 14 dec. 1674—*Fontes,* n. 1809.

[98] S. C. Ep. et Reg., *Parmen.,* 21 iul. 1648—*Fontes,* n. 1954.

[99] Cf. S.C.C., *Monopolitana, 27* sept. 1670—Ferraris, *Biblotheca,* s.v. *Eucharistia,* n. 19.

which existed in the pre-Code era with regard to the administration of the last sacraments by clerical religious superiors.[100] They have an explicit right and duty to administer Viaticum and Extreme Unction to their subjects. The term "subject" includes professed religious and novices, as well as lay persons who dwell day and night in the religious house for reasons of service, health, education or hospitality. According to a declaration of the Pontifical Commission for the Authentic Interpretation of the Code, the clerical superior or his delegate may administer the last sacraments to professed religious and novices even when they are confined by illness outside the precincts of the religious house, e.g., in a hospital.[101] The prescriptions of canon 848, §§ 1, 2, are to be observed in this regard. Consequently, the religious superior should bring Holy Viaticum privately to the sick religious, unless the superior feels justified in presuming the permission of the pastor or local ordinary to bring it publicly. The superior does not, however, enjoy the right in regard to the others mentioned in canon 514, § 1, namely, postulants, employees and guests, when these persons are confined outside the religious house. They are to look to the local pastor whose duty it is to bring them the last sacraments, unless the place of confinement has been withdrawn from the pastor's care and committed to a specially appointed priest.[102]

The expression *"diu noctuque"* in canon 514, § 1, indicates a certain permanence of residence. Authors commonly interpret it to imply at least a period of twenty-four hours residence, or that one has the manifest intention to visit the religious house at least for this period of time.[103]

In a case of necessity, any priest, religious or secular, may administer Extreme Unction to the faithful.[104] In fact, charity may even demand that he do so. When a sick person is in critical con-

---

[100] Can. 514, § 1.

[101] Cf. 16 iul. 1931—*AAS,* XXIII (1931), 353; Bouscaren, *Digest,* I, 294.

[102] Cf. cans. 462, n. 3; 850; 938, § 2.

[103] Cf. Vermeersch-Creusen, *Epitome,* I, n. 632, p. 471; Coronata, *Institutiones,* I, n. 540, p. 653; Augustine, *Commentary,* III, 142; Schaefer, *De Religiosis,* n. 565, p. 286; O'Brien, *Exemption of Religious,* p. 183; Beste, *Introductio in Codicem,* p. 341.

[104] Can. 938.

dition and spiritual distress, the obligation of the priest to assist is proportionate to the greater or lesser spiritual need of the person and the facility or difficulty entailed in giving the sacrament. Moreover, the obligation resting upon the extraordinary minister is a serious one when the sick person is in need of the sacraments and the priest may be obliged even to risk his life to fulfill his obligation.[105]

ARTICLE 4. ECCLESIASTICAL BURIAL AND THE CLERICAL RELIGIOUS HOUSE

Section 1. Religious and the Residents of the Religious House

Ecclesiastical burial consists in the transfer of the body to a church, the performance of the obsequies there, and the final transportation of the body to the place of interment.[106] Canon 1221 reflects the norms governing the funerals of religious. At their death, the bodies of the professed religious and of the novices may be transferred to the church or the oratory of the religious house to which they had been assigned in life. They may also, at the religious superior's discretion, be brought to another house of their institute. In either case, novices retain the right to choose another church for their funeral. When the body is at a place so distant that it cannot be transferred easily to any house of the institute, the funeral is to be conducted at the nearest parish church, unless a novice had indicated another church, or unless the superior chooses to transfer the body to a church of the institute despite the distance or expenses involved.[107] If the local parish is selected when the body of the religious is not removed to a church of the institute, the minister of the funeral is the pastor.[108]

The provisions of the Code regarding the burial of novices apply also to domestics who reside permanently on the premises

---

[105] Cf. Abbo-Hannan, *The Sacred Canons,* II, 939; Woywod-Smith, *Practical Commentary,* I, 545.

[106] Can. 1228, § 2.

[107] Cans. 1218, § 3; 1221, § 2; 1231, § 1.

[108] Cf. Schaefer, *De Religiosis,* n. 1383, p. 825; Fanfani, *De Iure Religiosorum,* n. 421, pp. 579-580.

of the religious house.[109] If these people should die while they are away from the religious house, their funerals are to be arranged like those of other lay people in accordance with the norms of canons 1216-1218. The funerals of postulants, scholastics, students, guests and patients are also governed by the norms of canons 1216-1218.[110] Such individuals, nevertheless, may exercise their right to select the church or oratory of the religious house for their funeral.[111]

Professed religious do not have the right to select their funeral church or cemetery.[112] Religious who are raised to the dignity of a cardinal, a bishop, or an abbot or a prelate *nullius,* however, enjoy this right.[113] Moreover, there is some probability for the opinion that professed religious who are vicars and prefects apostolic enjoy this right as well.[114] Such instances as these, however, are exceptions to the general denial of this choice to religious. Formerly, members of the regular clergy were permitted to have their funerals in the place of their choice when they died far away from their religious houses. This right is now revoked by the Code.[115]

Section 2. The Faithful in General

The faithful are free to select their funeral church and cemetery, unless this right is expressly restricted by law.[116] Religious, as indicated above, and those under the age of puberty do not have this right.[117] The faithful, however, may not select churches belonging to any religious institute, but only those which belong

[109] Can. 1221, § 3.

[110] Cf. Response of the Pontifical Commission for the Authentic Interpretation of the Code, 20 iul. 1929—*AAS,* XXI (1929), 573; Bouscaren, *Digest,* I, 572; cf. Ramos, "De conditione saecularium in domibus religiosorum," *CpR,* VI (1925), 479-481; Maroto, "Annotationes," *CpR,* X (1929), 334.

[111] Can. 1223, § 1.

[112] Cans. 1224, n. 2.

[113] Cf. cans. 215, § 2; 294, § 1; 1219, § 1.

[114] Cf. Coronata, *Institutiones,* II, n. 801 (b), p. 106; Beste, *Introductio in Codicem,* p. 604.

[115] Cf. Larraona, "Commentarium Codicis," *CpR,* IX (1928), 206.

[116] Can. 1223.

[117] Can. 1224.

to regulars. Other religious churches, even though they belong to exempt clerical institutes, may not be chosen unless the religious enjoy special permission to conduct the funeral services of lay people. Such a privilege may be had from the Holy See, the local ordinary, or legitimately prescribed custom.[118] In any case, when the selected church belongs to a religious institute, the permission of the proper superior is necessary before the choice becomes effective.[119]

The selection of a funeral church and cemetery may be made personally or by someone authorized to do so in behalf of the party in question.[120] The selection must be legally manifested before it enjoys juridic value. Even the relatives of the deceased require previous authorization, unless it be a matter of parents choosing a funeral church and cemetery for their deceased children who have not attained puberty.[121] Religious and secular clerics are strictly forbidden to attempt to induce the faithful to choose their church or cemetery for the funeral and burial. Moreover, they are forbidden to oblige the faithful to stand firmly by a choice previously made. Obligations derived from violations of these laws are invalid.[122]

Religious institutes may have their own cemeteries. Exempt religious communities are given this right by law,[123] while non-exempt institutes require the permission of the local ordinary.[214] When such permission is given by the local ordinary, he may place reasonable limitations on the use of the cemetery. Thus he may stipulate that the religious shall not bury lay persons in their cemetery unless they are benefactors of the institute. Religious may permit the faithful to select their cemetery as long as the ordinary does not forbid it. In any case, when a lay person selects

[118] Cf. can. 1225; Vermeersch-Creusen, *Epitome,* II, n. 534, p. 377; O'Brien, *Exemption of Religious,* p. 154.

[119] Can. 1228, §§ 1, 2; cf. Goyeneche, *Quaestiones Canonicae,* II, 330-331.

[120] Can. 1226, § 1.

[121] S.C.C., 15 nov. 1930—*AAS,* XXV (1930), 155; Bouscaren, *Digest,* I, 576; can. 1224, n. 1.

[122] Can. 1227.

[123] Can. 1208, § 2.

[124] Can. 1207, § 3.

the cemetery of religious, the proper superior may permit or refuse the execution of this choice.[125]

The local ordinary is to establish the proper offering for a funeral stipend unless custom has already fixed the amount. He may seek the advice of his diocesan consultors and the pastors of the episcopal city in drawing up a schedule of offerings.[126] The Pontifical Commission for the Authentic Interpretation of the Code has declared that the terms of such a list are binding upon all, even exempt religious.[127] This declaration is not merely a strict interpretation of canon 1234, § 1. It seems that the public welfare was the primary consideration and that parochial discord and the disedification of the faithful are thereby avoided.

The Code provides for the proper pastor's share of the funeral offering when the funeral of a parishioner is held in another church. This obligation is called the "parochial portion" or the canonical portion.[128] The pastor is to receive this offering unless particular law ordains otherwise, or unless the deceased could not have been conveniently brought to his proper parish for burial. The portion given to the pastor is stipulated by diocesan rule. It can be a third or a fourth of the stipend given for conducting the funeral. Suffice it to state, however, that we have a contrary custom in this regard in the United States, so that the "parochial portion" is of little practical concern in this study. As Fr. Beste notes: "*Apud nos, quantum scimus, consuetudine contraria, portio canonica non solvitur et cum haec consuetudo ad pacificum convictum non parum conferat, optandum ut retineatur.*"[129]

---

[125] Cans. 1209, § 1; 1228, § 2.

[126] Can. 1234, § 1.

[127] 6 martii 1927, ad II—*AAS,* XIX (1927), 161; Bouscaren, *Digest,* I, 582.

[128] Cans. 1236, § 1; 1237, § 1; cf. Goyeneche, *Quaestiones Canonicae,* II, 335-341.

[129] *Introductio in Codicem,* p. 615; cf. Augustine, *Commentary,* VI, 150; Woywod-Smith, *Practical Commentary,* II, 50.

CHAPTER VII

Parochial Assistance Given by the Religious Clergy to the Parish Clergy

ARTICLE 1. THE OBLIGATION TO RENDER ASSISTANCE

Section 1. The Subject of the Obligation

When parochial assistance is required by the local ordinary or pastors of the diocese, religious superiors should designate their priests to help care for the spiritual needs of the faithful. This sacerdotal assistance may be rendered within or outside of the churches and public oratories attached to clerical religious houses. It is especially fitting that it be given in the diocese where the religious reside. However, in all cases, the prescriptions of religious discipline should not be detrimentally affected.[1] Conversely, the ordinaries and pastors should make use of religious in the sacred ministry, especially in the administration of the sacrament of penance.[2] These prescriptions of canon 608, §§ 1, 2, are intended to foster mutual help and assistance between the religious and parish clergy in their common work, the honor and glory of God and the salvation of souls.

This canon is based on pre-Code legislation contained principally in the Constitution *Super cathedram of Boniface* VIII (1294-1303),[3] and the constitution *Dudum* of Clement V (1305-1314).[4] These papal constitutions were among the first and most

---

[1] "Curent Superiores ut religiosi subditi, a se designati, praesertim in dioecesi in qua degunt, cum a locorum Ordinariis vel parochis eorum ministerium requiritur ad consulendum populi necessitati, tum intra tum extra proprias ecclesias aut oratoria publica, illud, salva religiosa disciplina, libenter praestent."—can. 608, § 1.

[2] "Vicissim locorum Ordinarii ac parochi libenter utantur opera religiosorum, praesertim in dioecesi degentium, in sacro ministerio et maxime in administrando sacramento poenitentiae."—can. 608, § 2.

[3] 18 febr. 1300—c. 2, *de sepulturs,* III, 6, in Extravag. com.

[4] 6 maii 1312—c. 2, *de sepulturis,* III, 7, in Clem; Potthast, *Regesta,* n. 24913; cf. *supra,* pp. 37-45.

important expressions of general legislation concerning the parochial apostolate of religious priests. They were especially concerned with the use and extent of confessional and preaching jurisdiction or approbation. Subsequently, other constitutions and decrees of the Holy See were concerned with this same matter.[5]

Canon 608, § 1, has reference to local superiors of clerical religious houses. The subjects referred to in this canon are necessarily clerical subjects because the assistance specified is of a sacerdotal nature. Religious priests should be designated by their superior before they undertake any form of parochial assistance. The prescripts of canon 608, § 1, not only require the designation of the religious priest, but also presumes his presentation to the local ordinary when diocesan faculties are necessary for preaching and absolving the faithful.[6] Moreover, the religious may not use these faculties without at least the presumed permission of the superior. This is completely in accordance with religious discipline and the demands of good order. The religious superior is responsible for the discipline of the house and it is his right to judge what is best for the community. Consequently, the religious priest is not free to engage himself in clerical activity prior to the designation or approval of his proper superior. Nevertheless, the local ordinary and the pastor are free to request the assistance of specific priests.[7]

The local superior is certainly competent to designate priests for parochial assistance. This right is not necessarily reserved to a major superior. When the Code speaks of the rights and the obligations of religious superiors, the term "superior" is often used

---

[5] Cf. const. *Vas electionis,* 21 iul. 1321, of John XXII (1316-1334)—c. 2, *de hereticis,* V, 3, in Extravag. com.; const. *Gregis nobis,* 16 ian. 1446, of Eugene IV (1431-1447)—*Bull. Praed.,* III, 217; sess. V, *de ref.,* c. 2; sess. XXIII, *de ref.,* c. 15; sess. XXIV *de ref.,* c. 4; sess. XXV, *de regularibus,* c. 11.

[6] Cf. cans. 874, §§ 1, 2; 1339, § 2.

[7] "Ordinarius loci aut parochus, quominus Religisos sibi benevisos Superioribus proponant, non impediuntur. Religiosus subditus de ministeriis praestandis aliquid statuendi non habet ius independenter a Superiore."—Schaefer, *De Religiosis,* n. 1197, p. 712; Wernz-Vidal, *Ius Canonicum,* III, n. 384, p. 401.

without any qualification.[8] In such instances, all superiors are competent, unless the content of the law or the nature of the case indicates that a major superior is intended in the particular case.[9] In fact, after comparing canon 608 with other canons concerned with the presentation and approval of religious priests for diocesan faculties,[10] it appears that the proper superior is undoubtedly the local superior. He is the logical person to assign priests of his house to engage in the sacerdotal ministry. He can adequately judge the particular situation and determine the necessity of rendering parochial assistance. At times the circumstances will demand permission of higher authority. This, however, would appear to be an exceptional situation and certainly impractical as a general policy. Accordingly, the major superior may reserve the permission to himself when there is little necessity for offering such assistance; when the religious discipline is infringed upon; or when the particular activity would constitute a burden to the priests. Yet, if the ministry of religious priests is necessary and religious discipline is not affected, particular law should not reserve the right to supply priests for parochial assistance to a major superior. The common good of the Church and the welfare of souls might easily be impeded through useless restrictions on the power of the local superior.[11]

Section 2. The Extent of the Obligation

Religious superiors are to aid the diocesan and parish clergy in the *cura animarum* not only in the parish churches, but also in their own religious churches and public oratories.[12] When the local ordinary judges that their assistance is necessary for the catechetical instruction of the faithful, he may even require exempt religious to give this aid. Religious superiors can be obliged to give these instructions personally or through their subjects. They are

[8] E.g., cans. 454, § 5; 465, § 4; 514, § 1; 604, § 1; 609, § 3.

[9] Cf. Schaefer, *De Religiosis,* n. 429, p. 193.

[10] Cf. cans. 874-880; 1338, § 1; 1339-1340.

[11] Cf. O'Brien, *The Provincial Religious Superior,* The Catholic University of America Canon Law Studies, n. 258 (Washington, D. C.: The Catholic University of America Press, 1947), p. 138.

[12] Can. 608, § 1.

to do this certainly within their own churches. Religious discipline, however, is not to suffer from such assistance.[13]

Although it is the prerogative of the local ordinary to judge the need for such instructions, as is clear from canon 1344, it is still the right of the proper religious superior to ascertain whether harm may be done to religious discipline.[14] Consequently, when the superior decides assistance can not be given without detriment to the discipline of his house, he cannot be forced to give this aid. Moreover, when religious are required to leave their house in order to give these instructions, a more serious reason is required than to render such help in their proper churches and oratories.[15]

Besides the types of parochial assistance already mentioned, the religious must comply with the decrees of the local ordinary with reference to the recitation of certain prayers, the celebration of specified ceremonies, and the ringing of church bells when required for some public reason.[16]

Assistance by religious outside their houses and in the neighboring parishes may include all types of activity. Canon 608 mentions specifically only that type of help that is of a sacerdotal nature, namely assistance in the sacred ministry. The celebration of Masses in the parochial churches on Sundays and days of precept, preaching assignments,[17] and the administration of the sacraments are

---

[13] Can. 1344; It may be noted that canon 154, §§ 1, 2, of the Oriental Code corresponds almost verbatim to canon 608, §§ 1, 2, of the Latin Code, while canon 154, § 3, of that Code has its counterpart in our canon 1334. Therefore, the Oriental Code has joined the prescriptions regarding the parochial assistance of religious, as contained in two different canons and sections of the Latin Code, into one canon in the section concerned with religious. Cf. Motu Proprio *Postquam Apostolicis.*

[14] "Eximuntur seu excusantur autem Superiores ab hac obligatione, si institutio concedi nequeat sine regularis disciplinae detrimento, cuius rei iudicium ad ipsos religiosos Superiores pertinet."—Coronata, *Institutiones,* II, n. 918, p. 265; Blat, *Commentarium Textus Codicis Institutiones* (6 vols., Vol. II, 2. ed., Romae, 1921), II, n. 212, p. 265 (hereafter cited: *Commentarium*).

[15] Cf. Abbo-Hannan, *The Sacred Canons,* II, n. 1334, p. 570.

[16] Can. 612.

[17] Canon 154, § 2, of the Oriental Code makes special mention of this: ". . . et maxime in divino verbo tradendo atque in administrando sacramento poenitentiae."—Motu Proprio *Postquam Apostolicis.*

certainly included in the notion of priestly assistance. The sacrament of penance receives express mention in canon 608, § 2, because religious are presumed to be qualified especially as confessors and spiritual directors.[18] The Church desires that the faithful enjoy the greatest liberty possible in the matter of confession. By encouraging the local ordinary and the pastors to employ religious in such a capacity, the good of souls is evidently the primary consideration.

Religious superiors are to assign their priests to assist the parish clergy not only in the diocese where their religious houses are situated, but also in the neighboring dioceses.[19] This is evident from the use of the phrase *"praesertim in dioecesi degentium"* in canon 608, § 2. Although the local diocese is apparently given preference, the canon implies that such parochial help is not to be limited to the home diocese, but ought to be extended to other dioceses when it can be done conveniently.[20]

Particular circumstances are to be taken into consideration, but there are numerous occasions on which the religious clergy may assist the parish clergy. Although many religious are themselves engaged in the mission apostolate or in parish work, others are assigned to work which makes them available for the parish ministry on a part-time basis. Since many parish priests are burdened with overcrowded parishes, assistance by religious is a great charity and a help in furthering the ends of the Church.

Section 3. The Force of the Obligation

The whole tenor of canon 608 is one of exhortation. Its purpose is the stimulation of mutual co-operation and fraternal assistance between the religious and secular clergy. The use of such expressions in the canon as: *"Curent Superiores," "cum requiritur," "salva religiosa disciplina,"* and *"libenter praestent,"* manifest that an obligation in charity is imposed on religious superiors to allocate

[18] Cf. Vermeersch-Creusen, *Epitome,* I, n. 767, p. 579; Cocchi, *Commentarium in Codicem Iuris Canonici ad usum scholarum* (4. ed., 8 vols., Taurinorum Augustae: Marietti, 1931-1946; Vol. II, 1937), II, 208-209 (hereafter cited: *Commentarium in Codicem*).

[19] Can. 608, § 2.

[20] Cf. Blat, *Commentarium,* II, n. 683, p. 675.

their priests for such assistance. The force of this obligation depends on the particular needs and conditions of each case. Canon 608, § 1, expressly states that there be some need for assistance, that religious discipline be not harmed; and that help be generously proffered upon legitimate request. Consequently, dioceses with a shortage of priests to care for the faithful will have a greater need for help than other dioceses. Almost all dioceses, however, have the need of some parochial help at one time or another. Although the canon may impose a grave obligation in charity, it clearly does not intend to bind in justice.

In designating priests for parochial assistance, the religious superior should be inclined to use persuasive measures rather than precepts.[21] Yet, the superior may impose a strict precept when necessary, as long as the constitutions of the institute do not exclude such activity. Moreover, in a grave case, the superior may command his subject in virtue of the vow of obedience.[22] Certain institutes, nevertheless, by their very nature exclude external apostolic works. Institutes like the Trappists and Carthusians are strictly contemplative and cloistered. Their superiors can not oblige clerical subjects by the vow of obedience to enter the active ministry outside the monastery.

The obligation to supply priests for parochial assistance is placed by canon 608, § 1, on the religious superior. If he fails to comply when such help is necessary, it is questioned whether he can be forced to render such assistance. Certainly the pastor cannot force religious and, transcending from the obvious moral obligation imposed on the superior, it appears that the religious cannot be forced to give this assistance even by the local ordinary.[23]

The local ordinary certainly cannot force exempt religious, since

---

[21] Cf. Beste, *Introductio in Codicem*, p. 417; Wernz-Vidal, *Ius Canonicum*, III, n. 384, p. 400.

[22] "Superiores, Religione stricte contemplativa praetermissa, possunt subditos obligare etiam in virtute s. obedientiae ad ministeria sacra praestanda etiam extra ecclesias proprias. Imprimis, si Religio ex instituto curam animarum peragat."—Schaefer, *De Religiosis*, n. 1197, p. 712; cf. Augustine, *Commentary*, III, 323; Coronata, *Institutiones*, I, n. 615, p. 791.

[23] ". . . at neque a parocho neque ab Ordinario religiosi cogi possunt."—Fanfani, *De Iure Religiosorum*, n. 329, p. 483; "Vis directa ab Ordinario loci exerceri non potest."—Schaefer, *De Religiosis*, n. 417, p. 187.

they are not subject to his jurisdiction in this matter.[24] Non-exempt religious, however, are subject to his jurisdiction. They are subject to the local ordinary as clerics and as members of the faithful.[25] Moreover, diocesan institutes are fully subject to the jurisdiction of the local ordinary according to the norms of the law.[26] While it is maintained by some authors that the local ordinary may be considered a religious superior in virtue of canon 492, § 2, and that as a result he possesses dominative power over diocesan religious,[27] it would seem proper to deny him such power.

Dominative power has to do with the government of the institute and the internal affairs of the community. This power is certainly enjoyed by all religious superiors and Chapters of an institute. It is exercised according to the norms of each constitution and the general prescriptions of Canon Law.[28] Therefore, if the local ordinary enjoyed dominative power over a particular institute, he would have the right to assign its priests to give parochial assistance when the need arose.

The local ordinary has such authority over the internal regime of an institute only when the constitutions expressly concede it to him or when the religious profession expressly includes him. Otherwise, it is far too generous and unnecessary a concession to be substantiated canonically.[29] The Code gives no dominative power to the local ordinary. Canon 492, § 2, states only that diocesan institutes are subject to the jurisdiction of the local ordinary, not that he has dominative power over them. Although canon 499, § 1, states that religious are subject to the power of the Roman Pontiff, both in virtue of their vows and as members of the faithful, it does not extend this subjection to the bishop. There-

[24] Can. 615.

[25] Cf. Beste, *Introductio in Codicem,* p. 330; Bouscaren-Ellis, *Canon Law,* pp. 238-239.

[26] Can. 492, § 2.

[27] "*Si religio est tantum iuris dioecesani,* religiosi, sive viri sive mulieres, etiam quoad regimen internum ab Ordinario loci dependent."—Fanfani, *De Iure Religiosorum,* n. 46, p. 79; cf. Coronata, *Institutiones,* I, n. 530, p. 631; Schaefer, *De Religiosis,* n. 388, p. 171.

[28] Can. 501, § 1.

[29] Cf. Berutti, *Institutiones,* III, n. 48; Vermeersch-Creusen, *Epitome,* I, n. 614, p. 455.

fore, as Regatillo states, the free assertion that religious are subject to the dominative power of the local ordinary is something which must be proved before it can be admitted.[30] The assumption of such power by one outside the institute seems contrary to the independent and autonomous nature of the community.[31]

All religious institutes are moral persons and are to be directed by their own superiors according to their constitutions and the common law of the Church. It is not proper for the local ordinary to interfere in the internal life and government of a religious institute. The internal government and the exercise of dominative power over the members of religious communities is the prerogative and the reserved right of religious superiors.[32]

Since all religious institutes possess their own moral-juridical personality and the right to their own self government, it is not the will of the legislator that externs intervene in their affairs. The designating of religious priests for parochial assistance is reserved by canon 608, § 1, to the religious superior. This same canon expressly and clearly distinguishes between the religious superior who assigns his priests for such assistance and the local ordinary or pastor who require such help. The assigning of such duties is certainly beyond the power of the local ordinary.[33]

Consequently, it is the indisputable right of the religious superior to designate his subjects for parochial assistance. He may do this only after weighing the necessity for such assistance and the effect it will have on religious discipline. Therefore, the local ordinary cannot oblige the superior or the religious by vow, nor can he coerce them by threat of a penalty to give such assistance. Although there may possibly be a grave obligation on the religious superior

---

[30] Cf. "Relationes inter status canonicos perfectionis et alios status in Ecclesia," *Acta et Documenta Congressus Generalis de Statibus Perfectionis* (1950), I, n. 67, p. 553.

[31] Cf. Quinn, *Relation of the Local Ordinary to Religious of Diocesan Approval,* The Catholic University of America Canon Law Studies, n. 283 (Washington, D. C.: The Catholic University of America Press, 1949), pp. 74-76.

[32] Cf. Larraona, "Commentarium Codicis," *CpR,* VI (1925), 182; Bouscaren-Ellis, *Canon Law,* p. 239; Creusen, *Religious in the Code,* n. 53, p. 41.

[33] Cf. Creusen, *Religious in the Code,* n. 53, p. 41.

at times to designate his priests for this work, it is a moral obligation binding in charity, and not in strict justice.

Canon 297 may be considered a parallel canon in this matter. It states that vicars and prefects apostolic may compel religious, including the exempt, to perform pastoral work, but the co-operation of the religious must be necessary because of a shortage of secular priests in the vicariate or prefecture. Moreover, the religious superiors must be consulted and there must be no infringement on special statutes approved by the Holy See. When the above conditions exist, religious are obliged not only in charity, but in justice, to enter the ministry at the request of the vicar or prefect.[34]

A shortage of priests on the missions need not be the absolute norm in itself, but should be considered in relation to other circumstances in the vicariate or prefecture.[35] The judgment whether or not the help of religious is necessary, as canon 297 states, is reserved to the vicar or prefect. The obligation of justice binding religious to co-operate apparently arises from a quasi-contract which the religious enter by the mere fact of accepting the work of missionaries in the vicariate or prefecture.[36]

The unusual conditions and demands of foreign missionary work requires that vicars and prefects apostolic have a more extensive power over religious than is needed by ordinaries of established dioceses. Consequently, canon 297 expressly confers on them authority to compel religious to undertake active phases of the mission apostolate in certain circumstances. Therefore, the vicars and prefects have authority over religious by positive legislation, an authority which they would not enjoy except by express concession.

Canon 608, on the other hand, merely exhorts religious to assist the parish clergy in ministering to the needs of the faithful and, conversely, recommends that local ordinaries and pastors use the

---

[34] Cf. S. C. Prop. Fide, 30 sept. 1848—*Collectanea S. Congregationis de Propaganda Fide* (2 vols., Rome: Ex Typographia Polyglotta S. C. de Propaganda Fide, 1907), II, n. 1033, ad 3.

[35] Cf. Blat, *Commentarium,* II, n. 314, p. 314.

[36] ". . quae obligatio videtur habere explicationem ex quasi contractu quo acceptarunt munus missionarii."—Coronata, *Institutiones,* I, n. 373, p. 442.

assistance of religious. If an established diocese is placed in a situation where the need for priests is critical, it seems that the ordinary could petition higher religious authority or even the Holy See to compel unco-operative religious to undertake the *cura animarum* so as to relieve this need temporarily. Nevertheless, even in an exceptional case, it does not appear that the ordinary can coerce them without being given this authority by the Holy See.

When the text of canon 608, § 1, states: "*. . . cum . . . eorum ministerium requiritur ad consulendum populi necessitati . . . ,*" the legislator considers the parochial assistance of the religious clergy as required primarily for the spiritual good of the faithful, and not merely for the convenience of the parish clergy.[37] The necessity mentioned in the canon may certainly be interpreted in the wide sense as meaning anything which is beneficial or useful to the spiritual life of the people.[38] In fact, this is expressly noted in the parallel canon of the Oriental Code. Canon 154, § 1, of the Oriental Code is almost a repetition, verbatim, of canon 608, § 1. It expressly states that religious are to give parochial assistance "*. . . ad consulendum populi necessitati vel utilitati. . . .*" The spiritual need or benefit of the faithful may come about because of many different reasons. For example, an insufficient number of parish priests for the adequate care of the people and the need of religious to act as supplementary priests to offer Masses on Sundays and holy days of obligation may always be considered a true necessity. On the other hand, religious preachers and confessors may be helpful to the devotion of the parishioners, even though their assistance be not considered a real necessity in particular cases.

Section 4. Limitations on the Obligation

The obligation of religious superiors to make their priests available for parochial work must be weighed according to the conditions stated in the Code, as well as to certain regulations of the

---

[37] ". . . non ad fovendam commoditatem vel otium cleri saecularis."—Blat, *Commentarium,* II, n. 683, p. 675.

[38] ". . . sacrum ministerium, quum in utilitate populi fidelis . . ."—Toso, *Commentaria Minora,* II, 189.

Holy See. Canons 608, § 1, and 1334 make express mention concerning the effect such ministry will have on religious discipline. Moreover, the activities of certain religious priests will be limited because of their particular position or assignment. The Church has given definite instructions concerning the activities of priests who are novices, students, professors, or who are in other positions of special concern. Consequently, the superior will be restricted in the exercise of his right to designate priests for parochial assistance.

A) Religious Discipline

The canons which concern the parochial assistance to be given by religious priests are modified by the phrases *"salva religiosa disciplina"*[39] and *"sine tamen regularis disciplinae detrimento."*[40] Therefore, the type of assistance, the circumstances of time, place, and persons, as well as the necessity involved, must be considered in their relation to religious discipline. Not only do the general norms laid down by the Code, but also the constitution or rule of each religious institute determine what is to be understood by "religious discipline." Anything that is detrimental to this discipline must be considered detrimental to the religious institute and to the Church which has established and approved its specific mode of life.

Religious discipline is determined by the particular and general law which regulate the religious state. Certainly, the major obligations of religious are included. All matters which pertain to the observance and fostering of the vows of poverty, chastity, and obedience are part of this discipline.[41] The same may be said concerning the observance of the common life[42] and the maintenance of proper residence.[43] Religious clerics are also appropriately obliged to fulfill the duties common to all clerics, insofar as they are consonant with the religious life. The prescriptions of particular constitutions which prescribe the choral office, or perpetual

---

[39] Can. 608, § 1.

[40] Can. 1334.

[41] Can. 497.

[42] Can. 594.

[43] Cf. cans. 597; 604; 679, § 2.

residence within the monastic enclosure, also help determine the religious discipline to be observed in each institute.[44] Therefore, infractions of the established order, even by some activity otherwise commendable, can be considered detrimental to this discipline.

Consequently, religious discipline has a relative aspect when applied to different religious institutes and even to different religious houses within the same community. A practice which is not harmful to the discipline of one institute may be harmful to another. The particular constitutions, the nature and purposes of the institute, as well as approved customs and practices, will clearly outline the principles determining the extent to which the sacerdotal ministry and active apostolate may be undertaken.

It is the right and the duty of the proper superior to judge when this discipline is not observed and when certain practices are detrimental to it. Canon 608, § 1, gives the discretionary power to the superior. It is he who is to safeguard the discipline. It is solely his right to designate his subjects and assign them to the type of ministry required in each case of parochial assistance. Moreover, it is the personal obligation of every religious to observe faithfully and entirely the vows he has professed and the prescriptions of the constitutions of his particular institute. It is through this discipline that the religious tends toward perfection.[45]

As already stated, the nature of the institute may exclude certain works of the sacred ministry. For example, priests who are members of a strictly contemplative order may not be commanded by their superior to enter the sacerdotal ministry outside the monastery.[46] Nevertheless, even though the particular institute may exclude such an apostolate, pontifical authority can permit certain activities for the common good. This possibility arises from the fact that all religious institutes are completely subject to the authority of the Supreme Pontiff. Pope Pius XII noted this in his Constitution *Sponsa Christi* and in the general statutes attached to this document.[47] According to the norms established in this

---

[44] Can. 610.

[45] Can. 593.

[46] Cf. Coronata, *Institutiones,* I, n. 615, p. 794; Augustine, *Commentary,* III, 323.

[47] 21 nov. 1950—*AAS,* XXXXIII (1950), 5; Bouscaren, *Digest,* III, 221.

Constitution the exercise of apostolic works, when undertaken with due moderation and for sufficient reason, does no harm to the contemplative life, but may add an element which renders it more effective.

Even though religious institutes be of an active and apostolic nature, there are certain considerations which must be given to the demands of proper discipline. The prescriptions of religious discipline are meant also to protect the individual religious as well as his institute. Therefore, when the mental, physical, or psychological welfare of a religious subject is endangered by one or more duties, the superior is obliged to rectify the matter paternally. Although the absence of religious for reasons of the ministry is generally considered to be beneficial rather than an occasion of detriment, nevertheless it may have the latter result.

The ministry cannot be demanded nor prescribed when the ends of religion are compromised, nor when such activity is an occasion of grave harm to religious discipline.[48] Whatever may bring notable inconvenience to the particular community or whatever causes neglect of religious obligations may not be tolerated by the religious superior.[49] It is the positive will of the Church that religious discipline be safeguarded. Even though certain activities are commendable and praiseworthy, they must not conflict with the approved rule of life which the Church has recognized.

The Church has always manifested its concern for the discipline of her religious institutes. This discipline is a result of her own approbation and legislation expressed in the common law and in particular regulations. It has always been the fervent wish of the Church that this discipline be promoted and retained in its vigor. No less is this true among clerical religious institutes dedicated to an active mode of life, than it is among all other religious communities. Early legislation ordered all clerics and monks to refrain

---

[48] Cf. Beste, *Introductio in Codicem,* p. 417.

[49] "Singuli religiosi a propriis Superioribus dependent etiam quoad exercitium sacri ministerii, eisque proinde reservatur ius iudicandi quandonam et quomodo et a quibus religiosis opera dari possit confessionibus excipiendis et sacris concionibus habendis, praesertim extra propriam ecclesiam, quin notabile incommodum pro communitate exinde sequatur aut obligationes vitae regularis negligantur."—Berutti, *Institutiones,* III, 272.

from those activities foreign to their way of life.[50] The Council of Trent reminded religious superiors to guard their religious subjects and industriously to preserve and maintain with care the common life.[51] The pontiffs and the Sacred Congregations of the Holy See have consistently exhorted and encouraged the observance of a vigorous and healthy religious life.[52] All things being considered, the maintenance of this discipline is given preference over the exercise of some particular form of activity which is good and commendable, but harmful to the proper observance of an approved way of life.

B) Regulations Regarding the Ministry of Certain Priests

1) Novices

A priest who enters the religious life may not, during the course of his year in the canonical novitiate, be designated for the ministry of preaching, the hearing of confessions, or for any employment in the external activities of the ministry.[53] The expression *"ne destinentur"* in canon 565, § 3, does not mean that a priest-novice cannot hear confessions or preach once or twice,[54] or in a case of necessity.[55] However, the law excludes frequent and habitual employment of novices in such work. Certainly, this prohibition does not permit novices to be assigned to any form of parochial assistance, especially when it requires leaving the

---

[50] Cf. Pope Alexander III (1159-1181)—cc. 1, 4, 6, X, *ne clerici vel monachi saecularibus negotiis se immisceant,* II, 50.

[51] Sess. XXV, *de regularibus,* cc. 1, 2.

[52] Cf., e.g., Clement VIII (1592-1605), *Nullus omnino,* 25 iul. 1599—*Fontes,* n. 187; S. C. Ep. et Reg., decr. 22 aug. 1814—*Fontes,* n. 1893; Pius IX (1846-1878), decr. *Nostris et Nobiscum,* 8 dec. 1849—*Fontes,* n. 508; Pius XI (1922-1939), *Unigenitus,* 19 martii 1924—*AAS,* XVI (1924), 133; Pius XII, const. *Sedes Sapientiae,* 31 maii 1956—*AAS,* XXXXVIII (1956), 354.

[53] "Anno novitiatus ne destinentur novitii concionibus habendis aut audiendis confessionibus aut exterioribus religionis muniis, . . ."—can. 565, § 3.

[54] Cf. Schaefer, *De Religiosis,* n. 905, p. 512; Vermeersch-Creusen, *Epitome,* I, n. 712, p. 524.

[55] "Quoad alteram classem notanda sunt verba *destinentur* et *dedita opera,* quae non excludunt absolute omne ministerium, sive pro casu transeuntis necessitatis sive etiam ad modum probationis."—Wernz-Vidal, *Ius Canonicum,* III, n. 286, p. 244.

novitiate grounds. Such an assignment may be permitted in a particular case only. It should be the exception and tolerated only for unusual and grave reasons. In practice, priests should be entirely excluded from the ministry during the course of their canonical novitiate.

Today many religious institutes have a second term added to the canonical year of novitiate. This extended period is not required by the Code, but is approved for some religious communities. The Sacred Congregation of Religious has declared[56] that the novitiate discipline may be relaxed during this extended period and novices may be employed in the works of the institute, as long as this is not prohibited by the particular constitutions. A priest required to remain in the novitiate after his canonical year may be permitted to engage in some limited sacerdotal activity outside the novitiate. Novitiate discipline, however, requires that this activity remain the exception rather than the rule.

Recently, the Holy See recommended a year of final spiritual training which may be called a *tertianship,* "second novitiate," "apostolic novitiate," "year of perfection," or *schola affectus.* This recommendation was made in the Apostolic Constitution *Sedes Sapientiae* of Pius XII and in the General Statutes annexed to this document.[57] This period of spiritual training is not a canonical novitiate. The time and the program of this final spiritual training is left to the determination of each institute and to particular law. The type of ministry and the extent to which the participants in this training period may engage in the ministry is left to particular regulations.[58]

2) Professors and Students

Canon 589, § 2, states that religious superiors should not impose any office or duty on students or teachers in the seminary

[56] 3 nov. 1921—*AAS,* XIII (1921), 539.

[57] 31 maii, 1956—*AAS,* XXXXVIII (1956), 354-365; cf. Sole Official English Text (2. ed., Washington, D. C.: The Catholic University of America Press, 1957), p. 68.

[58] Articles 51-53 of the General Statutes attached to the Constitution *Sedes Sapientiae* by the Sacred Congregation of Religious.—Cf. Sole Official English Text, pp. 68-70.

which will impede their studies or be an obstacle to attendance at class. Although this canon is directly concerned with the major seminary, its prescriptions can also be applied to the minor seminary. This prohibition is a wise and practical norm. Progress and proficiency in study can result only from quietly conducted and duly limited courses in the seminary. Study and teaching require the application of the whole man.[59]

The prescriptions of the canon 589, § 2, however, do not apply to vacation periods. Moreover, the religious superiors are given power to dispense from all duties, community exercises, etc., which make it difficult to apply one's self completely to the work of study. Even the choir obligation may be dispensed with when such a dispensation is an aid to study. The dispensations and exemptions permitted by canon 589, § 2, may be granted to both professors and students also during vacation periods when such dispensations or exemptions serve the purpose of promoting study.[60]

Religious priests who are teachers and professors in seminaries and houses of study are not to be burdened with duties which occasion neglect of scholastic labors or distractions in the performance of their work. A modicum of sacerdotal work in the *cura animarum* is certainly not incompatible with this general prohibition. Whether or not "week end" assignments or other forms of parochial assistance occasion detriment to the training of seminarians is a matter that must be resolved by the proper superior. The circumstances of time and place, the health and temperament of the professor must be considered. That which is a healthy and refreshing sacerdotal exercise for one person may well be a fatiguing and burdensome assignment to another. It is not the intention of the Holy See to prohibit seminary professors

---

[59] "Opportunissima ista Codicis sanctio Superioribus maxime commendanda est. Non raro enim, propter utilitates practicas v. g. scholarum inferiorum, contra eam peccatur. Constat tamen, sine talia vacatione ab aliis negotiis, studia vix seria esse posse: totum hominem postulat."—Vermeersch-Creusen, *Epitome,* I, n. 743, p. 556.

[60] Cf. Beste, *Introductio in Codicem,* p. 407; Abbo-Hannan, *The Sacred Canons,* I, 607; Coronata, *Institutiones,* I, n. 596, p. 760.

from being of assistance to the parish clergy, but such a ministry must be subordinated to their primary duty of teaching.

As a general rule, it will probably be found that parochial assistance by professors is a welcome and refreshing opportunity to exercise their priestly powers. It is also a constant reminder to seminary teachers that they must reduce the theories of the classroom texts to the practical problems of parish and mission life. Therefore, all forms of sacerdotal labor and parochial assistance may be encouraged by the superior or the rector of the seminary, as long as it is not detrimental to the life of the seminary. The ministry can be a benefit to theological studies, when it is brief and moderately undertaken.[61]

The Holy See has given specific declarations concerning the ministry of student-priests who have not completed their fourth year of theological training. These priests are not to be assigned habitually to the sacred ministry. They should not be designated for the hearing of confessions, the work of preaching, nor are they to be employed in the exterior works of the particular religious institute.[62] This restriction imposes a grave obligation on the conscience of the proper superior. It is always presupposed, even though the dispensation for ordination at the end of the third year of theology be given personally by the Roman Pontiff. Nevertheless, occasional employment of student-priests is permitted. The words *"ne destinentur"* do not exclude completely the sacerdotal ministry of hearing confessions and of preaching the word of God.[63] Because this matter is one of great importance, the granting of permission for the student-priests to undertake this min-

---

[61] ". . . ministerium animarum, dummodo sit breve et valde moderatum, videtur potius prodesse quam obesse studio theologico . . ."—Prümmer, *Manuale,* q. 220, resp. 5

[62] S. C. de Rel., 27 oct. 1923; ". . . vetito interim quocumque animarum ministerio, id est, ne destinentur concionibus habendis aut audiendis confessionibus aut aliis exterioribus religionis muniis; super quibus Superiorum conscientia graviter onerata remaneat." *AAS,* XV (1923), 549; *Enchiridion de Statibus Perfectionis,* I, n. 347, p. 399; Bouscaren, *Digest,* I, 483.

[63] Cf. Schaefer, *De Religiosis,* nn. 1036-1037, pp. 616-617; Vermeersch, "Annotationes," *Periodica,* XII (1923), 156; Coronata, *Institutiones,* II, n. 589, p. 764.

istry seems to be reserved to the major superior. However, he may designate the local superior as his delegate.[64]

Prohibitions regarding the ministry of student-priests do not concern those who have completed their seminary course and are assigned to the year of "pastoral training" initiated by the Constitution *Sedes Sapientiae.* According to articles 47 and 48 of the General Statutes attached to this Apostolic Constitution, newly-ordained religious priests must spend a year after ordination in training which immediately prepares them for the active ministry. The year of pastoral training consists in classroom study and opportunities to exercise the sacred ministry moderately under the paternal direction of an experienced priest. The exact extent to which these priests may be employed in the sacred ministry is left to particular law and the discretion of the Director of this program.[65]

3) Masters of Novices and Spiritual Prefects

The Code also forbids religious superiors to burden the Master of Novices with duties that are incompatible with his position.[66] Moreover, the General Statutes of the Constitution *Sedes Sapientiae* specifically apply the norms of canon 589, § 2, regarding professors in the seminary, to the Spiritual Prefect of clerical students.[67] Consequently, superiors may not arbitrarily designate priests for parochial assistance. They must give serious consideration to the duties and positions of the priest. Seminary professors, student-priests, novices, etc., are not to be designated without assurance that their primary duties suffer no detriment from sacerdotal labor. Therefore, some priests will be excluded from entering all forms of parochial assistance. Other priests, because of the particular demands of their work or position, will be restricted in the assuming of assignments when there is any danger of interference with their more important tasks.

---

[64] Cf. O'Brien, *The Provincial Religious Superior,* p. 140.

[65] Cf. Sole Official English Text, p. 66.

[66] Can. 559, § 3.

[67] Article 28, § 7. Cf. Sole Official English Text, p. 39.

ARTICLE 2. TEMPORAL REMUNERATION FOR PAROCHIAL ASSISTANCE

Section 1. Mass Stipends and Compensation Arising from an Extrinsic Title

According to the established and approved practice of the Church, a priest who celebrates and applies a Mass for the intention of a donor may accept a pecuniary offering or stipend.[68] It is maintained that an innominate contract, *"do ut facias,"* arises between the donor of the stipend and the priest who accepts it. The priest is gravely bound in justice to offer the Mass according to the conditions specified or to make restitution, unless the stipend amounts to a mere token offering.[69]

A priest may celebrate only one Mass a day. He may offer more than one only by way of exception.[70] Whenever permitted to celebrate more than one Mass a day, the priest may not accept a stipend for another Mass when one Mass is applied under an obligation of justice. The Code notes certain exceptions to this general principle, for example, Masses celebrated on Christmas Day, or when an indult is received from the Holy See. Nevertheless, the priest may accept some compensation based on a claim extrinsic to the application of the Mass.[71]

An extrinsic title permits the priest to accept some remuneration for the celebration of a Mass for which he already has a stipend, or for which he may not accept a stipend. This title or claim may arise even though he celebrates only one Mass. However, an extrinsic claim must not be in the nature of a stipend given for the application of the special fruits of the Mass. Neither may it be a just claim which obliges the priest to apply a Mass out of justice, as is the case with regard to the obligation of pastors to offer the *missa pro populo.*[72]

There is a definite distinction between the Mass stipend and the remuneration that can be accepted for extrinsic labor or inconvenience involved in the celebration of a Mass. The stipend is

---

[68] Can. 824, § 1.

[69] Cf. Abbo-Hannan, *The Sacred Canons,* I, 823.

[70] Cf. can. 806, §§ 1, 2.

[71] Can. 824, § 2.

[72] Cf. cans. 306; 339; 466, § 1; Augustine, *Commentary,* IV, 178; 182-183.

for the application of the Mass alone. An extrinsic title arises as a consequence of circumstances surrounding the celebration of Mass. The donor, however, is able to offer a stipend with the stipulation that Mass be celebrated under certain conditions. Therefore, the priest accepting the stipend is obliged not only to apply the Mass for the specified intention, but bound in justice to fulfill the added conditions as well. Nevertheless, unless certain conditions are positively added by the donor, the presumption is that he wishes only the application of the Mass.[73]

An extrinsic title is certainly present when a pastor invites a priest to the parish to celebrate one or more Masses for the parishioners. When Masses are offered for the convenience of the faithful, especially on Sundays and holy days of obligation, pastors often require assistance from priests not attached to the parish. When a priest assists the parish clergy in this manner, he has a right to some equitable compensation even though he already has a stipend for the application of the Mass he celebrates. The fact that a priest is requested to come to a parish and celebrate one or more Masses, involves a contract separate and distinct from the application of the Mass. Even if the pastor intends that the priest apply Mass for his intentions, equity still demands that he receive some compensation for the inconveniences entailed in traveling to the parish and offering Mass at stated hours. This right is contemplated in the *"excepta aliqua retributione ex titulo extrinseco"* of canon 824, § 2, as well as the provisions of canon 832.[74]

In each diocese, it is the right of the local ordinary to fix the manual stipend for Mass. When possible, this is to be fixed by a synodal decree. Priests are not allowed to demand more than the amount defined.[75] When there is no decree, diocesan custom is to be observed.[76] Moreover, even exempt religious are obliged to obey the diocesan legislation or custom in this matter.[77] If a priest exacts more than the determined stipend, he violates not only the

---

[73] Cf. cans. 825, § 4; 833.

[74] Cf. S.C.C., decr. 16 ian. 1649—*Fontes,* n. 2691; Goyeneche, *Quaestiones Canonicae,* II, 250.

[75] Can. 831, § 1.

[76] Can. 831, § 2.

[77] Can. 831, § 3.

law, but commutative justice as well, and is obliged to make restitution.[78] The local ordinary can demand that even exempt clerics not accept less than the scheduled diocesan stipend.[79] This is obligatory only when it is accepted within the diocese, not when a stipend is received from outside the diocese.[80] If he does not expressly forbid this practice, a smaller stipend than is customary or specified may be accepted. Since stipends are a very nominal amount, however, it may be better to refuse the tendered stipend and inform the person that the Mass will be offered as a personal favor.

If an excessive stipend is demanded by a priest, he can be punished by the bishop. Exempt religious are expressly subject to the provisions of canon 831, § 1. Therefore, the local ordinary can penally coerce them for infractions. Unless it is expressly stated, however, that exempt religious are subject to a certain penalty they are considered to be excluded.[81] Canon 619 does not expressly revoke privileges in favor of religious with respect to this matter. Therefore, mendicants and others who are not subject to episcopal censures, except in certain specific cases, do not incur a censure for demanding an excessive stipend.[82] Practically speaking, it is advised that the diocesan statutes omit any reference to religious in this regard, unless the local ordinary especially desires to curb them. In this case the statute should mention them specifically and impose a vindictive penalty rather than a censure.[83]

Necessity demands that "bination" be a common occurrence in many parishes and mission stations within the United States. Often the only large group of priests who are available for parochial assistance on Sundays and holy days of obligations are those who belong to religious institutes. They are, along with the parish clergy, often required to binate and trinate on days of precept

[78] Cf. O'Brien, *Exemption of Religious,* p. 169; Abbo-Hannan, *The Sacred Canons,* I, 829-830.

[79] Can. 832.

[80] Cf. Goyeneche, *Quaestiones Canonicae,* II, 249.

[81] Cf. Coronata, *Institutiones,* I, n. 626, p. 816.

[82] Cf. Schaefer, *De Religiosis,* n. 1287, pp. 767-768; O'Brien, *Exemption of Religious,* p. 49.

[83] Cf. Hannan, "Exempt Religious and Penalty for Excessive Mass Stipend," *The Jurist,* VIII (1948), 244.

with a view to the adequate care of the people. Sometimes an indult is granted to the ordinary so that he may permit the acceptance of a stipend for a second Mass. He may permit this only for a serious reason, or on condition that this stipend is given to some charitable or educational institution within the diocese, as for example, for the support of the diocesan seminary.[84] In such a case even exempt religious who binate in one of the parish churches on Sunday have no right to retain the second stipend when the indult states that it is to be given to a specific charity or organization. The privilege to binate is not a personal privilege. It is given so that there will be sufficient opportunity for the faithful to attend Mass on Sundays and holy days of obligation. Diocesan and religious priests are treated the same way in this matter and have no right to the second stipend. Unless the local ordinary has such an indult, however, he may not oblige exempt religious to offer a bination Mass for his intentions, nor to accept a second stipend for a specified purpose. Canons 806 and 824 do not give the ordinary this right and he must have an apostolic indult to require this.[85]

Section 2. Synodal Legislation and Custom Concerning Honoraria

The primary purpose of the sacred ministry is the care of souls. In return for the spiritual administrations of the clergy, some material subsidy is certainly justified and frequently necessary for their support. This is normally provided by the faithful who benefit from the ministry of the priest. Therefore, canon 463, § 1, states that the pastor has a right to fees which are allotted him by legitimate custom or by the provincial schedule of fees enacted in accordance with canon 1507, § 1. These offerings are commonly termed "stole fees." Although one or more of the pastoral duties is performed by another priest, the fees and offerings belong to

[84] Cf. S. C. de Prop. Fide, decr. 24 maii 1870—*Fontes,* n. 4877; S.C.C., 9 maii 1920—*AAS,* XII (1920), 536; Bouscaren, *Digest,* I, 393; Augustine, *Commentary,* IV, 189; Abbo-Hannan, *The Sacred Canons,* I, 824-825.

[85] Cf. Goyeneche, *Quaestiones Canonicae,* II, 243; Donovan, "Regular Priests and the Application of a Bination Mass," *The Homiletic and Pastoral Review* (New York, 1900-), XLI (1940-1941), 1134.

the pastor untless it is certain that the donor wishes the excess over the established amount to go to the ministering priest.[86]

Common law does not absolutely require that the "stole fees" be allocated to the pastor. Custom and particular law may otherwise dispose of the whole or a part of the "stole fee."[87] When a non-reserved function is performed by another priest, the officiating priest has a right to the remuneration tendered, unless it be performed in the parish church. In the latter case, it appears that the pastor has a presumptive right to all offerings unless custom, law, or the intention of the donor state contrariwise.[88] If a priest acts in case of necessity, it appears that he may retain whatever offering is made.[89] In any case, even though a legitimately delegated priest may not have a right to the "stole fee" when he performs a pastoral function, he is still entitled to some compensation. This right may arise from an express contract or from a quasi-contract which is based on equity and sometimes called a "gentleman's agreement."[90]

The most frequent form of parochial assistance given by religious priests in the United States is what is commonly referred to as "week-end work." Although the parish clergy can cope with the pastoral work during week days, the influx of penitents for confessions on Saturdays and the necessity of extra Masses on Sundays often demand sacerdotal assistance from outside the parish.[91]

---

[86] Cf. can. 463, § 3; Goyeneche, *Quaestiones Canonicae,* I, 72.

[87] Cf. Hannan, "Alms for the Clergy," *The Jurist,* IX (1949), 303; Kay, "The Rights of the Parochial Beneficiary in the United States," *The Jurist,* XV (1955), 330-336.

[88] Cf. Bouscaren-Ellis, *Canon Law,* pp. 207-208; Augustine, *Commentary,* II, 542.

[89] Cf. Ferry, *Stole Fees,* The Catholic University of America Canon Law Series, n. 59 (Washington, D. C.: The Catholic University of America Press, 1930), p. 53.

[90] Cf. Berutti, *Institutiones,* III, 272; Piontek, "A Gentleman's Agreement," *The Jurist,* III (1943), 284-305.

[91] For a description of some of the practical pastoral problems that such assistance can entail, cf. Schwegler, "Sunday Help," *The Homiletic and Pastoral Review,* XLVIII (1947-1948), 40-44; 605-609.

Most secular priests are assigned to the parishes of their diocese and are not available for such temporary parish help. Priests from the diocesan seminary and other non-parochial institutions are often required to make themselves available for this work. Many religious priests are assigned to work that is non-parochial, such as the education of youth and the training of seminarians. Consequently, the parish clergy often rely on their assistance. The Code of Canon Law encourages this practice.[92]

It is only just and equitable, however, that priests who must leave their residence and travel to the parish where they are to assist the local clergy in the hearing of confessions, preaching, and the saying of Mass should receive some compensation. The religious cannot himself benefit from the honoraria or stipends he receives. He is obliged by his vow of poverty to turn these over to his superior unless he has permission to retain them.[93] The community, however, has a right to this temporal remuneration.

Equity demands that remuneration correspond to the type and the amount of work performed, as well as to the other inconveniences involved. A visiting priest should receive a larger honoraria for assistance on both Saturday and Sunday than for one day's help. The distance traveled and the inconveniences entailed are also to be considered. If more than one Mass is offered, or if some special or unusual service is asked and rendered, such as preaching at all the Masses on Sunday, then the reimbursement should be correspondingly regulated.

In the past, local or regional custom in the United States regulated the norm to be followed in the matter of reimbursing visiting priests for parochial assistance. Provincial councils and diocesan synods did not legislate regarding this, presumably leaving it to custom and the discretion of individual pastors. One of the first councils to refer to this expressly, but only in a general way, was the IV Council of Portland, Oregon, convened in 1932. In decree n. 364 of this council, it was stated that a priest who took the place of the pastor in the celebration of certain functions was to

---

[92] Cf. can. 608, § 1.

[93] Cf. can. 580, § 2.

receive some equitable remuneration even though he had no right to the tax which went to the pastor.[94]

One of the first synods actually to legislate on parochial assistance given by priests on week ends was the IX Diocesan Synod of Philadelphia, held in 1934. In its sixteenth statute it stated:

> a) Each compensation by the parish for an outside substitute, who hears confessions on Saturday afternoon and night, and also gives his services on Sunday for Masses, preaching, etc., shall be fifteen dollars; if however, he renders no assistance on Saturday, it shall be ten dollars. This regulation applies also to holy days of obligation and their vigils.
>
> b) It is understood that, if the outside substitute incurs extraordinary expenses for travel, he shall be compensated for the same by the parish.[95]

Since that time, the practice in diocesan synods has been to set up positive regulations on this matter. In 1936, the II Archdiocesan Synod of San Francisco in California stated: "*Salarium substituti . . . non residentialis quoties ad munera dominicalia vel festiva persolvenda venit, toties praeter itineris impendia, percipiet docem scutata.*"[96] In 1939, legislation appeared in the synodal statutes of the Dioceses of St. Cloud, Minnesota,[97] and of Savannah-Atlanta, Georgia.[98] The latter was rather detailed, stating the exact amounts that were to be rendered under various circumstances.

---

[94] "Decretum 364: Si sacerdos extraneus locum tenet parochi in functione sacra celebranda, taxa non illi qui functionem sacram peregerit sed titulari ecclesiae stricto iure est solvenda, salvo iure sacerdotis qui functionem sacram celebraverit ad aequam remunerationem pro opere praestito."—*Acta et Decreta Concilii Provincialis Portlandensis in Oregon Quarti, Anno MCMXXXII*, p. 127.

[95] *Synodus Dioecesana Philadelphiensis IX—1934*, Statute XVI, pp. 14-15.

[96] *Statuta Archidioecesis Sancti Francisci Secunda—1936* (Typis: The Monitor Publishing Co., San Francisco, California), Statutum 365, n. 2, p. 90.

[97] *Synodal Decrees of the Diocese of St. Cloud* (1939), Statute n. 20, p. 14.

[98] *Statuta Dioecesis Savannensis-Atlantensis necnon Facultates Sacerdotibus Concessae* (1939), n. 174.

Although this practice has become widespread, it is still not a general one. Examination of a number of recent synodal statutes shows that legislation is still often lacking, and that this matter is left up to the pastors and priests concerned.[99] In one case, a synodal decree of the Diocese of Fargo, North Dakota, expressly stated that the remuneration a priest is to receive for conducting a "mission," a retreat, a "triduum," or the like, is to be determined by a contract or mutual pact between the pastor and the visiting priest.[100]

One of the latest and most detailed examples of positive legislation in the United States concerning the remuneration to be given priests who assist the parish clergy is to be found in the statutes of the Archdiocese of Cincinnati, Ohio, in its V Synod, held in 1954:

> 249. A. Priests who assist parishes on Saturdays and Sundays, either occasionally as substitutes for the priests of the parish, or regularly because of the heavy demands of parochial work, are to receive the following stipends:
>
> | | |
> |---|---|
> | Sunday assistance only | $10.00 |
> | Saturday confessions only | 5.00 |
> | Saturday and Sunday assistance | 15.00 |
>
> B. In addition to the above stipends, an allowance of five cents (5c) a mile shall be given for traveling expenses.
>
> C. In order to avoid hardships for smaller parishes —it is strictly forbidden to give, upon any pretext whatsoever, more than the statutory stipend and traveling allowance for Saturday and Sunday parochial assistance, even if the additional amount is paid from personal funds.

---

[99] The following are some of the more recent diocesan synodal statutes that apparently leave the matter to be settled in some other manner: *Tenth Diocesan Synod, Diocese of Natchez-Jackson* (1957); *Synodal Statutes of the Archdiocese of Boston* (1952); *Acta et Statuta Synodi Neo-Eboracensis Decimae Septimae* (1950); *Statutes of the Diocese of Winona, First Diocesan Synod* (1950); *First Diocesan Synod, Diocese of Pueblo* (1948); *Third Synod of the Diocese of Nashville* (1947).

[100] "Summa certa in remunerationem sacerdotis missionibus sacris, exercitiis spiritualibus, exercitiis triduanis aliisque similibus habendis conducti pacto mutuo praefiniatur."—*Liber Synodalis Fargensis* II (1951), Statutum 599, p. 111.

> If more is given from parish funds, both donor and the recipient are bound *in solidum* to restore the excess to the parish treasury.
> 250. The remuneration for a priest who preaches sacred missions, novena services, and the like, is not to exceed $25.00 a day.

A footnote to number 249, A, defines exactly what is to be understood by the term "Sunday assistance":

> Sunday assistance is understood to include the saying of two Masses where bination is necessary and permitted, and the giving of a sermon at the Masses. If the helper says the Mass for the intention furnished by the pastor, he shall receive the regular stipend for that Mass.[101]

Statute n. 313 of the IV Diocesan Synod of the Diocese of Lafayette, Louisiana, held in the year 1953, sets up similar norms:

> The remuneration for priests helping on Sundays shall be $10.00 for one Mass, $15.00 for two Masses, $20.00 for three Masses, plus $5.00 for helping with confessions on Saturday afternoon; the priest replacing either the pastor or assistant shall receive $70.00 per month from the church revenues for a limit of two months per year; in cases of extended time, the pastor shall be personally responsible for the salary of his replacement.[102]

The Diocese of St. Louis, Missouri, in its VIII Diocesan Synod, convened in 1950, stated that the minimum stipends were to be fifteen dollars for Saturday and Sunday assistance, ten dollars for Sunday alone, plus remuneration for extraordinary traveling expenses.[103] Statute n. 115 of the I Synod of the Diocese of Scranton, Pennsylvania, convoked in 1949, stated that the honoraria for special substitutes on week ends, as well as for Sundays and holy days,

---

[101] *Fifth Synod of the Archdiocese of Cincinnati* (St. Anthony Guild Press, Paterson, New Jersey, 1954), Statute numbers 249 and 250, p. 67.

[102] *Fourth Diocesan Synod—Lafayette* (*1953*), Title XIX, n. 313, p. 46.

[103] *Synodus Dioecesana Sancti Ludovici Octava* (*1950*), Statutum 61.

was to be twenty and fifteen dollars respectively.[104] The III Synod of the Diocese of Sioux City, Iowa, held in the same year, stated:

> 229. Compensatio substituti specialis erit, praeter victum et hospitium, $15.00 pro officiis peractis die dominica vel festo. Summa pecuniae proportionata solvenda erit pro expensis itineris. Si substitutus officium mensile agit, compensatio erit $60.00, expensis additis.
> 231. Remuneratio sacerdotis ad missiones sacras vel ad exercitia novendialia et alia huiusmodi conducti ne excedat $15.00 per diem in paroeciis minoribus, $20.00 per diem in paroeciis maioribus, expensis additis. Contractus pro servitiis his inter parochum et Superiorem Religiosum antecedenter sit pactus.[105]

Many other recent synods legislate almost identical amounts with minor variations.[106]

Although this survey makes no pretense at being exhaustive, it does present a cross-section of the dioceses of our country and indicates the increasing trend to set up positive legislation concerning remuneration for parochial assistance. It indicates the present amount of the honoria, stipend, fee, or equitable remuneration given non-parochial priests for transitory parish help such as giving assistance on week ends, preaching sacred missions, or supplying for absent parish priests. Because these schedules are rather uniform and, moreover, represent dioceses from different sections of the country, they give a good indication of custom and practice in dioceses which do not have positive regulations in this regard.

---

[104] *First Synod of the Diocese of Scranton* (*1949*), Statute 115, p. 103.

[105] *Synodus Dioecesana Siouxormensis Tertia* (*1949*), art. xxxiv, statutum 229 et 231, pp. 39-40.

[106] Cf. *First Synod of Raleigh* (*1948*), statutes 95-96, p. 48, and statute 104, p. 50; *Ninth Synod of the Diocese of Harrisburg* (*1943*), n. 80, p. 62; *Synodus Detroitensis Nona Die XIV Decembris Anno Domini MCMLIV Celebrata* (Michigan Catholic Press, 1955), n. 73, p. 19; *Synodus Dioecesana Eriensis Septima* (*1942*), n. 120, p. 46; *Acta et Decreta Synodi Dioecesanae Toletanae Primae, MCMXLI*, nn. 397-401, pp. 120-121; *Synodal Statutes of the Archdiocese of Newark* (*1941*), n. 403, p. 100; *First Synod of Dubuque, 1957*, Statute n. 372; pp. 92-93.

Therefore, the average amount of remuneration for week end parish assistance, from Saturday afternoon to Sunday noon, is between fifteen and twenty dollars. When the assistance is for Sunday alone, the fee is ten or fifteen dollars. If the priest assists in the hearing of confessions only on Saturday, five dollars appears to be the average stipend. This sum is to be taken from the parish fund or treasury. Moreover, compensation for the inconveniences of traveling to and from the parish must be added. Almost all of the above mentioned statutes positively state this, and pastors must consider this even though not stated in the decrees or statutes of a particular diocese. Equity requires that this be given some attention in estimating the honoraria given for such parochial assistance.

Synodal statutes should be observed in this regard and the proper authorities are justified in punishing those who refuse to render the stated fee, as well as those who demand an excessive fee.[107] The schedule of fees for parochial help may well involve the general welfare of the diocese. Observance of the schedule may forestall unbecoming financial dealings between parish priests and visiting priests. Consequently, unless the amount of remuneration is clearly only the minimum fee to be given for assistance, the amount stated in synodal law or recognized by the legitimate custom must be given.

---

[107] Cf. cans. 362; 2220-2222.

CONCLUSIONS

1. Historically, the religious state has passed through a series of successive stages in which the active sacerdotal apostolate has received increasing emphasis. The primitive concept of the religious state placed emphasis on the ascetical life and considered all forms of an active and sacerdotal apostolate as entirely extraordinary. Now, however, many religious institutes are essentially clerical and oftentimes dedicated to one or more forms of the active sacerdotal apostolate. [Cf. pp. 3-6; 8-10; 12-28; 35-37; 45-46; 53-54; 64-78; 81-86.]

2. Religious clerics have rendered sacerdotal assistance to the parochial clergy from the earliest times, and this assistance especially parallels their relationship to the sacrament of penance and the mission of preaching. [Cf. pp. 14-17; 19-20; 22-23; 31-32; 39-41; 64-69; 74-76; 126-127; 130-131.]

3. One of the bases of parochial conflicts in the past, although occasioned by such things as the exemption and privileges of some religious, was the notion that religious were radically unqualified by their state to be participants in an active apostolate. When permitted to enter the apostolate, such activity was considered to be exceptional, transient and solely of a temporary and auxiliary nature. [Cf. pp. 4-5; 10-12; 16-20; 23-29; 34-39; 45-50; 77-78; 81-86.]

4. In any given era the Church is the sole judge of what activities harmonize with the sacerdotal and religious states. She has authoritatively sanctioned and approved of religious in parish and mission work so that this activity is not to be considered unusual, extraordinary, or temporary. [Cf. pp. 84-87.]

5. Canon 488, n. 4, classifies a clerical institute as one in which ". . . *plerique sodales sacerdotio augentur. . . .*" This is not a restrictive definition which excludes other obvious characteristics of a clerical institute. It is best interpreted as meaning that a clerical institute is one in which a notable part of the members

are destined for the reception of the priesthood. [Cf. pp. 82-84.]

6. The essential distinction between the multiple vocation of the religious priest and the vocation of the secular priest lies in the fact that the religious priest alone is called to live a completely sacerdotal life within a canonically approved state of achieving perfection. It is precisely the fact that a priest is a member of a specific religious institute that will determine when, where, how and to what extent the active sacerdotal ministry will be exercised. [Cf. pp. 87-90.]

7. Religious discipline is a relative norm. It is based not only on the prescriptions of the common law for all clerics and religious, but also on the regulations of particular law as found in the approved constitutions of individual religious institutes. The law makes the proper religious superior the competent judge and the guardian of this discipline. [Cf. pp. 157-160.]

8. The local ordinary is not required to consult or to obtain the consent of the pastor for the valid and lawful erection of a religious house within his parish boundaries. [Cf. pp. 91-94.]

9. The fact that the attendance of the faithful at the parish church will be lessened, or that a diminution of alms to the parish will be a consequence, has not been recognized as a canonical objection to the erection of a clerical religious house with its church or public oratory. [Cf. pp. 94-96; 102-104.]

10. It appears that the Code now grants all clerical religious the right to a church or public oratory in connection with their houses, not only because of the sacerdotal nature of their institutes, but also because of the spiritual benefits that will accrue to the faithful who have an acknowledged right to attend the services in these places. [Cf. pp. 99-101.]

11. The local ordinary is given the right to approve the site of the proposed church or public oratory in order that he may preclude any uncompensated detriment to the other churches in the vicinity. [Cf. pp. 101-104.]

12. Canons 609, § 3, and 1171 are the basic canons concerning the power of the local ordinary to supervise the sacred rites performed in the churches and public oratories of clerical religious houses. The local ordinary may schedule the time of services in all these places for any just reason, but he may not do so in exempt

churches for any reason. He does not have the power to prohibit, suppress, or limit the sacred functions themselves, except in so far as he may indirectly do this by regulating the time of services. [Cf. pp. 107-108.]

13. The obligation placed on religious superiors by canon 609, § 3, is a supervisory one which obliges them to see that sacred functions in their churches and oratories do not detrimentally affect the parochial catechetical instructions or gospel explanations. If, however, the religious have similar instructions during the services at which the faithful attend, the detriment is considered not to be present. [Cf. pp. 109-115.]

14. Clerical religious are removed from parochial jurisdiction and are not to be considered parishioners. Exempt religious are completely removed from parochial authority. This is a logical deduction from their exemption from the jurisdiction of the local ordinary. On the other hand, non-exempt clerical religious enjoy at least a partial exemption from parochial authority. This partial exemption appears to be implicitly given by the Code as a result of the privileges bestowed on clerical superiors and clerical institutes. [Cf. pp. 118-125.]

15. The obligation enunciated in canon 608, § 1, for religious superiors, namely, to designate their priests for parochial assistance, is an obligation that binds in charity, but not in justice. Although there may be a serious moral obligation for the superior to designate his subjects for such assistance, he can not be coerced into giving assistance through the threat of a penalty from the local ordinary. The Code gives the discretionary authority in this matter solely to the proper religious superior. Moreover, attempts by the local ordinary to assign religious priests for such parochial work would imply an interference into the internal government of the religious house. [Cf. pp. 147-156.]

16. The phrase ". . . *eorum ministerium requiritur ad consulendum populi necessitati* . . ." of canon 608, § 1, refers to a relative necessity. The necessity requiring the parochial assistance of religious priests is best interpreted in a broad sense so as to refer to anything which is beneficial to the spiritual welfare of the faithful. [Cf. pp. 156-157.]

17. The legislation of the Holy See has manifested special con-

cern about the activities of certain religious priests. Consequently, superiors are not entirely free to arbitrarily assign priests who are novices, students, professors, masters of novices or spiritual prefects, to every and all forms of the sacerdotal ministry or parochial assistance. [Cf. pp. 160-164.]

18. In the United States there has been an increasing trend to enact positive legislation regarding the remuneration to be offered extra-parochial priests for temporary assistance in parish work. When there is synodal legislation, or when an approved custom obtains in this regard, the stated amount should be rendered unless this amount reflects simply the minimum indicated offering. The diocesan synodal legislation in the United States is generally uniform in the amounts to be offered for parochial assistance, and it serves as a good indication of the custom observed in those dioceses which do not have positive legislation on this matter. [Cf. pp. 168-175.]

BIBLIOGRAPHY

Sources

Acta Apostolicae Sedis, Commentarium Officiale, Romae, 1909-1929; Civitate Vaticana, 1929-

Acta Congressus Iuridici Internationalis, 5 vols., Romae: Apud Custodiam Librariam Pontifici Instituti Utriuque Iuris, 1935-1937.

Acta et Decreta Concilii Plenarii Baltimorensis Tertii, Typis Joannis Murphy et Sociorum, Baltimorae, 1866.

Acta et Documenta Congressus Generalis de Statibus Perfectionis (1950), 4 vols., Typis Piae Societatis S. Pauli, Romae, 1952.

Acta Sancta Sedis, 41 vols., Romae, 1865-1908.

Bruns, Hermann, *Canones Apostolorum et Conciliorum Saeculorum* IV-VII, 2 vols., Berolini, 1839.

Bullarium Franciscanum, edidit, Joseph M. Pou Y Marti, O.F.M., Nova Series, Prope Florentiam, Ex Typographia Collegii S. Bonaventurae, Vol. III, 1949.

Bullarium Ordinis FF. Praedicatorum, Opera Revmi F. Thomae Ripoll, Magister Generalis, Editum, et a R. F. Antonio Bremond, S.T.M. Illustratum, 8 vols., Romae, 1729-1740.

Bullarum Diplomatum et Privilegiorum Romanorum Sanctorum Pontificum Tauriensis Editio, 25 vols., Augustae Taurinensis, 1857-1872.

Canones et Decreta Sacrosancti Oecumenici Concilii Tridentini, Romae, 1904.

Catholic Encyclopedia, 15 vols., Index and Supplement, New York, 1907-1922.

Codex Iuris Canonici Pii X Pontificis Maximi iussu digestus, Benedicti Papae XV auctoritate promulgatus, Praefatione, Fontium Annotatione et Indice Analytico-Alphabetici ab Emo Petro Card. Gasparri Auctus, Romae: Typis Polyglottis Vaticanis, 1917; reimpressio, 1934.

Codicis Iuris Canonici Fontes, cura Emi Petri Card. Gasparri editi, 9 vols., Romae (postea Civitate Vaticana): Typis Polyglottis Vaticanis, 1923-1939 (Vols. VII-IX, ed. cura et studio Emo Iustiniani Card. Serédi).

Collectanea in Usum Secretariae Sacrae Congregationis Episcoporum et Regularium, cura A. Bizzarri Archiepiscopi Philipensis Secretarii edita, Romae: Ex Typographia Rev. Camerae Apostolicae, 1863.

Collectanea S. Congregationis de Propaganda Fide, 2 vols., Romae: Ex Typographia Polyglotta S. C. de Propagande Fide, 1907.

Collectanea Sacrae Congregationis de Religiosis, Enchiridion de Statibus Perfectionis, Romae: Typis Polyglottis Vaticanis, 1949.

Collectio Omnium Conclusionum et Resolutionum Congregationis Concilii ab anno 1564 ad annum 1860, 18 vols., Salvator Pallottini, Romae: 1868-1893.

Concilii Plenarii Baltimorensis II, in Ecclesia Metropolitana Baltimorensis, a die VII ad diem XXI Octobris, A. D. MDCCCLXVI, Habiti et a Sede Apostolica Recogniti, Acta et Decreta, 2. ed., Baltimorae, John Murphy, 1894.

Corpus Iuris Canonici, editio Lipsiensis secunda, post Aemilii Ludovici Richteri curas instruxit Aemilius Friedberg, Lispsae: Ex officina Bernhardi Tauchnitz, 1879-1881; ed. anastatice repetita, 1928.

Decreta Authentica Congregationis Sacrorum Rituum, 6 vols., Romae: Ex Typographia Polyglotta, 1898-1927.

Decretales D. Gregorii Papae IX, suae integritati una cum glossis restitutae, cum privilegio Gregorii XIII, Pont. Max., et Aliorum Principum, Romae, 1582.

Decretum Gratiani emendatum et notationibus illustratum cum glossis, Gregorii XIII, Pont. Max., iussu editum, 2 vols., Romae, 1582.

Denzinger, H., Bannwart, C., Umberg, J. B., *Enchiridion Symbolorum, Definitionum, et Declarationum de Rebus Fidei et Morum,* 22-23. ed., Friburgi-Brisgoviae: Herder, 1947.

Hardouin, Jean, *Acta Conciliorum et Epistolae Decretales ac Constitutiones Summorum Pontificum,* 12 vols., Parisiis, 1714-1715.

Jaffé, Philippus, *Regesta Pontificum Romanorum ab condita Ecclesia ad annum post Christum natum MCXCVIII,* 2. ed. correctam et auctam auspiciis Gulielmi Wattenbach curaverunt, S. Loewenfeld, F. Kaltenbrunner, P. Ewald, 2 vols., Lipsiae, 1885-1888.

Liber Sextus Decretalium D. Bonifacii Papae VIII, suae integritati cum Clementinis Extravagantibus, earumque Glossis restitutis, Romae, 1582.

Litterae Apostolicae Motu Proprio Datae Ad Venerabiles Fratres Patriarchas, Archiepiscopos, Episcopos, Ceterosque Locorum Hierarchas Ecclesiarum Orientalium, Pacem et Communionem cum Apostolicae Sede Habentes: De Religiosis, De Bonis Ecclesiae Temporalibus et De Verborum Significatione Pro Ecclesiis Orientalibus, Adnotationibus Fontium Auctae cura Pontificii Consilii Codicis Iuris Canonici Orientalis Redigendo, Romae: Typis Polyglottis Vaticanis, 1952.

Mansi, Joannes, *Sacrorum Conciliorum Nova et Amplissima Collectio,* 53 vols. in 60, Paris, Arnhem, Leipzig, 1901-1927.

Monumenta Germaniae Historica, Legum Sectio III, *Concilia,* Tomus II, recensuit A. Werminghoff, Hannoverae et Lipsae, 1896.

———, *Gregorii I Papae Registrum Epistolarum,* edd. P. Ewald et L. Hartmann, Epistolorum Tomus I et II, Berolini, 1891-1899.

Potthast, A., *Regesta Pontificum Romanorum inde ab anno post Christum natum MCXCVIII ad annum MCCCIV,* 2 vols., Berolini, 1874-1875.

Schroeder, H., *Canons and Decrees of the Council of Trent,* St. Louis, Mo., Herder Co., 1941.

———, *Disciplinary Decrees of the General Councils,* St. Louis, Mo., Herder Co., 1937.

The Apostolic Constitutions Sedes Sapientiae and the General Statutes of the Sacred Congregation of Religious, 2. ed., Sole Official English Text, Washington, D. C.: The Catholic University of America Press, 1957.

Thesaurus Resolutionum Sacrae Congregationis Concilii, 167 vols., Romae, 1718-1908.

Synods:

Synodal Statutes of the Archdiocese of Boston (1952).

Fifth Synod of the Archdiocese of Cincinnati (1954), St. Anthony Guild Press, Paterson, New Jersey, 1954.

Synodus Detroitensis Nona Die XIV Decembris Anno Domini MCMLIV Celebrata, Michigan Catholic Press, 1955.

Eighth Synod of the Diocese of Dubuque (1947).

Synodus Dioecesana Eriensis Septima (1942).

Liber Synodalis Fargensis II (1951)

Ninth Synod of the Diocese of Harrisburg (1943).

Fourth Diocesan Synod—Lafayette (1953).

Third Synod of the Diocese of Nashville (1947).

Tenth Diocesan Synod, Diocese of Natchez-Jackson (1957).

Acta et Statuta Synodi Neo-Eboracensis Decimae Septimae (1950).

Synodal Statutes of the Archdiocese of Newark (1941).

Synodus Dioecesana Philadelphiensis IX—1934.

Acta et Decreta Concilii Provincialis Portlandensis in Oregon Quarti, Anno MCMXXXII.

First Diocesan Synod, Diocese of Pueblo (1948).

First Synod of Raleigh (1948).

Statuta Archidioecesis Sancti Francisci Secunda—1936, Typis: The Monitor Publishing Co., San Francisco, California.

Synodus Dioecesana Sancti Ludovici Octava (1950).

Statuta Dioecesis Savannensis-Atlantensis necnon Facultates Sacerdotibus Concessae (1939).

First Synod of the Diocese of Scranton (1949).

Synodus Dioecesana Siouxormensis Tertia (1949).

Synodal Decrees of the Diocese of St. Cloud (1939).

Acta et Secreta Synodi Dioecesanae Toletanae Primae, MCMXLI.

Statutes of the Diocese of Winona, First Diocesan Synod (1950).

Reference Works

A. Vasto, B., *De Communicatione Privilegiorum Praesertim Inter Religiones,* Schola Iuris Canonici Pontificiae Universitates Gregorianae, Aquilae in Vestinis-Italia, 1936.

Abbo, J.-Hannan, J., *The Sacred Canons,* 2 vols., St. Louis, Mo., B. Herder Book Co., 1952.

Agius, L., *Summarium Iurium et Officiorum Parochorum,* Neapoli: M. D'Auria, Pontificius Editor, 1953.

Allgeier, J., *The Canonical Obligation of Preaching in Parish Churches,* The Catholic University of America Canon Law Studies, n. 291, Washington, D. C.: The Catholic University of America Press, 1949.

Aquinas, T., *Sancti Thomae Aquinatis Doctoris Angelici Opera iussu Impensaque Leonis XIII, P. M. Edita, Summa Theologica,* Romae, 1882-

Augustine, C., *A Commentary on the New Code of Canon Law,* 8 vols., Vol. VI-VIII, 2. ed., 1923-1924; Vols. III-V, 3. ed., 1922-1923; Vols. I-II, 4. ed., 1921-1923, St. Louis: Herder.

Barbosa, A., *Collectanea Doctorum in Varia Concilii Tridentini et Canones,* Lugduni, 1657.

———, *De Officio et Potestate Parochi Descriptio,* ed. U. Giraldi a S. Cajetaneo, Romae, 1774.

Benedictus XIV, *De Synodo Dioecesana,* 3 vols., Romae, 1783.

Berutti, C., *Institutiones Iuris Canonici,* 6 vols., Taurini: Marietti, 1936.

Beste, U., *Introductio in Codicem,* 3. ed., Collegeville, Minn.: St. John's Abbey Press, 1946.

Blat, A., *Commentarium Textus Codicis Institutiones,* 6 vols., Vol. II, 2. ed., Romae: 1921.

Bouix, D., *Tractatus de Jure Regularium,* 2 vols., Parisiis, 1857.

Bouscaren, T. L., *The Canon Law Digest,* 3 vols., Vol. I, 7. printing, 1950; Vol. II, 5. printing, 1940; Vol. III, 1954, and Supplements 1953 through 1956, 1954-1957, Milwaukee: The Bruce Publishing Co.

Bouscaren, T. L.-Ellis, A. C., *Canon Law, A Text and Commentary,* Milwaukee: The Bruce Publishing Co., 1946, 3. printing, 1949.

Butler, C., *Benedictine Monachism,* 2. ed., London: Longmans, Green & Co., 1924.

———, *Sancti Benedicti Regula Monasteriorum,* 2. ed., Friburgi Brisgoviae, 1927.

Cappello, F., *Summa Iuris Canonici,* 4. ed., 3 vols., Romae: Aedes Universitatis Gregorianae, 1945-1955.

Cicognani, A. G., *Canon Law,* 2. ed., authorized English version by Joseph M. O'Hara and Francis J. Brennan, Westminster, Md.: The Newman Press, Reprint, 1949.

Claeys Boúúaert, F.-Simenon, G., *Manuale Iuris Canonici,* 3 vols., Gandae et Leodii; apud Auctores, 1939-1947; Vol. I, 5. ed., 1939; Vol. II, 3. ed., 1947; Vol. III, 5. ed., 1943.

Cocchi, G., *Commentarium in Codicem Iuris Canonici ad usum scholarum,* 4. ed., 8 vols., Taurinorum Augustae: Marietti, 1931-1946; Vol. II, 1937.

Conway, W., *The Time and Place of Baptism,* The Catholic University of America Canon Law Studies, n. 324, Washington, D. C.: The Catholic University of America Press, 1954.

Coronata, M. Conte a, *Institutiones Iuris Canonici ad usum utriusque cleri et scholarum,* 5 vols., Taurini-Romae: Marietti, Vol. II, *De Rebus,* 4. ed., 1951; Vol. IV, *De Delictis et Poenis,* 3. ed., 1948.

Creusen, J., *De Iuridica Status Religiosi Evolutione, Synopsis Historica,* Romae, Apud Aedes Pontificiae Universitatis Gregorianae, 1948.

———, *Religious Men and Women in the Code,* 5. ed., revised and edited by Adam Ellis to conform with the sixth French edition, Milwaukee: The Bruce Publishing Co., 1953.

De Meester, A., *Juris Canonici et Juris Canonico-Civilis Compendium,* 3 vols. in 4, Brugis, 1921-1928.

Denifle, C., *Chartularium Universitatis Parisiensis,* 5 vols., Parisiis, 1899-1907.

Deutsch, B., *Jurisdiction of Pastors in The External Forum,* The Catholic University of America Canon Law Studies, n. 378, Washington, D. C.: The Catholic University of America Press, 1957.

Duchesne, L., *The Early History of the Church,* 3. ed., 3 vols., John Murray Co., London, 1931.

Fanfani, L., *De Iure Parochorum ad normam Codicis Iuris Canonici,* Taurini-Romae, 1924.

———, *De Iure Religiosorum,* 3. ed., Rovigo: Istituto Pandano di Arti Grafiche, 1949.

Feldhaus, A., *Oratories,* The Catholic University of America Canon Law Studies, n. 42, Washington, D. C.: The Catholic University of America, 1927.

Ferraris, L., *Prompta Biblotheca, Canonica, Iuridica, Moralis, Theologica necnon Ascetica, Polemica, Rubricistica, Historica,* 9 vols., Romae, 1885-1899.

Ferry, W., *Stole Fees,* The Catholic University of America Canon Law Studies, n. 59, Washington, D. C.: The Catholic University of America Press, 1930.

Flanagan, B., *The Canonical Erection of Religious Houses,* The Catholic University of America Canon Law Studies, n. 179, Washington, D. C.: The Catholic University of America Press, 1943.

Goyeneche, S., *Quaestiones Canonicae de Iure Religiosorum,* 2 vols., Neapoli: M. D'Auria, Pontificius Editor, 1954-1955.

Hostiensis (Henricus de Segusio), *Commentaria in Quinque Libros Decretalium,* 3 vols., Venetiis, 1581.

Jone, H., *Commentarium in Codicem Iuris Canonici,* 3 vols., Paderborn: Officina Libraria F. Schöningh, 1950-1955.

Kelly, B., *The Functions Reserved to Pastors,* The Catholic University of America Canon Law Studies, n. 250, Washington, D. C.: The Catholic University of America Press, 1947.

Kindt, G., *De Potestate Dominativa in Religione,* Universitas Catholica Lovaniensis. Dissertationes, Series II, Tomus 34, Brugis-Parisiis-Romae: Desclée de Brouwer, 1945.

Lavelle, H., *The Obligation of Holding Sacred Missions in Parishes,* The

Catholic University of America Canon Law Studies, n. 295, Washington, D. C.: The Catholic University of America Press, 1949.

Lynch, T., *Contracts between Bishops and Religious Congregations,* The Catholic University of America Canon Law Studies, n. 239, Washington, D. C.: The Catholic University of America Press, 1946.

Many S., *De Locis Sacris,* Parisiis, 1904.

McCartney, M., *Faculties of Regular Confessors,* The Catholic University of America Canon Law Studies, n. 280, Washington, D. C.: The Catholic University of America Press, 1949.

McGrath, R., *The Local Superior in Non-Exempt Clerical Congregations,* The Catholic University of America Canon Law Studies, n. 351, Washington, D. C.: The Catholic University of America Press, 1954.

Melo, A., *De Exemptione Regularium,* The Catholic University of America Canon Law Studies, n. 12, Washington, D. C.: The Catholic University of America, 1921.

Migne, J., *Patrologiae Cursus Completus, Series Latina,* 221 vols., Parisiis: 1844-1864; *Series Graeca,* 161 vols., Parisiis, 1857-1866.

Mocchegiani, P., *Iurisprudentia Ecclesiastica,* 3 vols., Friburgi Brisgoviae: B. Herder Co., 1904-1905.

Montalembert, C. J., *The Monks of the West,* 2 vols., New York: Kenedy Co., 1912.

O'Brien, J. D., *The Exemption of Religious in Church Law,* Milwaukee: The Bruce Publishing Co., 1943.

O'Brien, R., *The Provincial Religious Superior,* The Catholic University of America Canon Law Studies, n. 258, Washington, D. C.: The Catholic University of America Press, 1947.

Ojetti, B., *Commentarium in Codicem Iuris Canonici,* 4 vols., Romae, 1927-1931.

———, *Synopsis Rerum Moralium et Iuris Pontificii,* 3. ed., 4 vols., Romae, 1909-1914.

Papi, H., *The Government of Religious Communities,* New York: Kenedy 1949.

Piatus, Montensis, *Praelectiones Iuris Regularis,* 2. ed., 2 vols., Parisiis, 1906.

Pignatelli, J., *Consultationes Canonicae,* 11 vols., Coloniae Allobrogum, 1700.

Pirhing, E., *Ius Canonicum Nova Methodo Explicatum,* 5 vols., Dilingae, 1674-1678.

Prümmer, D., *Manuale Iuris Canonici,* 4. ed., Friburgi Brisgoviae, 1927.

Quinn, S., *Relation of the Local Ordinary to Religious of Diocesan Approval,* The Catholic University of America Canon Law Studies, n. 283, Washington, D. C.: The Catholic University of America Press, 1949.

Regatillo, E., *Institutiones Iuris Canonici,* 2. ed., 4 vols., Santander: Sal Terrae, 1946.

Reiffenstuel, A., *Ius Canonicum Universum,* 7 vols., Venetiis, 1735.

Sartori, C., *Jurisprudentiae Ecclesiasticae Elementa,* 2. ed., Romae: Pontificium Athenaeum Antonianum, 1949.

Schaefer, T., *De Religiosis ad Normam Codicis Iuris Canonici,* Editio quarta aucta et emendata, Romae: Typis Polyglottis Vaticanis, 1947.

Schmalzgrueber, F., *Ius Ecclesiasticum Universum,* 5 vols. in 12, Romae, 1843-1845.

Sheehan, D., *The Minister of Holy Communion,* The Catholic University of America Canon Law Studies, n. 298, Washington, D. C.: The Catholic University of America Press, 1950.

Shuhler, R., *Privileges of Regulars to Absolve and Dispense,* The Catholic University of America Canon Law Studies, n. 186, Washington, D. C.: The Catholic University of America Press, 1943.

Sipos, S., *Enchiridion Iuris Canonici,* 6. ed. recognovit Ladislaus Galos, Romae, Orbis Catholicus-Herder, 1954.

Suarez, F., *Opera Omnia,* ed. nova, 28 vols., Parisiis, 1856-1878.

Thomassinus, L., *Vetus et Nova Ecclesiae Disciplina circa Beneficia et Beneficiarios,* 10 vols., Moguntiae, 1787.

Toso, A., *Ad Codicem Iuris Canonici . . . Commentaria Minora,* 5 vols. in 2, Taurini-Romae, 1920-1927.

Van Espen, Z. B., *Compendium Iuris Ecclesiastici,* 2 vols., Bassani, 1784.

Vermeersch, A.-Creusen, J., *Epitome Iuris Canonici cum Commentariis,* 3 vols., Vol. I, 7. ed., 1949; Vol. II, 7. ed., 1954; Vol. III, 6. ed., 1946, Mechliniae-Romae: Dessain, 1946-1954.

Vermeersch, A., *De Religiosis Institutis et Personis—Supplementa et Monumenta,* 4. ed., Brugis, 1909.

Wernz, F. X., *Ius Decretalium ad usum Praelectionum in Scholis Textus Iuris Canonici sive Iuris Decretalium,* 6 vols., Romae: 1898-1913, Vol. III, 1901.

Wernz, F.-Vidal, P., *Ius Canonicum ad Codicis Normam Exactum,* 3. ed., 7 vols. in 8, Romae: Apud Aedes Universitatis Gregorianae, 1923-1938, Vol. III, *De Religiosis,* 1933; Vol. IV, *De Rebus,* 1935.

Woywod, S.-Smith, C., *A Practical Commentary on the Code of Canon Law,* Revised and Enlarged Edition, 2 vols., New York; Joseph F. Wagner, Inc., 1948.

ARTICLES

Allaria, A., "Canons and Canonesses Regular," *The Catholic Encyclopedia,* III, 288-297.

Bastnagel, C., "Exempting Parishioners from the Pastor's Authority," *The Jurist,* X (1950), 58-59.

———, "Status of Religious Oratory after Waiver of Right to Public Oratory," *The Jurist,* IV (1944), 151-158.

Beyersbergen, H., "De monitione facienda fidelibus ut accedant ad ecclesias paroeciales proprias," *Periodica,* XXIX (1940), 16-23.

Donovan, J., "Regular Priest and the Application of a Bination Mass," *The Homiletic and Pastoral Review,* XLI (1940-1941), 1134.

Hannan, J., "Faculties for Retreat Conferences," *The Jurist*, X (1950), 391.

———, "Alms for the Clergy," *The Jurist*, IX (1949), 286-305.

———, "Exempt Religious and Penalty for Excessive Mass Stipend," *The Jurist*, VIII (1948), 243-244.

———, "The Obligation of Church Support," *The Jurist*, I (1941), 343-344.

Huizing, P., "De auctoritate Ordinariorum locorum in Missa Paroeciali Propaganda," *Periodica*, XLIV (1955), 175-195.

Kay, T., "The Rights of the Parochial Beneficiary in the United States," *The Jurist*, XV (1955), 318-336.

Larraona, A., "De potestate dominativa publica in iure canonico," *Acta Congressus Iuridici Internationalis*, IV, 145-180.

———, "De potestate paroeciali relate ad religiosos," *CpR*, VIII (1927), 36-41.

———, "Commentarium Codicis," *CpR*, II (1921), 284; III (1922), 47; V (1924), 323-334; 428-429; VI (1925), 182; IX (1928), 104; 206.

Maroto, P., "Annotationes," *CpR*, V (1924), 421; X (1929), 334.

McCarthy, J., "The New Regulations on Preaching," *The Ecclesiastical Review*, LVII (1917), 385.

Piontek, C., "A Gentleman's Agreement," *The Jurist*, III (1943), 284-305.

Ramos, D., "De conditione saecularium in domibus religiosorum," *CpR*, VI (1925), 479-481.

Regatillo, E., "Relationes inter status canonicos perfectionis et alios status in Ecclesia,"—*Acta et Documenta Congressus Generalis, De Statibus Perfectionis* (1950), I, n. 67, pp. 544-555.

Schwegler, E., "Sunday Help," *The Homiletic and Pastoral Review*, XLVIII (1947-1948), 40-44; 605-609.

Tocanel, P., "De facultate Ordinarii loci prohibendi divina officia in ecclesiis et oratoriis religiosorum," *Apollinaris*, XXVIII (1955), 316-353; XXIX (1956), 91-124.

Vermeersch, A., "Annotationes," *Periodica*, XII (1923), 156.

Periodicals

American Ecclesiastical Review, The, Vol. I-XXXII, Philadelphia, 1889-1905; *The Ecclesiastical Review*, Vols. XXXIII-CIX, Philadelphia, 1905-1943; *The American Ecclesiastical Review*, Vols. CX-, Washington, D. C., 1944-

Apollinaris, Romae, 1928-

Commentarium pro Religiosis, Romae, 1920-1934; *Commentarium pro Religiosis et Missionariis*, Romae, 1935-

Homiletic and Pastoral Review, The, New York, 1900-

Jurist, The, Washington, D. C., 1941-

Periodica de Religiosis et Missionariis, Brugis, 1905-1919; *Periodica de Re Canonica et Morali, utilia praesertim Religiosis et Missionariis*, Brugis, 1920-1927; *Periodica de Re Morali, Canonica, Liturgica*, Brugis, 1927-1936, Romae, 1937-

ALPHABETICAL INDEX

BIOGRAPHICAL NOTE

David O'Connor was born in Cambridge, Massachusetts, on August 7, 1928. He received his elementary education at Our Lady, Queen of Martyrs, and Queen of All Saints parochial schools in the Diocese of Brooklyn, New York. He was graduated from St. John's Preparatory School, Brooklyn, New York, in June, 1946. In September of that same year he entered St. Joseph's Preparatory Seminary at Holy Trinity, Alabama, an apostolic school of the Missionary Servants of the Most Holy Trinity. Upon completion of his junior college course, he entered Holy Ghost Novitiate, also located at Holy Trinity, Alabama, and made his religious profession on July 9, 1949. He continued his studies at the philosophical and theological houses of study of the Congregation at Silver Spring, Maryland, and Winchester, Virginia. He was ordained a priest on May 19, 1955. During the summers since his ordination, he was assigned to St. Joseph's Shrine at Stirling, New Jersey, and to work with the Diocesan Missionary Fathers, Richmond, Virginia. In the fall of 1955 he entered the School of Canon Law of the Catholic University of America, receiving the degree of Bachelor of Canon Law in June, 1956, and the degree of Licentiate in Canon Law in June, 1957.

CANON LAW STUDIES*

392. ADAMS, REV. DONALD E., A.B., J.C.L., The truth required in the *preces* for rescripts.
393. BÉGIN, REV. RAYMOND F., A.B., S.T.L., J.C.L., Natural law and positive law.
394. CLANCY, REV. WALTER B., A.B., J.C.L., The rites and ceremonies of sacred ordination.
395. COX, REV. RONALD J., S.T.L., J.C.L., A study of the juridic status of laymen in the writing of the medieval canonists.
396. DEMERS, REV. FRANCIS L., O.M.I., A.B., J.C.L., Temporal administration of the religious house in a non-exempt clerical pontifical institute.
397. DZIADOSZ, REV. HENRY J., M.A., S.T.L., J.C.L., The provisions of the Decree "Spiritus Sancti munera": the law for the extraordinary minister of confirmation.
398. GERHARDT, REV. BERNARD C., A.B., S.T.L., J.C.L., Interpretation of rescripts.
399. HACKETT, REV. JOHN H., A.B., J.C.L., The concept of public order.
400. MURPHY, REV. RICHARD J., O.M.I., S.T.L., J.C.L., The canonico-juridical status of a communist.
401. O'CONNOR, REV. DAVID, M.S.SS.T., J.C.L., Parochial relations and cooperation of the religious and the secular clergy.

*For a complete list of the available numbers of this series apply to the Catholic University of America Press, 620 Michigan Avenue, N.E., Washington (17), D. C., for a general catalogue.

www.ingramcontent.com/pod-product-compliance
Lightning Source LLC
LaVergne TN
LVHW050239080826
844660LV00012B/561

9780813225616